You Can Always Judge a Book by the Company It Keeps.

Read What These Top Achievers Are Saying About *The Power of Focus.*

"If you only read one book this millennium . . . *The Power of Focus* should be it!"

Harvey Mackay
author, *Swim with the Sharks*

"*The Power of Focus* is absolutely wonderful and is sure to make an impact on the business world for generations to come."
Ken Blanchard
coauthor, *The One-Minute Manager*

"A powerful, practical book that will inspire you to achieve your dreams."
Barbara De Angelis, Ph.D.
author, *Real Moments*

"The most successful individuals and companies use proven systems—*The Power of Focus* will teach you how to do the same."
Vic Conant
president, Nightingale-Conant

"Your ability to focus is the most important success skill you can ever develop. This book shows you how to develop this skill in every part of your life. It's outstanding!"

Brian Tracy
international seminar leader, consultant
and bestselling author

"You can be successful at anything in half the usual time by learning how to get focused and remain focused, and this book will show you how. *The Power of Focus* should be a business bible for anyone just starting out, as well as those already established who want to maximize their productivity and income. I own eleven Mexican restaurants. If YOU want the 'whole enchilada,' read this book!"

Tom Harken
author, *The Millionaire's Secret*
Horatio Alger Award recipient

"Many people don't focus very well. That's the reason they ultimately end up broke and disillusioned. This book will change all that."

Jim Rohn
America's foremost business philosopher

"This book will help your career go faster and further, while bringing you greater happiness and success in your personal life."

Somers White
president, Somers White Company,
international management and financial consultant

"For the first time, a book outlines in simple, easy-to-understand and usable terms, one of the most powerful yet overlooked principles that can help turn anyone into a money magnet. A must-read if you want to be a cash-generating machine."

Kevin Trudeau
founder, Shop America

"An important book for anyone who wants to succeed in anything! Outlines the master skill for achieving goals and realizing dreams. I not only got a lot out of it but thoroughly enjoyed reading it."

Robert Kriegel
author, *If it Ain't Broke . . . Break IT!*
commentator, NPR's *Marketplace* program

"This book can help anyone, in any profession, to make quantum leaps in personal, spiritual and vocational growth."

Rabbi Dov Peretz Elkins
The Jewish Center, Princeton, New Jersey

"This book is a clear, simple roadmap that shows you how to focus on the vital few, rather than the trivial many."

Dr. Tony Alessandra
author, *The Platinum Rule*

"*The Power of Focus* shows you how to define *your* path and start working *your* plan. It's an amazing compendium; inspiring as well as practical."

Jim Tunney
former NFL referee

"In this chaotic world, it's all too easy for focus to become blurred. For anyone brave enough to say, 'I want to be a better person,' this book offers a self-help method to discard those old habits which hold you back and to develop, instead, the new habits which promise successful change. To remain as you are denies who you can be. Life is what you make of it and achieving full potential is an everyday choice. *The Power of Focus* shows you how to choose nothing but the best!"

Larry Jones
president and founder, Feed The Children

"Use this book as you would a bridge to get from one shore to the other. If you are stuck on the side of 'Three to get ready' it will help you cross over to 'Four to go.' For me, the 'Ah Ha' was the connection between habits and focus. *The Power of Focus* will put you absolutely on target!"

Rosita Perez, CPAE
president, Creative Living Programs, Inc.

"The topic of focus is one that until now has been overlooked. Everyone in business can benefit by studying and implementing these strategies."

Richard Carlson
author, *Don't Sweat the Small Stuff
. . . and it's all small stuff*

"The strongest lenses in the world might give you perfect visual acuity, but they would not necessarily cause you to understand what you see. This book, unike those lenses, *will* give you that understanding."

Jim Cathcart, CSP, CPAE
author, *Relationship Selling*
past president, National Speakers Association

"Great practical advice! In this age of constant information, the ability to focus and weed out distractions is imperative to your success."

J. B. Fuqua
CEO, The Fuqua Companies

"The essence of personal power is captured in this unique must-read book. Focus on the content and questions. You will be amply rewarded."

Eileen McDargh
author, *Work for a Living and Still be Free to Live*

"A tremendous book packed with infinite wisdom."
Charlie "Tremendous" Jones
author, *Life Is Tremendous*

"Cameras, binoculars, microscopes—their functionality, and performance begin and end with focus. This book clearly and passionately applies focus to the boardroom, locker room and family room. *The Power of Focus* has changed my entire life!"

Dan Clark
international speaker, consultant, bestselling author

"A great step-by-step action plan that will help you get everything you want."

Ted Nicholas
author, *Magic Words That Bring You Riches*

"These acclaimed authors have brought the world a fantastic new book, that's certain to bring the power of focus to each of us as we enter an exciting new century."

Wyland
renowned marine life artist

"Clear, concise instructions for a better life."

Michael Gerber
author, *The E-Myth*

"If you're struggling with time pressures, financial pressures, or want to create an excellent balance in your life, read this book—and then do what it says."

George Thomson, CFP
region manager, Investors Group

"A powerful and inspiring book that you'll want to read again and again. *The Power of Focus* is a treasure trove of principles, methods, concepts, tips, techniques, and ideas that will change your life. Whatever other self-help books you may read in your lifetime, make this one your top priority."

Scott DeGarmo
former editor-in-chief and publisher,
Success and *Working at Home* magazines

"*The Power of Focus* will change your life. It will motivate you to take those small, daily, weekly and monthly actions, that will eventually compound your life into a masterpiece. Buy this book immediately—and get started."

Robert G. Allen
author, *No Money Down*

"To become truly successful, you must learn to focus. Make sure you read this book."

Patricia Fripp, CSP, CPAE
author, *Get What You Want*
past president, National Speakers Association

"I recommend *The Power of Focus* to all my clients. The topic is one of the most important for everyone in business. The information is clear, informative, and will benefit everyone who implements it."

Eldon Edwards
owner, Inco Business Sales

"If you are in sales or service, this book will change your life."

Doug Wead
special assistant to the president in the Bush White House

"This is the best book ever written on focus, targeting, and developing successful habits. Keep it close for frequent reference. It's a real winner."

Nido R. Qubein
chairman, Creative Services, Inc.

"Without focus, it's hard to build a successful business. This book is an effective road map that will really keep you on track."

Paul Orfalea
chairperson and founder, Kinko's, Inc.

"I have watched the life of a friend of mine transform and flourish. She has followed these focusing strategies for personal growth and success for four years. This is not theory—this is dynamite —it changed her life, and it will change yours!"

Lance H. K. Secretan
author, *Reclaiming Higher Ground*

The
Power
of
FOCUS

Jack Canfield
Mark Victor Hansen
Les Hewitt

VERMILION
LONDON

1 3 5 7 9 10 8 6 4 2

Copyright © 2000 Jack Canfield, Mark Victor Hansen and Les Hewitt

The authors have asserted their moral right to be identified as the author of this work in accordance with the Copyright, Designs and Patents Act 1998.

First published in the US in 2000 by Health Communications, Inc.

This edition first published in the United Kingdom
in 2001 by Vermilion,
an imprint of Ebury Press
Random House, 20 Vauxhall Bridge Road, London SW1V 2SA
www.randomhouse.co.uk

Random House Australia (Pty) Limited
20 Alfred Street, Milsons Point, Sydney
New South Wales 2061, Australia

Random House New Zealand Limited
18 Poland Road, Glenfield, Auckland 10, New Zealand

Random House South Africa (Pty) Limited
Endulini, 5a Jubilee Road, Parktown 2193, South Africa

The Random House Group Limited Reg. No. 954009

Papers used by Vermilion are natural, recyclable products
made from wood grown in sustainable forests.

Printed and bound in the UK by

A CIP catalogue record for this book is available from the British Library.

ISBN 0 09 187650 8

Cover design and inside text design/layout by Gail Pocock, Bulldog Communications, US.

Jack

To the teachers who have taught me the most
about *The Power of Focus* principles:

W. Clement Stone, Billy B. Sharp, Lacy Hall, Bob Resnick, Martha
Crampton, Jack Gibb, Ken Blanchard, Nathaniel Branden, Stewart
Emery, Tim Piering, Tracy Goss, Marshall Thurber, Russell Bishop,
Bob Proctor, Bernhard Dohrmann, Mark Victor Hansen, Les Hewitt,
Lee Pulos, Doug Kruschke, Martin Rutte, Michael Gerber,
Armand Bytton, Marti Glenn, and Ron Scolastico.

Mark

To Elisabeth and Melanie:

"The future is in safe hands."

Les

To Fran, Jennifer and Andrew:

"You are the focus of my life."

Contents

ACKNOWLEDGMENTS

This book has taken three years to write and many people encouraged us during the entire process. There were times when it seemed like we'd never get through it. However, with persistence and a keen focus, it is finally complete. We want to acknowledge everyone who participated for their help and support, without which this project would never have been finished.

Fran Hewitt, you are a pillar of strength. To put up with all the frustrations, crazy deadlines, and last-minute reviews required incredible fortitude. A heartfelt thank you. Jennifer and Andrew Hewitt, thank you for your encouragement, feedback and creative ideas. You are inspiring.

Dan Sullivan, thank you for your tremendous leadership in the world of business coaching, and for being a powerful influence and mentor. Thank you Jim Rohn, George Addair, Patricia Fripp, Ed Foreman, David McNally, Lance Secretan, Somers White, Rosita Perez, Danny Cox, Valerie Morse, Peter Daniels, Richard Flint, and many other great teachers too numerous to mention, for your combined wisdom and guidance over the last fifteen years.

To Tim Breithaupt for allowing your excellent book, *Take This Job and Love It!: The Joys of Professional Selling* to stimulate the completion of this one. Gail Pocock, you are a true champion. Thank you for your total dedication and immersion in this project. Your creativity and expertise in layout, text and cover design is outstanding. Thanks to Rod Chapman, whose editing skills have produced a superior product. We also acknowledge Georgina Forrest and Shirley Flaherty at Achievers for the wonderful typing and re-typing job, a miracle considering the almost unreadable scrawl they originally had to work from. To Elverina Laba for her enthusiasm and sales effort while Les was "absent."

A special cheer for all our clients in The Achievers Coaching Program who implemented these strategies, and proved they really work. Thanks also to the 1998 graduating class at Jack Canfield's Facilitating Skills Seminar—your enthusiasm and encouragement was greatly appreciated.

To Philip Keers and Ken Johnston, who carry the torch into the future, you are truly wonderful partners.

To everyone at Jack's office, a wonderful team whose synergy created momentum for many of our deadlines to be met. Special thanks to Deborah Hatchell for your calming influence and brilliant communication ability when things were particularly hectic. To Nancy Mitchell Autio for coordinating the exacting task of obtaining permissions with Shirley Flaherty. Shirley, your tenacity and persistence ensured we made our deadlines. Great job! Thanks to Ro Miller, "the switchboard queen," for your warmth and help with those endless phone calls. To Veronica Romero who made sure the readers' manuscripts went out on time, and more importantly, came back on time! Teresa Esparza for your wonderful positive attitude and willingness to help. Chris Smith, thank you for your muscle testing brilliance.

To Robin Yerian and Leslie Forbes Riskin, two back-room players whose high level of skill and commitment made sure all the details were expertly handled.

Thanks, Patty Aubery, for your keen insights and marketing knowledge. Your drive and energy make things happen.

Our gratitude also goes to Inga Mahoney and Christopher Canfield for allowing Jack to focus on the work and help maintain that all-important balance between business and family.

To the two people who have the most focus of anyone, anywhere, Elisabeth and Melanie Hansen.

To Patty Hansen for being an integral player in the day-to-day operations and decision-making process.

A big thank you to Laura Rush at Mark's office for being such an effective go-between and ensuring those important conference calls were scheduled (and often rescheduled!)

Thanks to everyone at Health Communications, our publisher, for totally supporting the project and ensuring that printing and distribution deadlines were handled smoothly.

To Peter Vegso, Tom Sand and Terry Burke for putting together and leading such a wonderful team.

A special thank you to Christine Belleris and Allison Janse for guiding us through the maze of details and responding promptly to every request. To Kim Weiss and Larry Getlen for heading up the public relations team and to Kelly Maragni opening many doors to enhance sales.

Thanks to Chuck Bush for cleaning up the final manuscript.

Heartfelt thanks to all those diligent people on our readers panel who took time to digest, peruse and analyze our ideas: Anna Alton, Barry Spilchuk, Eileen McDargh, David McNally, Philip Keers, Ken Johnston, Tim Breithaupt, Ralph Puertas, Steve Cashdollar, Bill Cowles, John P. Gardner, Walt Harasty, Keith Jacobsen, Tom Justin, Jeanne Kaufman, Audrey Kelliher, John Olsen, Elye Pitts and Dottie Walters. Your feedback and suggestions made an important contribution and helped create a much better product.

A special thanks to Fred Angelis who made an in-depth analysis and offered many excellent marketing ideas.

We also acknowledge the many examples and stories provided directly and indirectly by friends and clients. Because of the scope and duration of this project, we may have neglected to mention others who helped along the way. If so, please accept our apologies, and know that you are appreciated.

Writing and producing this book has truly been a team effort, proving once again that completing any successful venture doesn't require magic or hocus-pocus. It's simply learning how to focus.

The Purpose Of This Book: What's In It For You

"The individual who wants to
reach the top in business must appreciate
the might of the force of habit—and
must understand that practices are
what create habits. He must be quick to
break those habits that can break him
—and hasten to adopt those practices
that will become the habits that help him
achieve the success he desires."

—J. Paul Getty

Dear Reader, (or potential reader, if you're still browsing):

Our ongoing research clearly indicates that three of the biggest challenges facing business people today are: time pressures, financial pressures, and the struggle to maintain a healthy balance between work and home.

For many people the pace of life is too hectic, like being on a treadmill that just won't stop. Stress levels are at an all-time high. There's a growing need for people in business to be more well-rounded in order to avoid becoming burned-out workaholics who have little time for family and friends and the finer things in life. Many also carry a tremendous burden of guilt that adds even more stress. That's no way to live!

Is this something you can relate to?

The Power of Focus will help you in many ways. And the benefits apply whether you are a CEO, vice president, manager, supervisor, salesperson, entrepreneur, consultant, the owner of a professional practice or home-based business.

Here's Our GUARANTEE:

If you study and gradually implement the strategies we are about to share, you'll not only hit your business, personal and financial targets consistently, you'll far exceed the results you are currently experiencing. Specifically, we'll show you how to focus on your strengths, so that you can maximize your income, and at the same time enjoy a healthier, happier, well-balanced lifestyle.

In addition, you'll learn how to build a stronger foundation for the future, based on a little-used technique called Unusual Clarity. On top of that, you'll discover how to create financial peace of mind using proven methods from several multi-millionaires. There's also a smorgasbord of ideas to help nurture and enrich your most important relationships.

The reason we are so confident that the ideas in this book will work for you is because they have already worked for us and thousands of our clients. The three of us have seventy-nine years of combined business experience. This is real-world experience. It's been earned by making lots of mistakes, as well as by focusing on doing some things extremely well. We'll share some of our most important personal breakthroughs with you and tell you the way it really is instead of giving you vague theories and philosophies. This will help you avoid much of the trial and error in life and save you a lot of time, energy and unnecessary stress.

How to Get the Most Out of This Book.

Please note: If you are looking for a magic "quick-fix" formula, you won't find it here. In our experience, there's no such thing. It takes a real commitment to create positive transformation. That's why more than 90 percent of people who attend short-term seminars see no improvement in their lives. They don't take the time to implement what they learn and all of their notes usually end up collecting dust.

Our primary goal has been to make this information so compelling, it will galvanize you to take immediate action. This book is user-friendly—it's really easy to read. You'll even find cartoons along the way that make it fun.

Every chapter consists of a variety of strategies and techniques enhanced by anecdotes and inspiring stories. The first three chapters lay the foundation. Each subsequent chapter introduces a new set of strategies centered around a specific habit that will help you to focus and perform better. Individually, these habits are vitally important to your future success. In combination, they create a veritable fortress that will ensure you enjoy life to the fullest. At the end of each chapter you will find a series of Action Steps. These are designed to facilitate your progress. It is essential that you follow through and complete these if you want to enjoy a higher level of prosperity. You can initiate them one at a time. Use this book as a continuous work-in-progress that you can refer to over and over again.

We strongly suggest that you have a highlighter marker or pen and notepad beside you as you read. Use these to immediately capture the ideas that have the greatest impact.

Remember, it's all about focus. The main reason most people struggle professionally and personally is simply lack of focus.

They procrastinate or allow themselves to be easily distracted and interrupted. Now you have the opportunity to be different. The only purpose of this book is to inspire you to take action. That's it, pure and simple. There's a treasury of wisdom in the pages ahead. So let's get started. Use *The Power of Focus* to guarantee your better future. And may your life be truly enriched in the process.

Sincerely,

Mark Victor Hansen

P.S. If you are the owner of a business and are planning for rapid growth in the next few years, buy a copy of this book for everyone on your team. The momentum created by implementing these focusing strategies together, will ensure that you reach your targets much sooner than anticipated.

Your Habits Will Determine Your Future

"IT'S SO HARD WHEN CONTEMPLATED IN
ADVANCE, AND SO EASY WHEN YOU DO IT."

—Robert M. Pirsig

Brent Vouri knew he was going to die.
The severe asthmatic attack had deteriorated into adult respiratory distress syndrome. To put it simply, his lungs had completely seized, just like a car engine when it finally runs out of oil.

The last thing he remembered that night was the hospital floor rushing up to meet him, then, total blackness. The coma lasted for fifteen days, during which time his weight dropped by forty pounds. When he finally awoke, he was unable to speak for another two weeks. That was good, because for the first time in years it gave him time to think. Why, at only twenty years of age, had his life almost evaporated? The doctors had done a miraculous job keeping him alive, when others thought he had no chance for survival.

Brent reflected deeply. The asthma had been a part of his life since birth. He was well known at the hospital after numerous visits to stabilize his condition.

Despite having lots of energy as a child, he was never able to participate in any physical activities like other kids, such as skating or hockey. At age ten, his parents divorced and all of his pent-up frustrations finally boiled over. The next few years were a continuous downward spiral leading to drugs, alcohol abuse and a smoking habit that consumed thirty cigarettes per day.

He didn't finish school and aimlessly drifted from one part-time job to the next. Even though his health was steadily getting worse, he chose to ignore it—until that fateful night when his body said, "no more." With time to reflect, he came to this all-important conclusion: "I brought this on myself through years of making bad choices." His new resolve was, "Never again; I want a life."

Brent gradually became stronger and was eventually released from the hospital. Soon after, he mapped out a positive game plan to improve his life. First he enrolled in a fitness program. One of his initial goals was to win a T-shirt for completing twelve sessions. He did it. Three years later he was teaching aerobics. The momentum was building. Five years after that he competed in the National Aerobics Championships. Along the way he decided to further his education—first, completing his high school diploma and then successfully working his way through university.

Next, he and a friend started their own manufacturing business, Typhoon Sportswear Ltd. (*www.typhoonsports wear.com*), specializing in producing apparel for retail chains. Starting with only four employees, the company recently celebrated its fifteenth anniversary.

Today it's a multimillion-dollar enterprise with sixty-six people and an international distribution network supplying high-profile clients such as Nike. By deciding to make better choices and create better habits, Brent Vouri turned his life around—from yesterday's zero to today's hero!

Isn't that an inspiring story?

Here's what's important: Life doesn't just happen to you. It's all about choices and how you respond to every situation. If you are in the habit of continually making bad choices, disaster often occurs. Your everyday choices ultimately determine whether you end up living with abundance or living in poverty. However, life never completely closes the door to opportunity.

Consistent choices lay the foundation for your habits, as you'll find out in the next few pages. And your habits play a major role in how your future unfolds. This includes the habits you display to the business world every day, as well as the variety of behaviors that show up in your personal life. Throughout this book, you'll find strategies that can be applied to both work and home. Your job is to review all of them and implement the ones that will give you the greatest rewards. By the way, all of these strategies work equally well for men and women. They are not gender specific. If you haven't noticed, one of the most exciting developments in the marketplace today is the rapid growth of women entrepreneurs.

In this chapter, we've laid out the most important elements about habits. First you'll discover how habits really work. Then you'll learn how to identify bad habits and how to change them. This will allow you to check out your own specific habits and determine which ones are unproductive. Finally, we'll show you a unique **Successful Habits Formula,** a simple but powerful strategy that will help you transform your bad habits into successful habits. Using this technique will ensure that you stay focused on what works, instead of what doesn't work.

SUCCESSFUL PEOPLE HAVE SUCCESSFUL HABITS

Unsuccessful People Don't!

How HABITS Really Work

YOUR HABITS WILL DETERMINE YOUR FUTURE

What is a habit? Simply stated, a habit is something you do so often it becomes easy. In other words, it's a behavior that you keep repeating. If you persist at developing a new behavior, eventually it becomes automatic.

For example, if you learn to drive a car with a standard gearshift, the first few lessons are usually interesting. One of the big challenges is figuring out how to synchronize the clutch and accelerator pedals so you have a nice, smooth gear change. If you release the clutch too quickly, the car stalls. If you press down too hard on the accelerator without releasing the clutch, the engine roars but you don't go anywhere. Sometimes the car jumps down the street like a kangaroo, surging and stopping as the new driver struggles with the pedals. However, with practice, the gear change eventually becomes smooth and you don't think about it anymore.

> LES:
> We are all creatures of habit. When I drive home from my office every day, there are nine traffic lights along the route. Often I get home and don't remember any of the lights. It's like I'm unconscious as I drive. If my wife asks me to make a detour to pick up something on the way home, it's not uncommon for me to totally forget because I've programmed myself to take the same way home every night.

The great news is that you can reprogram yourself any time you choose to do so. If you're struggling financially, this is important to know!

Let's say you want to be financially independent. Doesn't it make sense to check your money-making habits? Are you in the habit of paying yourself first every month? Do you consistently save and invest at least 10 percent of your income? The answer is either "yes" or "no." Immediately you can see if you are moving in the right direction. The key word here is *consistent*. That means every month. And every month is a good habit. Most people dabble when it comes to growing their money. They are very inconsistent.

Suppose you start a savings and investment program. For the first six months you diligently put your 10 percent away according to plan. Then something happens. You borrow the money to take a vacation, and you tell yourself you'll make it up in the next few months. Of course you don't—and your financial independence program is stalled before it even gets off the ground! By the way, do you know how easy it is to become financially secure? Starting at age eighteen if you invest one hundred dollars per month compounding annually at ten percent, you will have more than $1.1 million tucked away at age sixty-five. Even if you don't start until you are forty years old, there's hope, although it will take more than a daily dollar to do it.

This is called a **no exceptions policy**. In other words, you commit to your better financial future every single day. It's what separates the people who have from the people who don't have. (In chapter 9, Taking Decisive Action, you'll learn a lot more about wealth creation.)

Let's look at another situation. If maintaining excellent health is high on your list of priorities, exercising three times a week may be the minimum standard to keep you in shape. A No Exceptions Policy means you will maintain this exercise habit no matter what happens, because you value the long-term benefits.

People who dabble at change will quit after a few weeks or months. And they usually have a long list of excuses why it didn't work out for them. **If you want to distance yourself from the masses and enjoy a unique lifestyle, understand this—your habits will determine your future.**

It's that important. Remember, successful people don't drift to the top. It takes focused action, personal discipline and lots of energy every day to make things happen. The habits you develop from this day forward will ultimately determine how your future works out. Rich or poor. Healthy or unhealthy. Fulfilled or unfulfilled. Happy or unhappy. It's your choice, so choose wisely.

YOUR HABITS WILL DETERMINE YOUR QUALITY OF LIFE

Many people today are concerned about their lifestyle. Phrases like, "I'm looking for a better quality of life," or "I just want to simplify my life," are now commonplace. It seems the headlong rush for material success and all the trappings of a so-called successful life are not enough. To be truly rich includes not only financial freedom, but developing rich, meaningful relationships, enriching your health, and enjoying a rich balance between your career and your personal life.

The nourishment of your own spirit or soul is also an essential requirement. This takes time to explore and expand. It is a never-ending process. The more you learn about yourself—how you think, how you feel, what your true purpose is and how you want to live—the more your life will flow.

Instead of just working hard every week, you will begin to make better choices based on intuition and instinctively knowing the right thing to do. It is this higher level of awareness that determines your daily quality of life. In chapter 10, Living On Purpose, we'll show you a unique system that will make all of this possible for you. It's a very exciting way to live.

THE RESULTS OF YOUR BAD HABITS USUALLY DON'T SHOW UP UNTIL MUCH LATER IN LIFE

Please make sure you are really alert before you read the next two paragraphs. If you're not, go splash some cold water on your face so you will not miss the importance of this fundamental concept.

More people than ever are living for immediate gratification. They buy things they can't really afford and put off payment as far down the road as possible. Cars, furniture, appliances, entertainment systems, or the latest "toy," just to name a few. People in the habit of doing this have a sense of playing catch-up all the time. There's always another payment next month. This often results in working longer hours or taking an additional job just to make ends meet, creating even more stress.

Taken to an extreme, if your expenses constantly exceed your income, you will have an ultimate outcome. It's called bankruptcy! When you develop a chronic bad habit, life will eventually give you consequences. And you may not like the consequences. Here's what you need to really understand: Life will still give you the consequences. Whether you like it or not isn't the issue. The fact is, if you keep on doing things a certain way you will always get a predictable result. **Negative habits breed negative consequences. Successful habits create positive rewards.** That's just the way life is.

Let's look at a few other examples. If you want to enjoy longevity, you must have healthy habits. Practicing good nutrition, exercising and studying longevity play a major role here. The reality? Most of the population in the Western world is overweight, under-exercised and undernourished. How would you explain that? Again, it's a live-for-the-moment attitude, with little or no thought given to future consequences. There's a long list when it comes to health. Here are a couple—working fourteen hours per day seven days a week will lead to eventual burnout. When you're eating fast foods or junk food on the run as a daily habit, the combination of stress and high cholesterol produces a much greater risk of heart attacks and strokes. These are life-threatening consequences, yet many people ignore the obvious and roll merrily along, undaunted by the fact that a major crisis may be looming just around the corner.

Look at relationships. Marriage is in trouble, with almost 50 percent ending up in divorce. If you are in the habit of starving your most important relationships of time, energy and love, how can you expect a happy outcome?

When it comes to money, your bad habits may lead you to a never-ending cycle of work in your later years, when you'd rather be enjoying more time off for fun.

Now here's some really good news:

YOU CAN TURN NEGATIVE CONSEQUENCES INTO POSITIVE REWARDS

Simply By Changing Your Habits Now.

Developing successful habits takes time

How long does it take to change a habit? The most common answers to this question are, "about twenty-one days," or "three to four weeks." This is probably true for making small adjustments in your behavior. Here's a personal example:

> LES:
> I remember losing my keys on a regular basis. At the end of the day I'd park the car in the garage, march into the house and toss my keys anywhere they happened to land. Later I'd be going out to a meeting and, of course, unable to find the keys. As the treasure hunt for my keys took place, my stress level would noticeably increase, and after the keys were finally found, I'd rush off to my meeting twenty-five minutes late, owning an attitude that would not be described as positive.
>
> The solution to this recurring problem was simple. One day I nailed a block of wood to the wall facing the garage door. It had two hooks on it and a large label that said, "keys."
>
> The next evening I came home, strode past my new parking spot for the keys, and tossed them in some remote corner of the room. Why? Because that's what I'd always done. It took me almost thirty days of forcing myself to hang them on the wall before my brain got the message: "I guess we're doing something different now," and a new habit was finally formed. I never lose my keys anymore, but it took a considerable effort to retrain myself.

What's fascinating is that after twenty-one to thirty experiences with a new habit, it's harder not to do it than to do it. Before you can change a habit, you need to first check how long you have owned it. If you have been doing something repeatedly for thirty years you may not be able to let go of it in a few short weeks. Acknowledge the fact that a deeply entrenched habit

9

has long roots. It's like trying to sever a multi-stranded fiber that has molded itself, over time, into a single powerful rope. It's very hard to break. Long-time smokers know how difficult it is to break the nicotine habit. Many never do, despite the overwhelming evidence that proves smoking can significantly shorten your life expectancy.

As well, people with a long history of low self-esteem won't transform themselves into highly confident individuals, ready to take on the world, in twenty-one days. It may take a year or more to develop positive belief systems. These important transitions can affect both your professional and personal life.

Another factor about changing habits is the potential for slipping back into your old patterns. This can happen when stress levels rise or an unexpected crisis occurs. The new habit may not be strong enough to resist these circumstances, and more time, energy and effort will be required. To ensure consistency, astronauts use a checklist for every single procedure to ensure the same results every time. You can create a similar fail-safe system. It just takes practice. And it's well worth the effort, as you'll see shortly.

Imagine if you only changed four habits every year. Five years from now you would have twenty positive new habits. Now, here's the thing—would twenty positive new habits make a difference in your results? Of course. Twenty successful habits can bring you all the money you want or need, wonderful loving relationships, a healthier and more energized physical body, plus all sorts of new opportunities. And what if you created more than four new habits every year? Think of the possibilities!

UP TO 90 PERCENT OF OUR NORMAL BEHAVIOR IS BASED ON HABITS

As mentioned earlier, many of our daily activities are simply routines. From the time you get up in the morning until you retire at night, there are hundreds of things you do the same way. These include the way you dress, get ready for the day, eat breakfast, read the newspaper, brush your teeth, drive to the office, greet people, arrange your desk, set up appointments, work on projects, attend meetings, answer the phone and so on. If you've been doing these same activities for years, you have a set of firmly entrenched habits. They involve every area of your life including your work, family, income, health, relationships and many more. The sum total of these habits determines how your life operates. Simply stated, this is your normal behavior.

As creatures of habit, we are very predictable. In many ways this is good because others may view us as reliable, dependable and consistent. (It's interesting to note that people who are very unpredictable also have a habit—the habit of inconsistency!)

However, with too much routine, complacency sets in and life becomes boring. We settle for less than we are capable of. In fact, many of the activities that make up our everyday normal behavior are performed unconsciously—without thinking. Here's the point: Your everyday normal behavior has a lot to do with the results in your life. If you're not happy with these results, something has to change.

QUALITY IS NOT AN ACT. IT IS A HABIT.

ONCE A NEW HABIT IS WELL-DEVELOPED, IT BECOMES YOUR NEW NORMAL BEHAVIOR

This is great news! By superimposing a new behavior on top of your present behavior, you can create an entirely new way of doing things. This new normal behavior then becomes your new standard of performance and productivity. In other words, you simply start replacing your old bad habits with new successful habits.

For example, if you always show up late for meetings, your stress levels are probably high and you feel unprepared. To improve this, make a commitment that you will arrive ten minutes early for every appointment during the next four weeks. If you discipline yourself to complete this process, you will notice two things:

1. The first week or two will be tough. In fact, you may need to give yourself a few mental pep talks just to keep yourself on track.

2. The more often you show up on time, the easier it becomes. Then one day it becomes normal behavior. It's like being re-programmed. And you'll discover that the benefits of the new program far outweigh the results of the old one.

By systematically improving one behavior at a time you can dramatically improve your overall lifestyle. This includes your health, income, relationships and time off for fun.

MARK:

I have a friend in his fifties who changed twenty-four eating habits over a two-year period. Before he decided to change, he was tired and overweight, had low energy and lacked motivation for his work. His bad habits included too many desserts, fast foods and a bottle of wine every day. Then he decided to change. It was a long process and required lots of self-discipline. With the help of an excellent nutritionist and a personal fitness trainer, he made a complete turnaround. He has stopped drinking, has no trouble avoiding desserts and eats smaller food portions that are well-balanced and provide maximum energy. He has a new zest for business and his confidence is at an all-time high.

If other people can make significant changes, why not you? Remember, nothing will change until you do. Embrace change as a positive catalyst, one that will give you more freedom and peace of mind.

IF YOU KEEP ON DOING
WHAT YOU'VE ALWAYS DONE

You'll Keep On Getting What You've Always Got.

How to IDENTIFY
Bad Habits

BE AWARE OF THE HABITS THAT
ARE NOT WORKING FOR YOU

Many of our habits, patterns, idiosyncrasies and quirks are invisible, causing renowned author Oliver Wendell Holmes to observe, "We all need an education in the obvious." So let's look more closely at the habits that are holding you back. You are probably conscious of a few right away. Here are some common ones we have received from clients in our workshops.

- Not returning phone calls on time.

- Being late for meetings and appointments.

- Poor communication between colleagues and staff.

- A lack of clarity about expected outcomes, monthly targets, goals, etc.

- Not allowing enough travel time for outside appointments.

- Not attending to paperwork quickly and efficiently.

- Handling the mail more than once.

- Allowing bills to go unpaid, resulting in interest penalties.

- Not following up consistently on overdue receivables.

- Talking instead of listening.

- Forgetting someone's name sixty seconds (or less) after being introduced.

- Hitting the snooze alarm several times in the morning before getting out of bed.

- Working long days with no exercise or regular breaks.

- Not spending enough time with your children.

- Having a fast-food meals program Monday to Friday.

- Eating at irregular times of the day.

- Leaving home in the morning without hugging your wife, husband, children and/or dog.

- Taking work home with you.

- Socializing too much on the telephone.

- Making reservations at the last minute (restaurant, travel plans, theatre, concerts).

- Not following through on time as promised, with other people's requests.

- Not taking enough time off for fun and family—guilt free!

- Having your cell phone on all the time.

- Answering the telephone during family mealtimes.

- Controlling every decision, especially the small stuff you need to let go of!

- Procrastinating on everything from filing taxes to cleaning out your garage.

Now check yourself out by making a list of all the habits that keep you unproductive. Block off an hour or more so you can really think through this process. And plan it so you won't be interrupted. It's a worthy exercise and will give you a strong foundation for improving your results in the years ahead. In fact, these bad habits, or obstacles to your goals, really act as a springboard to your future success. Until you clearly understand what is holding you back, it's difficult to create more productive habits. The Successful Habits Formula at the end of this chapter will show you a practical way to transform your bad habits into successful strategies.

Another way to identify your unproductive behavior is to ask for feedback. Talk to people you respect and admire, who know you well. Ask them what they observe about your bad habits. Look for consistency. If you talk to ten people and eight of them say you never return phone calls on time, pay attention. **Remember this—your outward behavior is the truth, whereas your inner perception of your behavior is often an illusion.** If you are open to good honest feedback, you can make adjustments quickly and eliminate bad habits permanently.

YOUR HABITS AND BELIEF SYSTEMS ARE A PRODUCT OF YOUR ENVIRONMENT

This is an extremely important insight. Understand that the people you hang around with and the environment you live in strongly influence what you do. A person brought up in a negative environment, continually subjected to physical or verbal abuse, has a different view of the world than a child reared in a warm, loving and supportive family. Their attitudes and levels of self-esteem are different. Abusive environments often produce feelings of unworthiness and a lack of confidence, not to mention fear. This negative belief system, if carried into adult life, can produce all sorts of unproductive habits including drug addiction, criminal activity and an inability to mold a steady career path.

Peer pressure also plays a negative or positive role. If you hang around people who are always complaining about how bad everything is, you may start believing what they say. On the other hand, if you surround yourself with people who are strong and positive, you're more likely to see a world full of opportunity and adventure.

In his excellent book, *NLP: The New Art and Science of Getting What You Want,* author Harry Alder explains further:

> Even small changes at the root level of belief will produce amazing changes in behavior and performance. This is seen more starkly in children than in adults, as they are more sensitive to suggestion and changing belief. So, for example, if children believe they are good at a sport, or a particular subject, they will actually perform better. The better performance will fuel the enhanced self-belief and they will go on to excel.
>
> In a few rare cases a person might have an overriding self-belief that says "I'm no good at anything," and this will have a very damaging effect on anything they try to accomplish—if they bother to try. But it is far more common to have a mixture of self-beliefs, some of which are positive or "empowering" and some of which are negative or "disempowering." A man might have a very low self-image in career terms and not see himself, for example, as being a good "manager" or "boss" or "leader". The same person, however, might see himself as a "natural" at sport, socializing, or in some hobby or pastime. Just as commonly, in a work situation, a woman might see herself highly in terms of professional ability —being able to do the job well technically—but be far

from happy about handling the "office politics" side of her career. Or vice versa. So we each have a range of self-beliefs, covering the many facets of our work, social and domestic life; and we need to be specific when identifying those that affect what we achieve. We need to replace disempowering ones with empowering ones.

Even if you were unfortunate enough to have a severely disadvantaged background, you can still make changes. And it may only take one person to help you make the transition. An excellent coach, teacher, therapist, mentor or positive role model can dramatically impact your future. **The only prerequisite is that you must commit to change.** When you are ready to do so, the right people will start showing up to help you. In our experience, that well-known saying, "When the pupil is ready the teacher appears," is true.

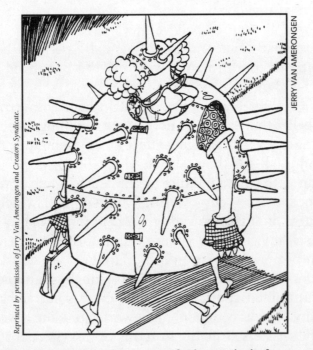

Harmony is no longer a part of Gloria's belief system.

How to CHANGE
Bad Habits

STUDY THE HABITS OF
SUCCESSFUL ROLE MODELS

As mentioned before, successful people have developed successful habits. Learn to observe what those habits are. Study successful people. As well-known business philosopher Jim Rohn says, "They leave clues." What if you were to interview one successful person every month? Take him or her out to breakfast or lunch and ask lots of good questions about their disciplines, routines and habits. What do they read? What clubs and associations do they belong to? How do they schedule their time? If you listen well and take good notes, you'll have a wealth of powerful ideas in a very short time. And if your request is sincere, truly successful people are happy to share their ideas. They enjoy the opportunity to be a coach to people who are genuinely interested in improving their lives.

JACK AND MARK:
When we finished writing the first *Chicken Soup for the Soul* book, we asked all of the bestselling authors we know—Barbara De Angelis, John Gray, Ken Blanchard, Harvey Mackay, Harold Bloomfield, Wayne Dyer and Scott Peck—what specific strategies would be required to assure that our book would become a bestseller. All of these people were generous with their ideas and their insights. We did everything we were told. We made a habit of doing a minimum of one radio interview a day, seven days a week, for two years. We retained our own publicist.

We sent out five books a day to reviewers and other potential opinion molders. We gave newspapers and magazines free reprint rights to our stories. We offered motivational seminars to all of the people responsible for selling our books. In short, we asked what our bestselling habits should be and we put them into action. As a result, we have sold fifty million books to date worldwide.

The trouble is, most people won't ask. Instead, they come up with all sorts of excuses. They're too busy, or they rationalize that successful people wouldn't have time for them, and how do you find these people anyway? Successful people aren't standing on every street corner waiting to be interviewed. That's right. Remember, it's a study. That means you need to be resourceful and come up with ways to find where these successful people work, live, eat and hang out. Make it a game. Have fun. It's worth it! (In chapter 5, which focuses on the habit of Building Excellent Relationships, you'll discover how to find and contact successful mentors.)

Here's another way to study successful people: Read their autobiographies and biographies. There are hundreds of them. These are wonderful true stories packed with ideas, and the books are in your local library and bookstores. Read one every month, and you'll gain more insights in a year than many university courses could offer.

Also, be alert for special television documentaries that feature successful people. Another habit the three of us have developed is listening to motivational and educational audiotapes when we are driving, walking or exercising. If you listen to an audiotape for thirty minutes each day, five days a week, in ten years you'll have been exposed to over thirteen hundred hours of new and useful information. This is a habit that almost all of the successful people we know have developed—they listen to audiotapes. (For some of the best, see our Resource Guide on page 303.)

Our friend Jim Rohn says, "If you read one book every month about your industry, in ten years you'll have read 120 books. That will put you in the top 1 percent of your field." Conversely, as Jim wisely notes, **"All the books you haven't read won't help you!"** Check out specialty stores that sell videos and cassette tapes featuring top personal development trainers and business leaders. All this terrific information is out there waiting for you. So feast on it, and watch your awareness soar. Pretty soon, if you apply what you learn, your income will soar too.

DEVELOP THE HABIT OF CHANGING YOUR HABITS

People who are rich in every sense of the word understand that life is a learning experience. It never stops. Learn to constantly refine your habits. There's always another level to reach for, no matter how good you are right now. When you constantly strive to improve, you build character. You become more as a person, and you have more to offer. It's an exciting journey that ultimately leads to fulfillment and prosperity. Unfortunately, sometimes we learn the lessons the hard way.

LES:
Have you ever experienced kidney stones? It's no fun, and a good example of how bad habits can make your life misery.

On consultation with my doctor it became evident that my suffering originated from poor eating habits. The consequences finally showed up in the form of several large stones. It was decided that a lithotrypsy was the best way to remove them. This is a laser technique that only takes about an hour and normally the patient fully recovers in a few days.

Prior to this I had booked a special father-and-son weekend in Toronto. My son had just turned nine and had never been there before. Our favorite football team was playing in the national championship final, plus the Los Angeles Kings, my son's favorite hockey team, were in town as well. We planned to fly out on Saturday morning. My lithotrypsy was on Tuesday of the same week, which I figured gave me lots of time to recuperate before the flight.

However, on Friday afternoon, after a severe bout of renal colic and three days of excruciating pain, dulled only by regular morphine shots, my surprise trip with my son was evaporating before my eyes. More consequences! Fortunately, at the last minute my doctor decided I was fit enough to travel and signed me out of the hospital.

The weekend was spectacular. Our football team won, we watched a great hockey game, and my son and I have memories we will treasure for a lifetime. And I almost lost that wonderful opportunity because of my bad habits.

I am now highly motivated to avoid future kidney stone problems. I drink ten glasses of water every day and choose not to eat certain stone-forming foods. It's a small price to pay. And my new habits have successfully kept me out of trouble, so far.

The point of this story is to illustrate how life will always give you consequences related to your actions. So before you embark on a specific course, look ahead. Are you creating negative consequences or potential rewards? Be clear in your thinking. Do some research. Ask questions before you start any new habits. If you do this, you'll enjoy more of life's pleasures, and not be screaming for morphine to kill your pain!

Now that you understand how habits really work and how to identify them, let's conclude with the most important part —how to permanently change your habits.

The Successful HABITS Formula

This is a step-by-step method to help you create better habits. It works because it's simple. You don't need complicated strategies. This template can be applied to any area of your life, business or personal. If applied consistently, it will help you achieve everything you want. There are three fundamental steps:

1. CLEARLY IDENTIFY YOUR BAD OR UNPRODUCTIVE HABITS

It's important that you really think about the future consequences of your bad habits. These may not show up tomorrow, next week or next month. The real impact could be years away. When you look at your unproductive behavior one day at a time, it may not look so bad. The smoker says, "What's a few cigarettes today? It helps me relax. I'm not wheezing and coughing." However, the days accumulate and twenty years later in the doctor's office, the X-rays are conclusive. Consider this: If you smoke ten cigarettes a day for twenty years, that's seventy-three thousand cigarettes. Do you think seventy-three-thousand cigarettes could have an impact on your lungs? Of course! In fact, the consequences can be deadly. **So when you examine your own bad habits, consider the long-term implications. Be totally honest. Your life may be at stake.**

2. DEFINE YOUR NEW
SUCCESSFUL HABIT

Usually this is just the opposite of your bad habit. In the smoker's example it would be, "Stop Smoking." What are you actually going to do? To motivate yourself, think about all the benefits and rewards for adopting your new successful habit. This helps you create a clear picture of what this new habit will do for you. **The more vividly you describe the benefits, the more likely you are to take action.**

3. CREATE A THREE-PART
ACTION PLAN

This is where the rubber meets the road. In the smoking example there are several options. Read how-to-stop-smoking literature. Start hypnosis therapy. Substitute something else when the desire for a cigarette arises. Place a bet with a friend to keep you accountable. Start a fresh air exercise program. Use a nicotine patch treatment. Stay away from other smokers. The important thing is to make a decision about which specific actions you are going to implement.

You must take action. Start with one habit that you really want to change. Focus on your three immediate action steps and put them into practice. Do it now. **Remember, nothing will change until you do.**

CONCLUSION

So now you know how habits really work and how to identify your bad ones. In addition, you have a proven formula that will jump-start your new successful habits. This will work equally well to improve your business habits as well as those in your personal life. We strongly encourage you to complete the Action Steps as described at the end of this chapter. Only when you commit to working through this Successful Habits Formula in writing will the true benefits become clear. Just keeping information in your head is short-lived. We want you to experience a transformation—in your results, and in your lifestyle. The next chapter will build on this strong foundation. It's all about focusing your power. Expect some major breakthroughs.

ACTION STEPS

Successful People I Want to Interview

The Successful Habits Formula

A. Successful People I Want to Interview

Make a list of people you respect, who have already done extremely well. Set a goal to invite each of them to breakfast, or lunch, or book an appointment at their office. Remember to take a notebook or a tape recorder with you to capture their best ideas.

	Name	Phone	Interview Date
1.	_____	_____	_____
2.	_____	_____	_____
3.	_____	_____	_____
4.	_____	_____	_____
5.	_____	_____	_____

B. The Successful Habits Formula

Look at the following examples. There are three sections—A, B and C. In section A, define the habit that is holding you back. Be specific. Then consider the consequences if you keep on repeating this behavior. Every action you take has consequences. Bad habits (negative behavior) produce negative consequences. Successful habits (positive behavior) produce benefits and rewards.

In section B, define your successful new habit. Usually all you need to do here is write the opposite of what you had in section A. If your bad habit was *No savings for the future*, your new habit could be *Save 10 percent of everything I earn*. In section C, list the three action steps you will take to turn your new habit into reality. Be specific. Pick a start date and then get going!

A. Habit That Is Holding Me Back

EXAMPLE:

No savings / investments for the future—spending all of my income.

CONSEQUENCES:

Unable to stop working in retirement years, no freedom of choice, poverty.

B. Successful New Habit

EXAMPLE:

Invest 10 percent of every dollar I earn.

BENEFITS:

Debt free, choose my own lifestyle, lots of time off, financial independence.

Three-Step Action Plan to Jump-Start My New Habit

1. Find an excellent financial planner to help me design a long-term game plan.

2. Set up a monthly automatic deduction investment account.

3. Make a list of where the money goes and eliminate unnecessary spending.

Start Date: Monday, March 5.

A. Habit That Is Holding Me Back

EXAMPLE:

Allowing distractions and interruptions throughout the day at work.

CONSEQUENCES:

Priority tasks never completed, less time for money-making activities, increased stress, longer work hours, reduced family time.

B. Successful New Habit

EXAMPLE:

Hire a personal assistant to screen phone calls, minimize interruptions and help with paperwork.

BENEFITS:

Able to complete projects, more time for money-making activities, reduced stress, more energy, better balance at home.

Three-Step Action Plan to Jump-Start My New Habit

1. Write up an ideal job description.

2. Advertise, interview and select the best candidate.

3. Train thoroughly.

Start Date: Tuesday, June 6.

On a separate sheet use the same format to record your own habits and action plans. DO IT NOW!

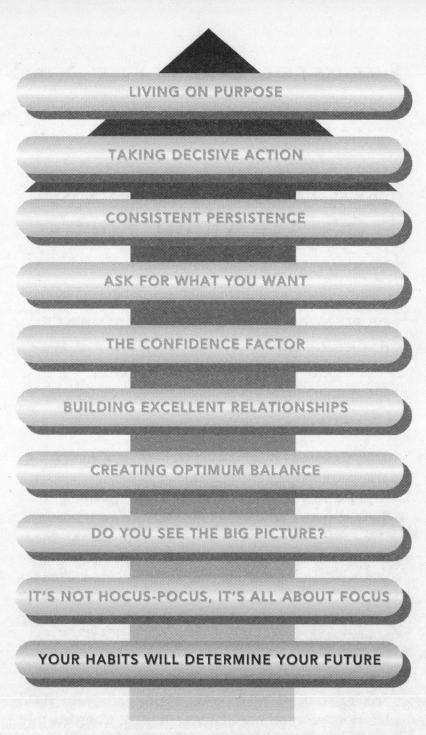

LIVING ON PURPOSE

TAKING DECISIVE ACTION

CONSISTENT PERSISTENCE

ASK FOR WHAT YOU WANT

THE CONFIDENCE FACTOR

BUILDING EXCELLENT RELATIONSHIPS

CREATING OPTIMUM BALANCE

DO YOU SEE THE BIG PICTURE?

IT'S NOT HOCUS-POCUS, IT'S ALL ABOUT FOCUS

YOUR HABITS WILL DETERMINE YOUR FUTURE

You've completed the first step—good effort!

FOCUSING STRATEGY NO. 2

It's Not Hocus-Pocus, It's All About Focus

"I NEVER COULD HAVE DONE WITHOUT THE HABITS
OF PUNCTUALITY, ORDER AND DILIGENCE...
THE DETERMINATION TO CONCENTRATE MYSELF
ON ONE SUBJECT AT A TIME."

—Charles Dickens

The entrepreneur's dilemma.
If you own your own business, or are planning to in
the near future, be aware of the Entrepreneur's Dilemma.
(You can also adapt this if you're in management
or any sort of supervisory role.) Here's the scenario:
You have this great idea for selling a new product
or providing a unique service. You visualize doing it
better than everyone else, and of course you're going
to make lots of money.

Initially, the main purpose of a business is to find
new customers and to keep the ones you already have.
Second, to make a fair profit. At the start, many small
business ventures are undercapitalized. Consequently,
the entrepreneur wears several hats, especially in the
first year, and puts in long days and nights, with not

much time for relaxing. However, it's an exciting time, putting deals together, meeting potential clients and improving the product line or service.

As a foundation is built, people and systems are put in place to create stability. Gradually the entrepreneur becomes more involved in day-to-day administrative duties. Paperwork increases and what started out as an exciting venture becomes a daily routine, with much more time spent putting out fires, handling people problems, tax challenges and monthly cash flow.

Does this sound familiar to you? Well, you're not alone. In our combined seventy-nine years of business experience, this is a very common situation. The dilemma is compounded because many entrepreneurs (and managers) are controllers. They find it difficult to let go, to allow other people to carry the load. Delegation is not their strength, and of course they are emotionally attached to their business. After all, they created it, weaned it and nurtured it. They understand every detail and, in their minds, nobody else can do these important everyday tasks as well as they can.

This is the ultimate Catch-22. There are more opportunities on the horizon, and bigger deals to close, but you can't get to them because you're stuck with the day-to-day routine. It's frustrating. So you think, "Maybe if I work harder and take a time management course, I can handle everything." This won't help. Working harder and longer hours will not solve your dilemma. Trust us, we've been there more than once. So what is the answer? Here it is in one sentence: **You must invest most of your time every week doing what you do best, and let others do what they do best.**

That's it in a nutshell.

Carl's one of those people who looked at the hand
he was dealt and began playing the cards.

Focus on those activities you do brilliantly, and from which
you produce extraordinary results. If you don't, you'll probably
create higher stress levels and ultimate burnout. Not a pleasant
picture. Your brilliant activities give you energy, keep you
excited and free you up to chase those new opportunities. But
you're probably wondering how to handle all that stuff that's
holding you back. You're right. It won't just disappear. Later in
this chapter, you'll find out specifically how to deal with those
monkeys and get them off your back.

Focus on Your
NATURAL Talents

It's critically important that you understand this. To help you get
the picture, let's take a look at the world of rock and roll music.

The Rolling Stones are one of the most prolific and enduring
rock-and-roll bands in history. To date, their career has spanned
almost forty years. Mick Jagger and his three friends are

now well into their fifties and still performing to sold-out stadiums around the world. You may not like their music, but it's hard to deny their success.

Let's go behind the scenes just before their concert begins. . . . The stage is set. It took over two hundred people to build this mammoth structure several stories tall and half the length of a football field. A convoy of more than twenty semi-trailers was required to haul it from the last location. Two private planes jet the key people, including the band, between cities. It's a huge operation. Their 1994 world tour earned more than $80 million profit, so it's obviously worth the effort!

A limousine pulls up back of the stage. The four band members step out and wait expectantly for their cue call. They exhibit a hint of nervousness mixed with excitement as seventy-thousand people erupt into a deafening roar when their names are announced. The Stones walk on stage and pick up their instruments. For the next two hours they perform brilliantly, sending their legions of fans home happy and satisfied. After the final encore they wave good-bye, step into the waiting limousine and exit the stadium.

They are masters at applying the habit of Priority Focus. That means they only do the things they are brilliant at— recording and performing on stage—period. Notice this. After the initial planning, they don't get involved with hauling equipment, figuring out the complex itinerary, setting up the stage or doing the hundreds of other tasks that need to be performed efficiently to make the tour a smooth operation, and ultimately profitable. Other skilled people look after the details. The Stones simply concentrate on what they do best —singing and performing.

There's a great message here for you, dear reader, and it's this: **When you focus most of your time and energy doing the things you are truly brilliant at, you eventually reap big rewards.** This is a fundamental truth. And it's critical to your future success.

PRACTICE, PRACTICE, PRACTICE

Let's take a look at a few other examples. Sports is a good one. Every champion athlete focuses on his or her unique talents and continually refines them to an ever-higher level of performance. No matter which sport you choose, the big winners all have one thing in common. They spend most of their time focusing on their strengths, the things they are naturally good at. Very little time is wasted on unproductive activities. And they practice, practice, practice, often several hours every day, honing their skills.

Basketball superstar Michael Jordan made hundreds of jump shots per day, every day, no matter what. George Best, one of the world's greatest soccer stars in the sixties, often stayed long after the other players had finished training. George knew his greatest assets were his feet. He would line up balls at varying distances from the goal posts and practice his scoring touch time after time. As a result he was Manchester United's top goal scorer for six consecutive seasons. It's this type of discipline that creates brilliance.

Notice how these top performers spend very little time on their weaknesses. Many of our school systems could learn from this. Often, children are told to focus on their weaker subjects and not spend so much time on the ones they do well in. The rationale is to develop a broad level of competency in many subjects instead of focusing on a few. Wrong! As business coach Dan Sullivan says, "If you spend too much time working on your weaknesses, all you end up with is a lot of strong weaknesses!" This doesn't give you a competitive edge in the marketplace or position you to be wealthy. It just keeps you average. In fact, it's an absolute insult to your integrity to major in minor things.

It's important to clearly differentiate your areas of brilliance from your weaknesses. You are probably good at a lot of things, even excellent in some. Others you are competent at, and if you are honest, there are some things you are totally useless at doing. On a scale of one to ten, you could plot your entire range of talents, one being your weakest and ten being your most brilliant. All your biggest rewards in life will come from spending the vast majority of your time in the areas that score a ten on your talent scale.

To clearly define your areas of brilliance, ask yourself a few questions. What do you do effortlessly—without a lot of study or preparation? And what do you do that other people find difficult? They marvel at your ability and can't come close to matching it. What opportunities exist in today's marketplace for your areas of brilliance? What could you create using your unique talents?

DISCOVER YOUR BRILLIANCE

We are all blessed with a few God-given talents. A big part of your life is discovering what these are, then utilizing and applying them to the best of your ability. The discovery process takes years for many people, and some never truly grasp what their greatest talents are. Consequently, their lives are less fulfilling. These people tend to struggle because they spend most of their time in jobs or businesses not suited to their strengths. It's like trying to force a square peg into a round hole. It doesn't work, and it causes a lot of stress and frustration.

Jim Carrey, the comedian and movie star who now commands twenty million dollars or more per picture, has a unique talent. He can twist and contort his face and body into the most unusual positions. At times it looks like he's made of rubber.

As a teenager, he spent hours every day practicing in front of the mirror. He also realized that he was brilliant at doing impersonations, and this became his early routine on the comedy circuit.

Carrey had many challenges along the road to stardom. At one point he took two years off as he battled low levels of confidence and uncertainty. However, he was so convinced of his comedic brilliance that he kept persisting until he was finally offered the main role in a movie called *Ace Ventura—Pet Detective*. This part gave him an opportunity to be totally bizarre. The movie became a huge box office hit and launched him on the path to super-stardom. Notice, in the early stages of his career he didn't attempt to play serious dramatic roles. His supreme talent was unusual comedy. The combination of a strong belief in his ability plus hours of daily practice eventually paid off big time.

Carrey improved his focus using visualization. He wrote himself a check for ten million dollars "For Services Rendered," dated it, and kept it in his pocket. When times were tough he would sit on a quiet hillside overlooking Los Angeles and imagine himself as a movie star. Then he'd reread the check as a reminder of his upcoming good fortune. Interestingly enough, a few years later he signed a deal for more than ten million dollars to star in *The Mask*. The date? Almost identical to the one written on the check he kept for so long in his pocket.

Priority focus works. Make it a part of your everyday plan and you'll experience dramatic jumps in productivity and income. We have a practical method that will make this easy for you and will also clarify your unique talents. It's called the Priority Focus Workshop, and is outlined on page 54. You need to be absolutely clear about what really goes on during your typical week. This reality check is usually very revealing. Basically, you make a list of all the activities you do at work in a typical week.

Most people, when they add up their total, score between ten and twenty. One of our clients had forty! It doesn't take a genius to figure out you can't do forty things each week and be truly focused. Even twenty activities is far too many. You'll be scattered and more prone to interruptions and distractions.

Many people are in shock when they see how much of their week is fragmented. "Overwhelmed," "out of control" and "stressed out" are typical phrases we hear a lot. However, completing the Priority Focus Workshop at the end of this chapter is a good starting point. At least you'll know where your time really goes. If you have trouble remembering all the things you do (another sign of doing too much) you can create a time-log. Simply record everything you do at fifteen-minute intervals. Just keep a notepad beside you. Do this for four or five days and you'll have a super-accurate record. It takes a little discipline, but you'll find it well worth the effort. This will clearly demonstrate how you are investing or wasting your time.

After completing the Priority Focus Workshop, the next step is to list three things you are brilliant at doing in your business. Remember the definition of brilliant? These are activities you do effortlessly, that give you energy, and that produce the greatest results and income for your business. By the way, if you are not directly involved with income-generating activities, who is? And are they doing a brilliant job of it? If not, you probably need to make some major decisions in the near future.

Now here's the next important question: In a typical week, what percentage of your time do you spend on your brilliant activities? Be totally honest. Often the answer is 15 to 25 percent. Even if 60 to 70 percent of your time is being used profitably, there's still a lot of room for improvement. What if you could refine this to 80 or 90 percent? Remember, your bottom-line income is directly linked to the amount of time spent in your areas of brilliance.

YOUR LEVEL OF BRILLIANCE WILL DETERMINE
THE SIZE OF YOUR OPPORTUNITIES IN LIFE.

The next step is to look at your original list of weekly activities and select three things you don't like doing, resist doing or are just no good at. There's no shame in admitting you have a few weaknesses. The most common answers here are paperwork, bookkeeping, setting up appointments or doing follow-up calls. All the little details that bring a project to completion are usually found on this list. Of course these need to be done, but not necessarily by you.

Have you noticed how these activities tend to drain your energy instead of expanding it? If this is true for you, wake up! When you keep on doing work that you detest, you need to remind yourself that this is futile. As well-known speaker Rosita Perez explains: "When the horse is dead, get off!" Stop flogging yourself. There are other options.

Are You a STARTER
or a Finisher?

This is a good time to consider why you like doing certain things and not others. Ask yourself this question: *Am I a starter or a finisher?* You probably do both to a degree, but what do you do more often? If you are a starter, you enjoy creating new projects, products and ideas that make things work better. The trouble with starters is that they aren't very good at finishing. All those little details we talked about earlier? That's boring stuff for starters. Most entrepreneurs are great starters. But after they get the ball rolling they tend to leave it and go on to something new. And what they often leave in their wake is a mess. Other people are then required to clean it all up. They are called finishers. Finishers love taking projects to completion. Often they aren't good at initiating the project (starters do that best); however, they are great at organizing what needs to be done and ensuring that the details are handled effectively.

So identify yourself. Knowing what your natural tendencies are is really helpful. If you're a starter, you can release the guilt you have about never getting things finished. Here's the key: Find a brilliant finisher to handle the details, and between you a lot more projects will be initiated and completed.

Let's give you a practical example. This book you're reading started out as an idea. Getting the book written—outlining the chapters, developing the content and having it all flow properly—is essentially the starter's job. Each of the three coauthors played an important role in this. However, to produce a finished product—including editing, printing, publishing and establishing distribution channels—required a lot of other people who are great finishers. Without them the original text would be collecting dust somewhere for years. So here's the next important question for you to consider: Who else could do the tasks you don't enjoy doing?

For example, if you don't enjoy doing the books, find an excellent bookkeeper. If you don't enjoy setting up appointments, have an experienced telemarketer or telemarketing service help you. You don't like selling, or "motivating" people? Maybe you need a great sales manager who can recruit, train and track results of the sales team every week. If tax time frustrates you, use the services of an outstanding tax specialist.

Now, before you start thinking, "I can't afford all these people— it will cost too much," think again. How much time will you free up by effectively delegating the work you don't like doing in the first place? Either you delegate or you'll stagnate. You can plan to phase this help in gradually, or consider contracting the work out using part-time services to keep your overhead low.

One of our clients with a thriving home-based business found a unique combination. She hired a woman to come in on Wednesday mornings to do her books. The same person then cleaned her home in the afternoon. She really enjoyed both types of work, always did a great job, and it was cost-effective.

If You're Feeling SWAMPED, Get Help!

LEARN TO LET GO OF THE "STUFF" IN YOUR LIFE

If you're in a situation where your business is expanding and your role in the company requires you to focus better, a great way to handle the expanded workload is to hire a personal assistant. If you find the right person, your life will dramatically change for the better, guaranteed. So let's take a closer look at this key strategy. First, a personal assistant is not a receptionist, secretary or someone whose duties you share with two or three other people. A true personal assistant is someone who is totally dedicated to you. He or she is brilliant at doing the tasks you don't like to do, or shouldn't be doing in the first place. The main role of this person is to free you up from all of the mundane jobs and stuff that clutter up your week. Their role is to protect you so that you can focus entirely on your most brilliant activities.

The careful selection of this key person is critical to your future health. Select the right person and your life will become a lot simpler, your stress levels will noticeably diminish and you'll have a lot more fun. Select the wrong person and you will only compound your current problems.

Here are a few tips: First, make a list of all the tasks you want your assistant to be 100 percent responsible for. Most of these are the activities you want to discard from your own weekly list. When you interview, have the top three applicants complete a personal profile evaluation. There are several good ones on the market. (See Resource Guide, page 303.)

You can have a profile made up of the ideal candidate before you start your selection campaign. Run profiles on your top three interviews and compare these to the ideal candidate profile. Usually the person who is the closest match to your ideal profile will do the best job. Of course, you must take into account other factors, such as attitude, honesty, integrity, previous track record and so on.

Be careful not to select someone just like you. Remember, you want this person to complement your skills. Hiring someone with the same likes and dislikes as yourself will probably create a bigger mess.

A couple of other points worth noting: If you are a controller, someone who won't let go of things easily, it is essential that you surrender to your personal assistant! Before you panic about the word *surrender,* take a closer look. Controllers typically have a mindset that says nobody can do these things as well as they can. That may be true. However, what if your assistant could do these tasks 75 percent as well initially? With proper training and good communication every week, your well-chosen assistant will eventually do these activities as well as you, and will outperform you in many of them. So give up the need for total control—it's holding you back. Gleefully surrender to someone with better organizational ability and a passion for looking after the details.

DILBERT *reprinted by permission of United Feature Syndicate, Inc.*

Just in case you're still hanging on to the notion that you can do it all, ask yourself, "How much am I worth per hour?" If you have never taken the time to do this, do it now. Check out the chart below.

How Much Are You Really Worth?

Your Income	Income Per Hour	Your Income	Income Per Hour
$30,000	$15	$120,000	$60
$40,000	$20	$130,000	$65
$50,000	$25	$140,000	$70
$60,000	$30	$150,000	$75
$70,000	$35	$160,000	$80
$80,000	$40	$170,000	$85
$90,000	$45	$180,000	$90
$100,000	$50	$190,000	$95
$110,000	$55	$200,000	$100

Based on working 250 days per year, eight hours per day.

Hopefully your dollar figure is high. Then why are you running around doing low-income activities? Give them up!

Last comment on personal assistants: It is absolutely imperative that you schedule time each day or at least once a week to discuss your agenda with your personal assistant. Communicate, communicate, communicate! The number-one reason these potentially great relationships fall apart is simply a lack of communication. Make sure your assistant knows what you want to spend your time on.

Also, allow reasonable time for your new "partner" to learn your systems. Indicate the key people you want to spend time with. Set up screening methods with your assistant that protect you from all the potential distractions and interruptions, so you can focus on what you do best. Be open to all input and feedback. Often, your assistant will create better ways to organize your office. Rejoice if this happens—you've found a real winner.

Now let's consider how you can implement the habit of Priority Focus into your personal life, so you have more time to relax with family and friends, or enjoy a particular hobby or sport.

No matter where you live, keeping a home in first-class condition requires maintenance. If you have kids, the problem is magnified three or four times, depending on their age and ability to destroy! Think of all the time spent in a typical week cooking and cleaning, washing up, fixing things, cutting grass, servicing the car, running errands and so on. Have you noticed there's no end to this? These activities have a habit of being continually recycled. It's the ongoing stuff of life. Depending on your mood, you either enjoy it, put up with it or resent it.

What if you could find a way to minimize it, or even better, eliminate it? How would you feel? Free, more relaxed, able to enjoy more of the things you'd prefer to do? Of course!

What you're about to read in the next few minutes may require a new way of thinking, a leap of faith to some degree. However, focus on the rewards and benefits instead of the initial cost. They will far outweigh any investment you make. To put it simply, if you want to free up your time—get help. There's all sorts of good help available. Most of the help you require will be part time. For example, hire someone to do house cleaning once a week, or every other week.

LES:
We found a wonderful couple who have cleaned our home for twelve years. They love their work. They are honest, caring people. Not surprisingly, they do a fantastic job. The house is cleaned from top to bottom. The investment? Only sixty dollars per visit. The benefit? Several hours freed up and more energy to enjoy the week.

Is there a handyman in your neighborhood who is semi-retired and loves to fix things? Many experienced older people have terrific skills and are looking for little part-time jobs to keep them busy. These activities give them a sense of fulfillment. Usually, money isn't their primary need.

Make a list of all the things at home that need servicing, fixing or upgrading. You know, all those little jobs that you never seem to get around to because your time is all used up. Release your stress and hire someone.

You'll be making a contribution so that someone else can continue to use their skills. And you can eliminate hours and hours of frustration trying to do all those fix-up jobs that you're no good at, and don't even have the tools for. Maybe you weren't supposed to be a plumber, electrician, carpenter and all-around handyman.

What about outside the house? Cutting grass, weeding, trimming, watering plants and bushes, raking. Now here's a great opportunity for you. Check out the neighborhood. Look for an enterprising kid who wants to earn some money so he or she can buy a new bike, Rollerblades or the latest CDs. Contrary to popular opinion, there are lots of young people who work hard and get the job done right. Find one. It's inexpensive, compared to the professionals. And don't be cheap. A job well done deserves fair compensation.

If you are mentally blocking this idea, consider again. Think of all the extra time you'll have. You could reinvest those valuable hours into your own best money-making activities, or have real time to relax and re-energize with your family and friends. Maybe this new freedom from weekly "stuff" allows you to embark on that hobby you've always wanted to pursue, or enjoy more time for sports. And please, do it without feeling guilty. After all, you deserve time off, don't you?

Remember, you only have so much time every week. Life becomes more enjoyable when you are operating on a highly efficient, low-maintenance schedule. Now if you genuinely enjoy doing some of these tasks around the house (and you need to be totally honest about this), then go ahead. But only if it's truly relaxing or gives you a feeling of contentment.

The 4-D Solution

It's vital that you effectively separate so-called urgent tasks from your most important priorities. Putting out fires all day long in your office is, as time management expert Harold Taylor says, "Giving in to the tyranny of the urgent." That means every time a telephone rings you jump to answer it. When a letter or fax shows up on your desk you react to the request immediately, even if it does not require an immediate answer.

Instead, focus on your priorities. Whenever a choice to do or not do something has to be made, use the 4-D Formula to help you prioritize. You have four options to choose from:

1. Dump It
Learn to say "No, I choose not to do this." Be firm.

2. Delegate It
These are tasks that need to be done, but you are not the person to do them. Hand them over to someone else, with no guilt or regrets. Simply ask, "Who else could do this?"

3. Defer It
These are issues that you do need to work on, but not right away. They can genuinely be deferred. Schedule a specific time at a later date to handle this type of work.

4. Do It
Do it now. Important projects need your attention right away, so get started today. Move forward. Give yourself a reward for completing these projects. Don't make excuses. Remember, if you don't take prompt action you'll end up with all those nasty consequences.

Boundaries of
BRILLIANCE

Priority Focus is all about setting new boundaries that you do not cross. First you need to decide very clearly what those boundaries are, in the office and at home. Discuss these new parameters with the most important people in your life. They need to understand why you are making these improvements. You will also need their support to keep you on track. Most business people get into trouble because they spend too much time on things they don't know much about. Stick to what you know best and keep refining these talents. (This is especially good advice when it comes to investing your money!)

To give you a clearer picture of setting boundaries, picture a small child on a sandy beach at the ocean. There is a safe area of water cordoned off by a series of plastic buoys connected by a thick rope. Attached to the rope, a heavy-duty net ensures that the child cannot go beyond this point. The water within this area is only a few feet deep. It's calm, and the child can play happily without any concerns.

On the other side of the rope there are strong currents, and a steep underwater slope increases the depth to twenty feet. Powerboats and jet skis zoom up and down this stretch of water. Warning signs proclaim, "Danger. No Swimming. Do Not Enter." As long as the child stays within the boundaries, everything is fine. Beyond that point it's dangerous. Here's the message: When you play around in areas that destroy your focus, you go beyond safe boundaries. It's very dangerous to your mental and financial health out there. When you stay within your boundaries of brilliance, that is, focus on what you do best, you can splash around safely all day long.

The Power of NO

Staying within these boundaries requires a new level of self-discipline. That means being more conscious every day of the activities you choose to spend your time on. To avoid drifting away from your focus, ask yourself at regular intervals, "Is what I'm doing right now helping me to achieve my goals?" This takes practice. It also means saying "No" a lot more. There are three areas to examine:

1. Yourself
The biggest battle going on every day is between your own ears. We talk ourselves in and out of situations constantly. Put a stop to this. When that little negative voice in the back of your head demands attention and tries to get to the forefront of your thinking, take a time-out. Give yourself a quick mental pep talk. Focus on the benefits and rewards of sticking to your priorities, and remind yourself of the negative consequences if you don't.

2. Other People
A variety of other people may attempt to destroy your focus. Sometimes they wander into your office for a chat because you have an open-door policy. Here's how to fix that—change your policy. Close your door for at least part of the day when you want to be left alone so you can concentrate on your next big project. If that doesn't work you might put up a sign that says, "Do Not Disturb. Any Intruders Will Be Fired!"

Top California business consultant and best-selling author Danny Cox uses this vivid analogy when it comes to focusing on priorities. He says, "If you gotta frog to swaller, don't look at it too long. If you've got more than one to swaller, swaller the biggest one first!" In other words, tackle your most important priorities immediately.

Don't be like most people, who have six things on their daily To-Do list and start doing the easiest, low-priority tasks first. At the end of the day the number-one priority, the biggest frog, is still sitting there untouched.

Here's an idea. Buy yourself a big plastic frog and place it on your desk when you are working on a top-priority project. Alert your staff that the green frog means absolutely no interruptions. Who knows, maybe this will spread to the rest of your team and you'll have a more productive office.

3. The telephone

Perhaps the most insidious intrusion of all is the telephone. Isn't it amazing how people allow this little piece of hardware to control their day? If you require two hours of uninterrupted time, unplug the phone. And turn off your cellular or any other device that may distract you. E-mail, voice mail and answering machines can help you avoid these annoying interruptions. Use them wisely—obviously there are times when you need to be available. Pre-schedule your appointments just like a doctor—2 P.M. to 5 P.M. on Mondays, 9 A.M. to 12 noon on Tuesdays. Then choose the most productive time to make your phone calls, for example, 8 A.M. to 10 A.M. If you want to enjoy bigger results, there are times when you need to be secluded from the outside world. Give up the habit of automatically reaching for the phone every time it rings. Say "No." And take charge at home, too.

Our time-management friend Harold Taylor recalls an incident in the days when he was "addicted" to a ringing telephone. On arriving home he heard the phone ring. In his haste to get there before it stopped, he broke down the screen door, gashing his leg in the process. Undaunted, he hurdled several pieces of furniture in a desperate bid to find out who was calling. Just before the final ring, he lifted the receiver, gasping, and said "Hello?" A demure voice replied, "Do you subscribe to the *Globe and Mail*?"

Here's another suggestion: To avoid those telemarketing calls, unplug your home phone at mealtimes. Isn't that when they call most often? Your family will appreciate the opportunity for some real discussion instead of these annoying intrusions. Don't allow your better future and your peace of mind to be put on hold through constant interruptions. Consciously stop yourself when you start doing things that are not in your best interest. From now on those wasteful activities are off limits. You don't go there anymore.

Setting New
BOUNDARIES

This section is all about implementing these new boundaries. It requires a change in your thinking. And most important, it requires action. So get started right away. Here's a good example to help you. In the medical profession doctors have become particularly proactive in defining boundaries. Because of the large number of patients, many doctors need to streamline their activities. One of the best focusing experts is Dr. Kent Remington. Kent is a highly respected dermatologist specializing in laser therapy. Over the years his practice has grown steadily because of the excellent results his patients enjoy. Consequently, efficient time-management strategies and the ability to focus on his areas of brilliance are essential.

Dr. Remington sees his first patient at 7:30 A.M. (Yes, top achievers are usually up early.) On arrival, patients are checked in and then directed to one of several waiting rooms. A medical assistant reviews the file and then briefs the patient, at the same time asking questions to get an update on his current condition. Instructions are given in readiness for Dr. Remington's arrival. He appears a few minutes later, having first read the file placed on the door by his assistant.

This team approach allows Dr. Remington to focus on treating the patient. The preliminaries are all handled ahead of time. After his visit, further instructions are carried out by his capable staff. In this manner, many more patients are able to be treated, and waiting time is minimal. Every person on the team is focused on the few things they do extremely well, resulting in a superbly efficient enterprise. How does this compare to other offices? Well, you probably know the answer to that one!

What else can you do to jump to the next level of efficiency and better focus? Here's an important tip:

Be aware of old habits that may be pulling you away from your focus.

For example, excessive TV watching. If you're used to lying on the couch for three hours every night and your only exercise is pushing the remote control, you may want to take a look at that. Some parents understand the consequences of this and limit TV watching for their kids to a few hours on the weekend. Why don't you do the same for yourself? Here's a challenge for you. Take a whole week off from watching TV and see how much you can get done. You'll be amazed.

A study by the Nielsen Company, which specializes in recording how many people watch TV, what they watch and how often they watch, offers some interesting statistics. On average, people watch TV 6.5 hours per day! The key word in the last sentence is *average*. That means some people watch even more than that. At this rate, in an average life span you would spend about eleven years of your life watching TV! By the way, if you just stopped watching the commercials, you'd save about three years. Yes, we know old habits die hard, but this life is not a practice session. It's the real thing. If you want to make the most of it, start kicking your old habits out the door. Develop a fresh set of strategies that will help you create a lifestyle that's rich in every dimension.

JACK:

When I went to work for W. Clement Stone in 1969, he sat me down for a one-hour interview. His first question was, "Do you watch television?" He then asked me, "How many hours a day do you think you watch?" After a short calculation I answered, "About three hours a day."

Mr. Stone looked me directly in the eye and said, "I want you to cut out one hour a day; reduce your TV-watching time to two hours per day. If you do that, you'll be saving 365 hours per year. If you divide that by a forty-hour work week, you'll see that you'll have added about nine and a half additional weeks of productivity to your life. That's like getting two additional months every year!"

I agreed that this was a great leveraging concept, and then I asked Mr. Stone what he thought I should do with this extra hour every day. He suggested I read books in my field of motivation, psychology, education, training and self-esteem. He also suggested I listen to educational and motivational cassettes, take classes and study a foreign language.

I took his advice and it has made a profound difference in my life.

There are no magic formulas.

We hope you are getting the message that achieving what you want in life does not require magic formulas or secret ingredients. It's simply focusing on what works versus what doesn't work. However, many people focus on the wrong things. Those who live from paycheck to paycheck every month have not studied how to acquire financial intelligence. They have focused more on spending instead of acquiring a strong asset base for the future.

Many people are stuck in a job or career they don't enjoy because they have not focused on developing their areas of brilliance. There's a similar lack of awareness with health issues. The American Medical Association recently announced that 63 percent of American men and 55 percent of American women (greater than twenty-five years of age) are overweight. Obviously there's a lot of people out there focused on eating too much and exercising too little!

Here's the point. Carefully study what's working and what's not working in your life. What creates your biggest victories? What are you focusing on that's giving you poor results? This requires clear thinking.

In the next chapter, we'll show you step by step how to develop what we call *unusual clarity*. You'll also learn how to set "big picture" goals. Then we'll equip you with a unique focusing system to ensure you achieve them. These strategies have worked wonderfully well for us. They will work equally well for you too.

SUCCESS ISN'T MAGIC OR HOCUS-POCUS

It's Simply Learning How To Focus.

CONCLUSION

We've covered a lot in this chapter. Read over this material several times until you are thoroughly familiar with these concepts. Adapt these ideas to your own situation and then take action. Again we emphasize the importance of doing the Action Steps that follow. These are essential tools to help you make priority focus a habit. In a few weeks you will really notice the difference. Productivity will surge and your personal relationships will be enriched. You'll feel healthier, and of course you will be making a significant contribution to other people. As well, you'll have more fun and the opportunity to reach some personal targets that you didn't have time for before.

As a bonus, your new focus will put more money in your bank account. You'll discover that the benefits and rewards are huge when you choose to be a master of priority focus. Start today!

ACTION STEPS

**The Priority Focus
Workshop**

The Priority Focus Workshop

A practical six-step guide to maximize your time and productivity.

A. List all of the business activities at work that use up your time.

For example: phone calls, meetings, paperwork, projects, sales, follow-up procedures. Subdivide major categories such as phone calls and meetings. Include everything, even the five-minute tasks. Be specific, clear and brief. Use additional paper if you have more than ten.

1. _____

2. _____

3. _____

4. _____

5. _____

6. _____

7. _____

8. _____

9. _____

10. _____

B. Describe three things that you are brilliant at doing in business.

1. _____

2. _____

3. _____

C. Name the three most important activities that produce income for your business.

1. _____

2. _____

3. _____

D. Name the three most important activities that you don't like to do or are weak at doing.

1. _____

2. _____

3. _____

E. Who could do these for you?

1. _____

2. _____

3. _____

F. What one time-consuming activity are you going to say "No" to or delegate right away?

_____

What immediate benefit will result from this decision?

_____

_____

LIVING ON PURPOSE

TAKING DECISIVE ACTION

CONSISTENT PERSISTENCE

ASK FOR WHAT YOU WANT

THE CONFIDENCE FACTOR

BUILDING EXCELLENT RELATIONSHIPS

CREATING OPTIMUM BALANCE

DO YOU SEE THE BIG PICTURE?

IT'S NOT HOCUS-POCUS, IT'S ALL ABOUT FOCUS

YOUR HABITS WILL DETERMINE YOUR FUTURE

Your momentum is picking up—on to number three.

Do You See The Big Picture?

"THE LIFE WHICH IS UNEXAMINED IS
NOT WORTH LIVING."

—Socrates

**Peter Daniels is an unusual man whose life reads like
a Horatio Alger story.**
Born in Australia, his parents were third-generation
welfare recipients used to being poor. Peter attended
elementary school in Adelaide. Because of a learning
disability, he found it difficult to understand and assemble
words. Consequently he was labeled stupid by teachers
who were either too busy or didn't care enough to
find out why he struggled. One teacher in particular,
Miss Phillips, would make Peter stand in front of the
class where she would berate him with, "Peter Daniels,
you're a bad boy and you'll never amount to anything."

Of course this did nothing for his self-esteem. As a
result, he failed every grade in school. One of his
earliest career choices was to become a bricklayer.
A few years later, married with a young family, he
decided to go into business for himself. The first
venture failed miserably and he was broke within

a year. Undaunted, he saw another opportunity and channeled his energy into making it a success. A similar fate awaited him; he was broke within eighteen months. With steely determination to overcome these setbacks, Peter again launched himself into the competitive world of business, only to end up broke for a third time. He now had the unbelievable track record of going broke three times within five years.

Most people would give up at this point. Not Peter Daniels. His attitude was, "I'm learning and I haven't made the same mistake twice. This is excellent experience." Asking his wife Robena to support him one more time, he decided to sell residential and commercial real estate. One skill Peter had honed over the years was his ability to persuade. He was a naturally good promoter. Much of this came from the necessity to deal with a constant stream of creditors who wanted payment. During the next ten years the name Peter Daniels became synonymous with residential and commercial real estate. Through careful selection and astute negotiation he accumulated a portfolio worth several million dollars.

Today Peter Daniels is an internationally acclaimed businessman who has created successful ventures in many countries around the world. His friends include royalty, heads of state, and the leading movers and shakers of the commercial world. He is also a philanthropist who is passionate about helping others, and whose generosity has funded many Christian endeavors.

When asked what turned his life from triple indebtedness to unprecedented success, he replied, "I scheduled time to think. In fact, I reserve one day a week on my calendar just to think. All of my greatest ideas, opportunities and money-making ventures started with the days I took off to think. I used to lock myself away in my den with strict instructions to my family that under no circumstances was I to be disturbed." The same strategy worked for Einstein who actually did his pondering in a special thinking chair.

And it transformed the life of Peter Daniels from school failure to multimillionaire. By the way, Peter has now written several bestselling books, one of which was titled *Miss Phillips, You Were Wrong!*, a reminder to his old teacher not to give up too quickly on her students.

Developing Unusual
CLARITY

Another reason why Peter Daniels enjoys continuous success, is his ability to create exciting pictures of the future. Most people don't have a clear picture of what they want. At best it's fuzzy. What about you?

Do you schedule time regularly to think about your better future? You may say, "It's okay for Peter Daniels, but I could never find a day each week to think. I need an extra day just to keep up with my present commitments."

Well, could you start with five minutes and gradually build it to an hour? Wouldn't that be a good use of your time, spending sixty minutes each week creating an exciting picture of your future? Most people spend more time planning a two-week vacation than they do designing their life, especially their financial future.

Here's a promise: If you make the effort to develop the habit of unusual clarity, the payoff for you down the road will be tremendous. Whether your desire is to be debt-free, financially independent, enjoy more time off for fun or build wonderful loving relationships, you can achieve all of this, and more, if you have a crystal-clear picture of what you want.

In the next few pages, you'll discover a comprehensive strategy that will give you a "big screen" picture of the years ahead. In the following chapters you'll also learn how to strengthen and support this future vision through the use of weekly game plans, Mastermind Groups and specific mentors. In fact, you'll develop a solid fortress of support that will render you impenetrable to negativity and doubt. So let's get started.

BY THE WAY, HAVE YOU NOTICED THAT KIDS HAVE UNUSUAL CLARITY? HERE'S SOME PROOF:

 "I've learned that you can be in love with four girls at the same time."

—Age nine

"I've learned that just when I get my room the way I like it, Mom makes me clean it up."

—Age thirteen

 "I've learned that you can't hide a piece of broccoli in a glass of milk."

—Age seven

SOURCE: *Live and Learn and Pass It On* by H. Jackson Brown Jr.

The Purpose of
GOALS

Are you a conscious goal-setter? If you are, great. However, please read the information we are about to share. Chances are you'll benefit from the reinforcement, plus this expanded vision of setting goals may give you new insights.

If you don't consciously set goals, that is, you don't plan on paper or set targets for the weeks, months and years ahead, then pay very close attention to this information. It can dramatically improve your life.

First, what is the definition of a goal? If you're not clear on this, you may get derailed before you start. We've heard lots of answers over the years. Here's one of the best:

A GOAL IS THE ONGOING PURSUIT OF A
WORTHY OBJECTIVE UNTIL ACCOMPLISHED

Consider the individual words that make up this sentence. "Ongoing" means it's a process, because goals take time. "Pursuit" indicates a chase may be involved. There will likely be some obstacles and hurdles to overcome. "Worthy" shows that the chase will be worthwhile, that there's a big enough reward at the end to endure the tough times. "Until accomplished" suggests you'll do whatever it takes to get the job done. Not always easy, but essential if you want a life full of outstanding accomplishments.

Setting and achieving goals is one of the best ways to measure your life's progress and create unusual clarity. Consider the alternative—just drifting along aimlessly, hoping that one day good fortune will fall into your lap with little or no effort on your part. Wake up! You've got more chance of finding a grain of sugar on a sandy beach.

The Top-10 Goals
CHECKLIST

Talk show host David Letterman has wacky top-10 lists that people actually pay money for. Here's a list that has a lot more value—a checklist to make sure you're using a successful framework to set goals. It's like a smorgasbord. So pick out what seems to fit you best and use it.

1. Your most important goals must be yours.

This sounds obvious. However, a common mistake made by thousands of people across the country is to allow their main goals to be designed by someone else. This could be the company you work for, your industry, your boss, your bank or mortgage company, or your friends and neighbors.

In our workshops, we teach people to ask themselves the question, "What do I really want?" At the end of one of these sessions a man came up to us and said, "I'm a dentist. I only went into this profession because my mother wanted me to. I hated it. One day I drilled through the side of a patient's mouth and ended up having to pay him $475,000."

Here's the point: When you let other people or society determine your definition of success, you're sabotaging your future. So put a stop to that right away.

Think about this for a moment. The media has one of the strongest influences on you when it comes to making decisions. And most people buy into it daily. In fact, if you live in a fairly large city you are bombarded with at least twenty-seven hundred advertising messages every day. There are constant radio and TV commercials, plus billboards, newspapers and magazines contributing to this onslaught. Our thinking is consciously and subliminally being influenced non-stop. The media defines success as the clothes we wear, the cars we drive, the homes we live in and the vacations we take. Depending on how you measure up in these categories, you're branded a success or a failure.

Do you want more evidence? What's on the front of most popular magazines? A cover girl—someone whose glamorous figure and hairstyle are perfect, with not a wrinkle in sight. Or a male hunk whose muscular torso wasn't formed by merely working out five minutes a day on an Ab-Roller. What's the message? If you don't look like this you're a failure. Is it any wonder that many teenagers struggle with eating disorders like bulimia and anorexia, when society's peer pressure doesn't tolerate anyone who's remotely out of shape or who has average looks. This is ridiculous!

Decide now to create *your* definition of success and stop worrying about what the rest of the world thinks. For years, Sam Walton, the founder of Wal-Mart, currently the largest and most successful retail store chain in history, enjoyed driving an old Ford pickup truck even though he was one of the wealthiest men in the country. When asked why he didn't drive a vehicle better suited to his position, he'd reply, "Well, I just like my old truck." So forget about image and set goals that are right for you.

And by the way, if you really want to drive a luxury car, or live in a beautiful home or create an exciting lifestyle, go for it! Just make sure that it's what *you* want, and that you're doing it for the right reasons.

2. Your goals must be meaningful.

Well-known speaker Charlie "Tremendous" Jones recalls the early days of his career like this: "I remember when I was struggling to get my business off the ground. There were long nights at the office when I'd take my jacket off, roll it up to make a pillow and grab a few hours sleep on my desk." Charlie's goals were so meaningful that he did whatever it took to help his business grow. If that meant spending a few nights sleeping in the office, so be it. That's total commitment, a crucial ingredient if you want to become the best you can be. In his early thirties, Charlie went on to build an insurance brokerage that produced more than $100 million per year in revenue. And that was back in the early 1960s, when $100 million was still a lot of money! (Have you noticed that big company revenues are now measured in billions?)

When you prepare to write down your future goals, ask yourself, "What's really important to me? What's the purpose of doing this? What am I prepared to give up to make this happen?" This thinking process will increase your clarity. It's critically important that you do this. Your reasons for charting a new course of action are what give you the drive and energy to get up in the morning, even on the days you don't feel like it.

Ask yourself, "What are the rewards and benefits for this new discipline?" Focus on the exciting new lifestyle you can enjoy by committing yourself now to consistent action.

If this doesn't get your adrenaline pumping, visualize the alternative. If you just keep on doing the same things that you've always done, what will your lifestyle be like five years from now, ten years from now, twenty years from now? What words will describe your future financial picture if you don't make any changes? What about your health, relationships and the amount of time you have off for fun? Will you be enjoying a lot more freedom or still be working too many hours a week?

AVOID THE "IF ONLY" SYNDROME.

Master philosopher Jim Rohn astutely observes that there are two major pains in life. One is the pain of discipline, the other is the pain of regret. Discipline weighs ounces, but regret weighs tons when you allow your life to drift along unfulfilled. You don't want to look back years later, saying, "If only I had taken that business opportunity; if only I had saved and invested regularly; if only I had spent more time with my family; if only I had taken care of my health. . . ." Remember, it's your choice. Ultimately, you are responsible for every choice you make, so choose wisely. Commit yourself now to creating goals that will guarantee your future freedom and success.

3. Your goals must be specific and measurable.

Here's where most people lose it. It's one of the main reasons individuals never achieve what they're capable of. They never accurately define what they want. Vague generalizations and wishy-washy statements aren't good enough. For example, if someone says, "My goal is to be financially independent," what does that really mean? For some people financial independence is having $50 million saved and invested. For others it's earning $100,000 a year. For someone else it's being debt-free. What is it for you? What's your number? If this is an important goal for you, take the time now to figure it out.

Your definition of happiness requires the same scrutiny. Just "wanting more time with my family," doesn't cut it. How much time, when, how often, what will you do with it, with whom? Here are three words that will help you tremendously: **Be more specific.**

LES:
One of our clients in The Achievers Coaching Program indicated his goal for better health was to start exercising. He was feeling sluggish and wanted more energy. "Start exercising" is a very poor definition of this goal. It's too

general. There's no way to measure it. So we said, "Be more specific." He added, "I want to exercise thirty minutes a day, four times a week."

Guess what we said next? You're right. "Be more specific." By repeating this question several times his health goal was redefined as follows: To exercise for thirty minutes a day, four times a week, Monday, Wednesday, Friday and Saturday from 7 A.M. to 7:30 A.M. His routine consists of ten minutes stretching and twenty minutes on his exercise bike. What a difference! Now we can easily track his progress. If we show up at the scheduled times to observe, he will either be doing what he says, or not. Now he's accountable for results.

Here's the point: When you set a goal, challenge yourself with the words, "Be more specific." Keep repeating this until your goal is crystal-clear and measurable. By doing this, you'll dramatically increase your chances of achieving the desired result.

REMEMBER, A GOAL WITHOUT A NUMBER IS JUST A SLOGAN

It's important that you have a system for measuring your progress. The Achievers Focusing System is a unique game plan we use that will make this easy for you. It's laid out in detail in the Action Steps at the end of this chapter.

4. Your goals must be flexible.

Why is this important? There are a couple of reasons. First, you don't want to design a system that is so rigid and cast in stone that you feel suffocated by it. For example, if you design an exercise program for better health, you may want to vary the times during the week and the type of exercise, so it doesn't get boring. An experienced personal fitness coach can help you customize a program that's fun, has lots of variety and still guarantees the results you want.

Here's the second reason: A flexible plan allows you the freedom to change course if a genuine opportunity comes along that is so good you'd be crazy not to pursue it. A word of caution here. This doesn't mean you start chasing after every idea that comes by your door. Entrepreneurs are famous for getting distracted and losing their focus. Remember, you don't need to be involved with every new idea—just focusing on one or two can make you happy and wealthy.

© 1974 JIM UNGER

"D'yer ever feel you're on the verge of an incredible breakthrough?"

5. Your goals must be challenging and exciting.

Many business owners seem to "plateau" a few years after the start of a new venture. They lose the early excitement that was originally fueled by uncertainty and the risks involved to

67

get their product or service into the marketplace. They become operators and administrators and much of the work seems repetitive and uninspiring.

When you set goals that are exciting and challenging, you acquire an edge that prevents you from settling into a life of boredom. To do this you must force yourself to jump out of your comfort zone. This might be a little scary because you never know for sure if you'll land on your feet. Here's a good reason to push yourself—you will always learn more about life and your capacity to succeed when you are uncomfortable. Often when your back is up against the wall of fear, the greatest breakthroughs occur.

John Goddard, the famous explorer and adventurer, the man *Reader's Digest* calls "the real Indiana Jones," is a wonderful role model for this concept. At the tender age of fifteen he sat down and made a list of 127 challenging lifetime goals he wanted to accomplish. Here are a few of them: Explore eight of the world's major rivers including the Nile, the Amazon and the Congo; climb sixteen of the highest mountains including Mount Everest, Mount Kenya and the Matterhorn; learn to fly a plane, circumnavigate the globe (he's done this four times); visit the North and South Poles; read the Bible from cover to cover; play the flute and violin; and study primitive cultures in twelve countries including Borneo, the Sudan and Brazil. By the time he turned fifty he had successfully completed more than one hundred of the goals on his list.

When asked what caused him to create this fascinating list in the first place, he replied, "Two reasons. First, I was fed up with adults telling me what to do and what not to do with my life. Second, I didn't want to be fifty years old and realize I hadn't really accomplished anything."[1]

---

[1] Mark did an in-depth audio recording about John Goddard accomplishing the impossible. For more details call toll free 800-433-2314.

You may not want to challenge yourself the way John Goddard has done, but don't settle for mediocrity. Think big. Create goals that get you so excited you can hardly sleep at night. Life has a lot to offer—why shouldn't you enjoy your fair share?

6. Your goals must be in alignment with your values.

Synergy and flow are two words that describe any process moving effortlessly forward to completion. When your goals are in synch with your core values, the mechanism for this harmony is set in motion. What are your core values? Anything you feel strongly about that resonates at a deeper level of your being. These are fundamental beliefs that are well-developed and have molded your character for years. Honesty and integrity, for example. (You can make your own list on page 84.) When you do something that contradicts these values, your intuition, or gut feeling, will serve as a reminder that something isn't right.

Suppose you owed a lot of money and there is incredible pressure on you to repay the loan. In fact, the situation is almost unbearable. One day a friend approaches you and says, "I've figured out a way for us to make some easy money. All we need to do is rob the bank! The biggest monthly deposits are being made tomorrow. I've got a foolproof plan—we'll be in and out of there in twenty minutes." You now have an interesting dilemma. On the one hand, your desire to ease your financial concerns is strong and getting your hands on that much money may be very appealing. However, if your honesty value is stronger than your desire for the money, you won't rob the bank because you know it's not the right thing to do.

And even if your "friend" did a super sales job and actually convinced you to go ahead with the heist, afterwards you'd be churning inside. That's your honesty factor reacting. The guilt would haunt you forever.

When you harness your core values to positive, exciting, purposeful goals, decision-making becomes easy. There is no internal conflict holding you back—this creates an energy surge that will propel you to much higher levels of success.

7. Your goals must be well balanced.

If you had to live your life over again, what would you do differently? When people in their eighties are asked this question, they never say, "I'd spend more time at the office," or "I'd go to more board meetings."

No, instead they clearly indicate they'd travel more, spend more time with their family and have a lot more fun. So when you're setting goals make sure you include areas that give you time to relax and enjoy the finer things in life. Working yourself to a standstill every week is a surefire way to create burnout and ill health. Life's too short to miss the good stuff.

In chapter 4, Creating Optimum Balance, you'll discover an excellent strategy that will make it easy for you to enjoy a well-balanced lifestyle.

8. Your goals must be realistic.

At first this sounds contradictory to the previous comments about thinking big. However, a measure of reality will ensure that you get better results. Where most people are unrealistic about their goals is in determining the amount of time it will take to achieve them. Make a point of remembering this sentence:

THERE ARE NO SUCH THINGS AS UNREALISTIC GOALS, ONLY UNREALISTIC TIME FRAMES.

If you're earning thirty-thousand dollars a year and your goal is to be a millionaire in three months, that's definitely unrealistic. When it comes to new business ventures, a good rule of thumb is to double the time you think it will take for the initial start-up. Usually there are legal holdups, government red tape, financing challenges and a multitude of other things that tend to slow you down.

Sometimes people set goals that are pure fantasy. If you're four feet tall, you probably will never play professional basketball. So by all means think big and create an exciting picture of the future. Just make sure your plan isn't far-fetched and that you allow a reasonable amount of time to get there.

9. Your goals must include contribution.

There's a well-known Bible phrase that says, "Whatever a man sows, that he will also reap." (Galatians 6:7). This is a fundamental truth. It seems if you hand out good things and you consistently sow well, your rewards are guaranteed. That's a pretty good deal, isn't it?

Unfortunately many people who strive for success—usually defined as money and things—miss the boat. There's just no time, or room in their lives, to give something back to society. Simply put, they are takers, not givers. And if you always keep taking, you will eventually lose out in the long run.

Contribution can take many forms. You can give your time, your expertise and you can, of course, give financially. So make it a part of your ongoing goals program. And do it unconditionally. Don't expect a payback immediately. That will come in due course, often in the most unexpected ways.

10. Your goals need to be supported.

This last part of your goals checklist is controversial. There are three points of view. Some people advocate telling the whole world about what they are going to do. They rationalize that it makes them more accountable. It's pretty hard to back down when the world is watching to see if you'll really do what you said. There's a lot of pressure when you choose this strategy, and certain individuals thrive on it.

Dr. Robert H. Schuller is a good example. He told the world he was going to build a beautiful Crystal Cathedral in Garden Grove, California, at a cost of more than twenty million dollars. Many observers laughed and scoffed at his idea and said he couldn't do it. He went ahead and did it anyway—the Crystal Cathedral was dedicated debt-free. The cost? Just under thirty million dollars.

One of Schuller's comments said it all "I think when you have big dreams you attract other big dreamers." And he did. In fact, several people donated more than one million dollars each to help the project succeed.

Here's the second option. Set your own goals, keep them to yourself and get on with the job. Actions speak louder than words, and you'll surprise a lot of people.

HERB STANSBURY

"Your strategic plan, brilliant in concept and magnificent in execution, isn't working."

Third, and this may be the wisest strategy, selectively share your dreams with a few people you trust. These are carefully chosen proactive individuals who will support and encourage you when the going gets tough. And if you have big plans you'll need their help, because you are bound to run into a few roadblocks along the way.

Your Master PLAN

Now that we have laid the groundwork, it's time to get started on your own master plan. This is the exciting part—actually creating your better future, and the clarity to go with it. This is your big picture. There are six major steps. We suggest you read through all six first and then set time aside to implement each strategy. Use the Action Steps at the end of the chapter as a guide. Steps five and six will be dealt with in greater detail in chapters 4 and 5.

1. Review the Top-10 Goals Checklist.
Use this checklist as your frame of reference when you sit down to create your actual goals. It will help you design a crystal-clear picture. It is summarized on page 84.

2. Go for the gusto—101 goals.
To get your juices flowing, make a list of 101 things you want to accomplish in the next ten years. Have fun with this, and open your mind to all the possibilities. Create a childlike enthusiasm—do not place any restrictions on your thinking. Be specific and personalize your list by starting each sentence with "I am" or "I will." For example—"I am taking a six-week vacation in Europe," or "I will save or invest 10 percent of my net income every month." To help you, here are a few important questions to help you focus:

- What do I want to do?

- What do I want to have?

- Where do I want to go?

- What contribution do I want to make?

- What do I want to become?

- What do I want to learn?

- Who do I want to spend my time with?

- How much do I want to earn, save and invest?

- How much time do I want off for fun?

- What will I do to create optimum health?

To ensure that you enjoy excellent balance in your life, choose some goals in each of the following areas—career and business, financial, fun time, health and fitness, relationships, personal, and contribution, plus any others that are of special significance.

PRIORITIZING YOUR LIST

Now that you have stretched your imagination, the next step is to prioritize. Take a look at each of your 101 goals and determine a realistic time frame for accomplishment.

Write a number beside each goal—one, three, five or ten years. This will give you a general framework to work from. In his great book, *The On-Purpose Person*, author Kevin W. McCarthy describes an excellent technique to help you prioritize. He calls it the tournament draw. This is a format used for all sorts of competitions—from spelling bees to tennis tournaments to the Super Bowl playoffs. Prioritize your choices by making separate draw sheets for your one-year, three-year, five-year and ten-year goals.

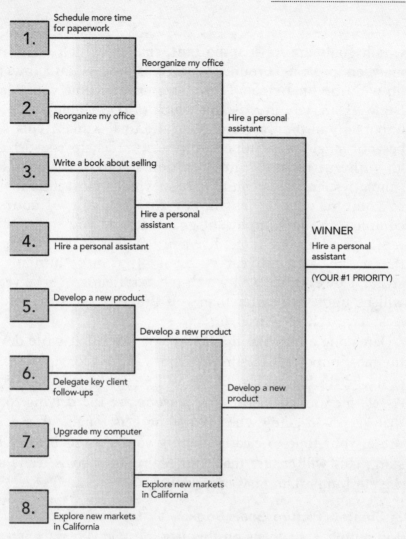

1. Schedule more time for paperwork

2. Reorganize my office

Reorganize my office

3. Write a book about selling

4. Hire a personal assistant

Hire a personal assistant

Hire a personal assistant

WINNER

Hire a personal assistant

(YOUR #1 PRIORITY)

5. Develop a new product

6. Delegate key client follow-ups

Develop a new product

7. Upgrade my computer

8. Explore new markets in California

Explore new markets in California

Develop a new product

THE MAIN DRAW [2]

List each of your one-year goals on the left-hand side of the sheet. Make the draw sheet big enough to accommodate all of the items on your list—sixteen, thirty-two or sixty-four lines deep. (We are assuming you will have more than eight one-year goals.) This is the preliminary draw. Now you decide

[2] The Main Draw concept: *The On-Purpose Person*, Kevin McCarthy, 1992, used by permission of NavPress. All rights reserved. 1-800-366-7788.

which goals are most important; that is, which ones will move on to the next round. Repeat this process until you end up with the final eight. These have now become your Main Draw. Again, you must select which of these eight are more important, all the way through to the final winner. This will be your single most important priority. To help you decide, go with gut feeling. Your intuition is rarely wrong. This simple system forces you to choose what is most meaningful to you and what is less important. You can, of course, complete the less important goals later as you wish. Now repeat this for your three, five and ten-year goals. We know that a five- and ten-year vision is often more difficult to create. However, it's well worth the extra effort. Those years will be upon you faster than you think! Make sure you at least have a three-year plan.

Here's one other vital tip: Before you prioritize, write down the most important reason that you want to accomplish each goal, and the biggest benefit you will receive upon completion. As we mentioned before, big reasons are the driving force that keep you going when the going gets tough. It's a good use of your time to clearly identify your reasons before you start. This will ensure that your Main Draw goals really are the most important ones on your list.

3. Create a Picture Goals Book.
To improve your focus on the new lifestyle you want, create a picture book of your most important goals. This is an enjoyable process and the whole family can join in.

Buy a large photo album and start collecting pictures. For example, if one of your goals is to have a holiday in London, England, get some travel brochures and cut out three or four pictures of the attractions you want to see. If it's a family vacation, place a bold heading at the top of the page that reads, "I am enjoying a three-week holiday with my family in London, England," and include the date you want to go.

You can divide your Picture Goals Book into lifestyle sections. Make sure you include all the areas we mentioned in step 2. Our friend Glenna Salsbury consistently uses this strategy with great success. Earlier in her career, Glenna was a single mother with three young daughters, a house payment, a car payment and a need to rekindle some dreams. Here's her story:

One evening, I attended a seminar on the I x V = R Principle. (Imagination mixed with Vividness becomes Reality.) The speaker pointed out that the mind thinks in pictures, not in words. And as we vividly picture in our minds what we desire, it will become a reality.

This concept struck a chord of creativity in my heart. I knew the biblical truth that the Lord gives us 'the desires of our heart' (Psalm 37:4) and that 'as a man thinketh in his heart, so is he' (Proverbs 23:7).

I was determined to take my written list of desires and turn it into pictures. So I cut up old magazines and gathered pictures that depicted the 'desires of my heart.' Then I arranged them in an attractive photo album and waited expectantly.

My pictures were specific. They included: 1. A woman in a wedding gown and a good-looking man in a tuxedo. 2. Bouquets of flowers. 3. An island in the sparkling blue Caribbean. 4. College diplomas for my girls. 5. A woman vice president of a company. (I was working for a company that had no female officers. I wanted to be the first woman vice president.) 6. A mortar-board hat—representing my desire to earn a master's degree from Fuller Theological Seminary so that I could influence others spiritually.

Eight weeks later I was driving down a California freeway. While I was admiring a beautiful red and white car next to mine, the driver looked at me and smiled. I smiled back. The next thing I knew, he was following me. I pretended to ignore him, but he followed me for fifteen miles. Almost scared me to death! I drove for a few more miles, he drove a few more miles. I parked, he parked . . . and eventually I married him!

After our first date, Jim sent me a dozen roses. We dated for about two years. Every Monday, he sent me a red rose and a love note. Before we married, Jim said, 'I've found the perfect place for our honeymoon —St. John's Island in the Caribbean.' I did not confess the truth about my picture book until Jim and I were moving into our new home, which I had also pictured in the album.

Soon after, I became vice president of human resources in the company where I worked. After completing my master's degree, I was one of the first women admitted as a doctoral candidate at Fuller Seminary. Not only did my daughters earn college degrees, but they created their own photo albums, and have seen God at work in their own lives through this principle.

This sounds like a fairy tale, but it is absolutely true. Since then, Jim and I have made many picture books. I've discovered there are no impossible dreams —you really can have the desires of your heart.

SOURCE: *Chicken Soup for the Soul*

Today, Glenna Salsbury is one of the top professional speakers in the country and a former president of the National Speakers Association.

The clearer and more specific your pictures are, the more likely you are to stay focused on them, and attract the results you want. So be creative. Explore different ways to reinforce your vision. A Picture Goals Book is a great way to start.

In chapter 4, Creating Optimum Balance, you'll learn how to develop a specific action plan that will transform your pictures into reality. Before we get to that, though, here are the three remaining strategies to help you create unusual clarity.

4. Use an Ideas Book.

This is simply a notebook where you jot down your day-to-day observations and insights. It is a powerful tool to expand your awareness. Did you ever have a big idea in the middle of the night? You sit straight up in bed and your mind is racing. Usually, you only have a few seconds to capture that idea before you lose it, or your body says, "Go back to sleep, it's three o'clock in the morning!" In fact, you may drift back to sleep, wake up hours later and have completely forgotten what your great idea was.

A BRILLIANT IDEA WITHOUT ACTION
IS LIKE MARK McGWIRE PLAYING
BASEBALL WITHOUT A BAT![3]

This is why an Ideas Book is so valuable. By recording your best thoughts in writing, you never need to rely on your memory. You can review your ideas any time you want. Use your book for business ideas, sales tips, presentation skills, money-making projects, quotes you have read or stories that will help you explain something better. Just keep your ears and eyes open every day, and listen to your own intuition.

For example, if you have just finished a great sales presentation where everything went exactly as planned and you closed a big deal, capture it in your Ideas Book. What did you say that worked so well? Maybe you asked a specific question that prompted the buying decision, or gave a better explanation of your benefits and services. Replay the presentation in your mind and write down what worked.

It's also beneficial to tape-record your presentation. Invite someone who you really respect to go over it with you and then

[3] Mark McGwire won Major League Baseball's home-run title in 1998 and 1999, hitting seventy and sixty-five home runs, respectively.

you can brainstorm how to improve it. Keep practicing. Movie star Robin Williams averages thirty takes per scene, until both he and the director are satisfied with his performance.

Did you ever screw up an important presentation? That's also a good time to open your Ideas Book and record what you did wrong. You might underline it in red ink and add, "Never say this again!" In both examples, by writing down your thoughts while they are fresh in your mind, you reinforce what worked and what didn't work. This gives you incredible clarity.

Here's another valuable suggestion for your book. First thing in the morning, for ten minutes, record your feelings. Words to describe feelings include anxious, sad, happy, excited, bored, angry, enthusiastic, frustrated, energized. Write in the present tense as if you are having a conversation with yourself. Use "I" language: "I am feeling anxious today because my daughter is driving on her own for the first time," or "I feel excited because I'm starting a new job this morning." When you consistently get in touch with your feelings you are more connected to everyday situations and more aware of what's really going on in your life.

5. Visualize, think, reflect and review.
The power of visualization is often seen in sports. Olympic athletes mentally run the event in their minds several times just before they perform. They totally focus on a positive result.

Olympic gold medalist Mark Tewksbury, the Canadian who won the 200-meter backstroke swim at the 1992 Olympic Games in Barcelona, Spain, actually stood on the winners' podium on the eve of the race and visualized a come-from-behind winning performance. He heard the roar of the crowd, could see where his family was sitting in the stands and saw himself triumphantly accepting the gold medal. The next day he swam the race exactly as imagined and won by a fingertip!

Remember, if you copy the techniques of champions you too can become a champion. Use your positive imagination to create these winning pictures.

The sharper these images are and the more intense you feel, the more likely you are to create the desired result. It's a powerful process. In chapter 4, Creating Optimum Balance, you'll learn how to think at a deeper level and how to reflect and review your progress every day. All of these techniques help to produce unusual clarity, one that will give you a distinct edge in the marketplace.

6. Develop mentors and Mastermind Groups.

Another wonderful way to ensure major improvements in your productivity and vision is to enlist the aid of people who have vast experience in areas where you need the most help. When you surround yourself with a carefully chosen team of experts, your learning curve increases rapidly. Very few people do this consistently. Again, if you dare to be different you'll reap the rewards down the road. The alternative is to figure everything out yourself using trial and error. It's a slow way to move forward because you run into many roadblocks and distractions. On the other hand, cultivating advice and wisdom from specific mentors propels you to faster results.

A Mastermind Group consists of four to six people who meet regularly to share ideas and support each other. These are powerful alliances. They are designed to foster long-lasting relationships. You'll learn all about this in chapter 5, Building Excellent Relationships.

Now that you have a complete framework to create your long-term goals, here's the final piece of the puzzle—we call it the Achievers Focusing System.

The Achievers Focusing System

This simple but highly effective focusing method makes it easy for you to measure progress and stay on track. It's used by all of our most successful clients. Essentially it breaks your goals into seven categories and forces you to enjoy an excellent balance.

You can decide the time frame for achieving these results. A two-month cycle is good. It's not too far away, yet it gives you enough time to set some meaningful targets.

The seven goal categories are as follows:

- FINANCIAL

- BUSINESS/CAREER

- FUN TIME!

- HEALTH AND FITNESS

- RELATIONSHIPS

- PERSONAL

- CONTRIBUTION

When you dedicate a portion of your time to accomplishing one significant goal in each of these areas every sixty days, you will start enjoying what most people are desperately striving for—balance. And with balance comes peace of mind. All the details of this are laid out in the Action Steps at the end of this chapter. The Achievers Focusing System is the backbone of your overall game plan. Initially it may seem a bit unrealistic to complete seven goals in sixty days, but with practice you can do it. Start with small increments and gradually increase the size of your goals. When you start this process it's more important to create seven mini-victories for yourself than to set your targets too high. To keep these in the forefront of your mind, review them daily. Most people don't do this. In fact, most people don't even have an action plan for their goals. Be smarter, and give yourself a jump on the competition. It will pay off handsomely.

CONCLUSION

Like all successful habits, developing the habit of unusual clarity takes effort and daily discipline. Remember, it's an ongoing process. The key points are:

1. Use the Top-10 Goals Checklist as a framework.
2. Design a master plan to prioritize your goals.
3. Create a Picture Goals Book.
4. Use an Ideas Book.
5. Visualize, think, reflect and review.
   (Chapter 4 will cover these in detail)
6. Develop unique mentor and Mastermind Group alliances. (*We will show you how in chapter 5*)
7. Use the Achievers Focusing System to measure weekly progress.

DO THIS AND YOU'LL HAVE EXCEPTIONAL CLARITY, GUARANTEED!

If you're feeling a bit overwhelmed right now, don't worry. That's quite normal. Take it one step at a time. Schedule sufficient time to work through each of these strategies. Commit to getting started. Take the first step. Then focus on accomplishing your short-term goals. Creating a successful future takes energy, effort and concentrated thinking. That's the reason most people don't do it. However, by deciding to read this book you have taken the first step to rise above the crowd. Accept the challenge. Focus. The rewards will be worth it. Make the effort now!

ACTION STEPS

Your Personal
Master Plan

The Achievers
Focusing System

Below is a complete review to help you implement your personal "big picture" Master Plan as well as your short-term action plan.

To maximize your results, we strongly recommend that you schedule at least one full day to do this.

Top-10 Goals Checklist
To maximize your results remember your goals must be:

1. Yours.
2. Meaningful.
3. Specific and measurable.
4. Flexible.
5. Challenging and exciting.
6. In alignment with your core values.
7. Well balanced.
8. Contributing to society.
9. Realistic.
10. Supported.

LIST YOUR CORE VALUES BELOW:

e.g., Honesty, integrity, living a win-win philosophy, experiencing joy and love.

_____

_____

Your 101 Goals

To do this use your own notebook. Before writing out your list of all the things you want to accomplish, turn back to step two on page 73. Read through this section again. Jot down your initial thoughts to the questions. This will help you develop a framework. Take as much time as you need. Then make your actual list of 101 Goals. Next, prioritize your list by using a Tournament Draw sheet similiar to the one on page 75.

Your Personal Master Plan

Use the sample worksheet on page 86 as a guide. Enlarge this as necessary, depending on the number of goals you have in each area. Make sure you complete the reasons and benefits column. Your reasons are the driving force behind your goals. Also, select a specific completion date. We use The Essential Goals framework—seven key areas that create an excellent balanced lifestyle. If you want, you can add other areas that are of special significance to you. Use a similar sheet for your three-year, five-year and ten-year goals.

Create a Picture Goals Book

Review step three (Page 76). The key here is to have fun and to be creative. The more impact your pictures have, the better. Choose ones that are big, bold and brightly colored. If one of your goals is to own a brand-new car, visit the local dealership and have a picture taken with you in the driver's seat. One of our male clients wanted to have a fine physique, so he cut out a picture of an athlete, lopped off the head and replaced it with a cut-out of his own head!

Use an Ideas Book

Review step four (Page 79). You can select anything from a simple notebook to an elaborate engraved journal. There are plenty to choose from—check your local stationery store.

Number each page if not already numbered. When the book is almost finished, you may want to create an index at the back, to help you find specific entries later. Develop the habit of capturing your best ideas, thoughts and insights. This is not a "Dear Diary." Use it for business strategies, money-making ideas, stories that illustrate a point, marketing concepts and whatever else you think is important. If you enjoy structure, create tabs for specific topics. The most important thing, however, is to train yourself to start writing. Start this week.

MY PERSONAL MASTER PLAN

Sample sheet for one-year goals. Create a similiar worksheet for your longer-term goals.

From _____ To _____

	Specific Goal	Reason for Accomplishing This Goal	Date Accomplished
FINANCIAL Total Income $ 150,000 Savings/Investments $ 20,000 Debt elimination $ 25,000	1. I will be mortgage-free on January 1, 2001. 2. I am earning $150,000 (pre-tax) by Aug. 31, 2001. 3. I will find a wealthy mentor to advise me by Nov. 30, 2000.	1. To be debt free after twenty years of paying loans/interest. 2. A six-figure income will boost my confidence/reinforce my business. 3. I plan to be wealthy six years from now and a mentor will guide me.	
CAREER & BUSINESS New projects, partnerships, expansion, new products/services, sales, new ventures, relationships.	1. I am starting my own computer software company by Aug. 31, 2001. 2. I am finding a financial partner who will invest $1 million by May 30, 2001. 3. I will have two new software products developed by July 30, 2001.	1. I want the freedom of being my own boss instead of working for a salary. 2. Being well capitalized will give me a strong foundation. 3. To prove that my creative ability can produce unique solutions.	
FUN TIME! Vacations, trips, sports, reunions, special events. Number of weeks off ___4___	1. I am taking a one-week vacation in Colorado, Jan. 22-29, 2001. 2. I am organizing and attending a 25th anniversary family reunion. 3. I am going on a two-week hiking tour of the Rockies, June 1–14, 2001.	1. An opportunity to spend significant time with my two best friends. 2. To thank my parents for their support and guidance. 3. To meet new people, spend time reflecting and enjoy nature.	

© The Achievers Coaching program.

Category	Goals	Outcomes
HEALTH & FITNESS Lose/gain weight, exercise programs, nutritional habits, medical, sports, martial arts.	1. I will be at my ideal weight of 165 lbs. by Feb. 21, 2001. 2. I am running forty minutes per day, four times per week. 3. I am starting Tai Chi on Nov. 15, 2001.	1. I will enjoy better health, look better and feel better. 2. I will boost my energy and stamina and enjoy the fresh air. 3. I will feel more relaxed, focused and aware.
RELATIONSHIPS 1. Family—spouse, children, parents, siblings. 2. Personal—friends (local & long distance), mentors. 3. Business—strategic alliances, mentors, partners, clients, staff, colleagues.	1. I will call my sister Gloria every week. 2. I am developing six clients for my new business by Aug. 31, 2001. 3. I will set up a personal Mastermind Group (six people) by March 1, 2001.	1. To support and help her through her divorce. 2. To establish a strong foundation for my new business. 3. To surround myself with ambitious, fun-loving, positive-thinking people.
PERSONAL 1. Anything I personally want to have, be or do. 2. Education—courses, professional speaking, consulting, reading, etc. 3. Spiritual—courses, Bible study, church, relationships, retreats.	1. I will attend three major concerts by June 30, 2001. 2. I will complete a ten-week public speaking course by April 1, 2001. 3. I will read four books that will increase my spiritual awareness by Aug. 31, 2001.	1. To appreciate and enjoy great music. 2. To significantly improve my presentation skills. 3. To become more aware of my life's purpose.
CONTRIBUTION Charitable, community, mentoring, church.	1. I will mentor a high school student one hour per week, starting Oct. 14, 2001. 2. I will tithe 10 percent of my income to my two favorite charities and our church. 3. I will volunteer to help with the annual United Way campaign.	1. To help and encourage someone who may be struggling. 2. To continually experience the joy of unconditional giving. 3. To help people less fortunate.

The Achievers Focusing System

This is the weekly game plan that ensures you hit the bigger targets listed in your long-term Master Plan. The categories are identical. Refer to the sample sheets on pages 90–91. The first step is to write down your single most important goal in each of the seven areas. Remember, be specific.

1. FINANCIAL—this is divided into total income and the amount of money you want to save or invest during this time. If you are paying down debt, you can also record the amount here.

2. BUSINESS/CAREER—you will probably complete several business goals in this time frame. However, select the one that will help you progress most, and focus on this. Maybe it's a sales target, or a new project or joint venture, or hiring (or firing) a key person.

3. FUN TIME!—this is your goal for time off, totally away from work. Record the number of days and remember, you deserve it.

4. HEALTH AND FITNESS——there are three major components to consider here—physical, mental and spiritual. What will you do to improve your overall health? Consider exercise, nutritional habits, new knowledge and spiritual awareness.

5. RELATIONSHIPS—what one important relationship will you work on during this period of time? Maybe more time with a family member, a mentor, or key employee or client. Obviously you will interact with a lot of people every week; however, just focus on significantly expanding one of these relationships.

6. PERSONAL—this is a wide-open choice involving something that gives you personal satisfaction. It might include buying something, developing a new skill like playing guitar, or planning a special vacation.

7. CONTRIBUTION—what are you going to contribute back to society during this time? Perhaps it's a financial contribution to your favorite charity or church organization. Maybe you'll contribute your time to the community or local sports team, or simply help someone out by being a willing listener.

When you have written out your seven major goals, shift your focus to the week ahead—we call it The Seven-Day Focus. Here's how it works: At the beginning of each week select the three most important things you want to accomplish. Be sure to choose activities that move you toward the completion of your seven major goals.

For example, if your health and fitness goal is to set up a new exercise program, the first step might be to join a fitness club. If your major relationship goal is to spend more time with your children on the weekends, your first step could be scheduling time in your weekly planner. If your overall business goal is to reach a specific sales volume, you might target a certain number of appointments in the next seven days to get you off to a good start.

Of course you will be doing other things every week in your business and personal life. This action plan will help you focus on the most important activities. Make sure you monitor your progress. Whatever gets measured gets done! It's fun checking off your list each week, and it will boost your confidence as you get closer to reaching your bigger targets. We highly recommend having a focusing partner to keep you accountable for your results. This could be a business colleague who would also enjoy using the Achievers Focusing System.

Phone your partner at the beginning of the week and share your three most important activities. Seven days later discuss your results, victories and challenges, and start the process for the following week. By supporting and challenging each other you are less likely to procrastinate during the week. There is an expectation when you reconnect that progress has been made. You can also create some incentives for each other that will stimulate you to stay focused. For example, one of our clients is an avid skier. She had booked a day off at her favorite resort as a reward for achieving her weekly goal. As an added incentive, if she did not complete her three most important objectives, she promised to give her ski passes to her focusing partner. Another client said he would phone his biggest competitor and give him three hot business leads if he did not finish his goals for the week. That was all the motivation he needed!

THE ACHIEVERS FOCUSING SYSTEM

FROM _____ TO _____

Goals: select one goal in each of the seven areas. For clarity keep it simple and specific.

THE SEVEN-DAY FOCUS: At the beginning of each week select the three most important things you want to accomplish. Choose activities that will move you toward the completion of your seven major goals. Make contact with your focusing partner to review your progress.

Focusing Partner:
Name: Linda Martin
Phone: 555-4000
Fax: 555-9045

Goal Area	Goal	WEEK 1 — Focusing Partner contacted: ☒ yes ☐ no	WEEK 2 — Focusing Partner contacted: ☒ yes ☐ no	WEEK 3 — Focusing Partner contacted: ☒ yes ☐ no	WEEK 7 — Focusing Partner contacted: ☒ yes ☐ no	WEEK 8 — Focusing Partner contacted: ☒ yes ☐ no	WEEK 9 — Focusing Partner contacted: ☒ yes ☐ no
FINANCIAL	I am earning a total income of $12,000 I am saving or investing $2,000 I am reducing my debt by $1,000	1. Specific game plan for sales contest.	1. Set up ten sales appointments.	1. Outline chapter one of book.	1. Set up customer focus group launch.	1. Final check for product launch Friday.	1. Outline chapter three of book.
BUSINESS (e.g., Projects, sales or new ventures)	I am celebrating our new product launch on Friday, February 22.	2. Start walking program.	2. Finalize new product brochure.	2. Complete first mentoring appointment.	2. Extend mentoring schedule one month.	2. Set up eight sales appointments.	2. Call financial coach; invest $2,000 bonus.
FUN TIME! (Total days off for relaxation, vacation and rejuvenation)	I am enjoying seventeen days off for fun.	3. Contact high school, re: mentoring student.	3. Call Core Clients.	3. Set up media presentations on new product.	3. Pick up surprise gift for Fran.	3. Call Core Clients.	3. Set up eight sales appointments.
HEALTH (e.g., Physical, mental or spiritual)	I am enjoying a thirty-minute walk four days per week.						

		WEEK 4 — Focusing Partner contacted: ☒ yes ☐ no	WEEK 10 — Focusing Partner contacted: ☐ yes ☐ no
RELATIONSHIPS (e.g., Family, personal or business)	I am concentrating on my top three Core Clients; minimum two personal contacts every other week.	1. Call Core Clients. 2. Maintain walking program, increase time. 3. Set up eight sales appointments.	
PERSONAL (e.g., Projects, purchases or learning)	I am outlining the first three chapters of my new book.	**WEEK 5 — Focusing Partner contacted: ☒ yes ☐ no** 1. Plan long weekend getaway Feb. 23–25. 2. Confirm new product delivery date. 3. Pay down credit card $1,000.	**WEEK 11 — Focusing Partner contacted: ☐ yes ☐ no**
CONTRIBUTION (e.g., Charitable, community, or donations)	I am mentoring a high school student one hour per week for six weeks.	**WEEK 6 — Focusing Partner contacted: ☒ yes ☐ no** 1. Call Core Clients. 2. Set up eight sales appointments. 3. Outline chapter two of book.	**WEEK 12 — Focusing Partner contacted: ☐ yes ☐ no**

Suggested time frame, sixty or ninety days.

© The Achievers Coaching program.

LIVING ON PURPOSE

TAKING DECISIVE ACTION

CONSISTENT PERSISTENCE

ASK FOR WHAT YOU WANT

THE CONFIDENCE FACTOR

BUILDING EXCELLENT RELATIONSHIPS

CREATING OPTIMUM BALANCE

DO YOU SEE THE BIG PICTURE?

IT'S NOT HOCUS-POCUS, IT'S ALL ABOUT FOCUS

YOUR HABITS WILL DETERMINE YOUR FUTURE

You've built a solid foundation—well done!

Creating Optimum Balance

"WHEN YOU WORK, WORK, AND WHEN YOU
PLAY, PLAY. DON'T GET THE TWO MIXED UP."

—Jim Rohn

Gerry is a design architect, and he's busy.
As a partner in his business he works long hours. Every
morning he's up early—no later than 6 A.M. Breakfast is a
cup of coffee consumed hurriedly in the car. Occasionally
he manages a sticky doughnut to go with it.

Jane, his wife, also works full-time, so their two
children, Paul, four, and Sarah, two, are dropped off at a
daycare center. Gerry doesn't see his kids very often. He
has already left for the office before they get up, and it's
usually after 7:30 P.M. when he returns home. By then
they are usually asleep. Even on weekends the business
consumes a lot of Gerry's time. There's always something
more to be done at the office, and when Jane chastises
him for "living" there, he bundles up the paperwork
and brings it home, usually to burn the midnight oil
for a few hours after everyone is asleep.

Gerry's kids have a neat way of communicating with
him. They leave little pictures or Post-It notes on his
bathroom mirror. Gerry feels guilty when he sees them

stuck there, especially when he reads the ones that say how much they miss him. But what can he do? The business is at a critical point. After three years of long hours, he and his two partners are initiating a major expansion. Being the junior partner, much of the extra work falls on his shoulders.

Even with two incomes, money is tight. Jane wants to take the kids to Disneyland but with no budget for savings, this isn't likely to happen soon.

Do you relate at all to this family scene? It's becoming more and more common, as people struggle to create a healthy balance between their career, personal and family lives. Often the greater pressures are on women, who work full time building a career and are still expected to cook, clean and somehow cater to most of the children's needs at the same time. In fact these multiple pressures have become one of the biggest reasons for divorce and family breakdown today. How long can Gerry, Jane, Sarah and Paul continue with the "ships passing in the night" routine? Eventually something has to give, and it will probably be sooner than later.

If you have any stress or concern about the quality of life you currently enjoy, then study this chapter carefully. In the next few pages you will find answers to your concerns. More importantly, we will share with you a unique system that will guarantee you a healthy, well-balanced lifestyle. There *is* a better way. Being stuck like Gerry is no way to live. So follow along. Read and reread the following information, and be prepared to make changes.

First, let us emphasize that some people really do enjoy optimum balance in their daily lives. Here's one example. Their names are John and Jennifer. Like Gerry in the previous story, John is thirty-eight years old. He's been happily married to Jennifer for fifteen years. They have three children, David, three, Joanne, seven, and Charlene, nine. John also works hard in his own electrical contracting company, which he started six years ago. Unlike Gerry, John and his family enjoy annual vacations. In fact, they take six weeks off for fun every year. Both John and Jennifer had parents with strong values and undoubtedly this influenced them growing up. One of these values was an excellent work ethic: "If you are going to do a job, do it to the best of your ability." Another was the value of saving and investing money. By the time they married, both had a savings plan in place, and they maximized their joint savings potential during those early years to create a well-diversified portfolio. With the help of a carefully chosen financial adviser, their investment plan is now worth two hundred thousand dollars. They also have an education fund set up that will eventually pay for their children's college expenses.

At work, John has a first-class personal assistant who allows him to focus on what he does best. Consequently he does not get caught up in unnecessary paperwork or become distracted by people who could waste valuable chunks of his time. Because of this ability to be well-organized, he enjoys most weekends off. Although he starts the day early, John is rarely home later than 6 P.M., allowing him special time with his family.

At the beginning of each new year, John and Jennifer sit down and plan their personal and family goals. This includes scheduling specific time for vacations, including one major holiday together as a family and mini-breaks for three or four days for John and Jennifer, with no kids. Twice a year John enjoys a long weekend away with his Mastermind Group to golf. Jennifer also plans a few ski trips with a group of women friends.

REMEMBER, IF YOU WANT A DIFFERENT RESULT

Do Something Different.

Through self-discipline and good advice, John and Jennifer have created a healthy balance in their lives. They have not succumbed to the workaholic syndrome that strains so many relationships. And John has no guilt about taking time off. His attitude is, "I work hard and smart at my business, so I deserve my time for fun." As a result, he creates a high income. That, combined with their habit of consistent investing, minimizes any financial pressure. Interestingly, John and his family are not consumption oriented. They don't spend a lot of money on typical consumer goods. Instead they prefer to save for memorable vacations. Their kids don't get everything they ask for, but they don't suffer either. John is more than happy driving his four-year-old car, unlike Gerry, who prefers a new model every other year, even though he really can't afford it.

When you look at the lifestyles of John and Gerry, where do you fit in? It's not difficult to figure out who has the healthier lifestyle. Now, you may not run your own business or be in the same age group. You may not even be married or have a family. That's not the point. The question here is: "Do you enjoy a healthy, well-balanced lifestyle, doing work that you love, and that gives you an excellent financial return and allows you to have significant time off to pursue your other interests?" The answer is either "Yes" or "No."

The B-Alert SYSTEM

If your answer is "No," we are now going to give you a system that will keep you focused and balanced. Even if you answered "Yes," this unique system will elevate your awareness to a new level. It's called The **B-ALERT** System for Optimum Balance. With this system, you will be more alert every day to those subtle pressures that can so easily push you off-target.

If you check the word *alert* in the dictionary, it says, "At the ready, mindful, using intelligence, on guard, conscious, and prepared."

Obviously, being at the ready every day and using intelligence will keep you mindful of your priorities and your state of balance. When you are truly alert you are more conscious of what is going on. What is the opposite of alert? Mindless, unprepared, unconscious, off-guard and stupid! If you had a choice, which side of the scale would you choose to sit on— alert or unprepared and stupid? You *have* the choice, and you can exercise it every day. Selecting alertness over the negative option is an obvious choice. Why then, if it's an easy choice to make, do most people hang out on the opposite side of the scale? The truth is, old habits die hard. It's uncomfortable to make changes, and there never seems to be enough time. It's easier doing it the old way, even though the long-term consequences may be disastrous. When it comes to enjoying an excellent balance in their lives, most people are wholly unprepared, easily caught off-guard, and not very smart.

Now let's discover what your reality is. We're going to analyze your daily behavior in detail, using the acronym **B-ALERT**. These six letters add up to a powerful formula that will help you create a well-balanced day. Repeat the process seven times and you'll have a well-balanced week. Persevere for just four weeks and you'll have a great month. Make it a habit every month, and before you know it you'll have a terrific year, with a lot more time off, and a lot more money to go with it. As you go through each of the six steps, monitor your emotions. Be aware of any resistance you feel. Think about the reasons for this potential resistance. Letting go of any mental blocks will assist you tremendously in creating your new habit of Optimum Balance.

> EVERY WELL-BUILT HOUSE STARTED WITH A
> DEFINITE PLAN IN THE FORM OF BLUEPRINTS.
>
> —Napoleon Hill

B Is for Blueprint

This is how you prepare for the day. You do prepare, don't you? A blueprint is simply a map for the day. It helps you prioritize the important tasks on your agenda. To illustrate this, imagine a tall, beautiful building in a major city. It has stunning architecture. There's marble and glass everywhere with opulent details to complement the unique design. Before the first stone was laid, a detailed blueprint was prepared and approved. The owners of the building didn't say to the contractor, "We'd like a big, tall building with lots of glass and marble—here's the money. See what you can throw together for us." No, every last detail was meticulously planned and clearly visualized in advance.

If you ask a printer to print a brochure, you must approve the blueline before the job is put on the press. This allows you to carefully go over everything before the work is started, just in case there are any errors or omissions. It's the last check before action is taken.

There are two options for preparing your blueprint for the day. Either do it the night before, or early in the morning before your day has started. You only need ten to fifteen minutes to do this.

Recent research indicates that if you create your blueprint the night before, rather than in the morning, your unconscious mind will actually work during the night figuring out how to fulfill your next day's plan, i.e., preparing the best sales presentation, handling potential objections, or solving any conflicts or problems that need to be addressed. So if you can, take time each evening to plan for the next day, and review your plan before bedtime. This review should focus on your most important activities, such as whom you will meet with and the purpose and objective of each appointment. Set specific time limits for your appointments. Also go over what projects must be worked on, and determine if you have reserved enough time to deal with them.

It's important to have your own blueprint recording system. This could be a standard daily journal or time planner, or you may prefer an electronic organizer or computer software program to create your blueprint. Just choose a system that works well for you. For best results keep it simple. Customize it to suit your own style.

Have you ever observed people who are not in the habit of designing a blueprint for the day? You'll find a few in most sales organizations. They tend to hang around the coffee pot first thing in the morning. And for many of these non-planners "first thing" is sometime after 9 A.M. Socializing and reviewing the newspaper are high on their agenda. Perhaps the first sales call happens around 11 A.M., so you can imagine how productive the rest of their day is likely to be.

A well-planned blueprint allows you to take charge of the day. You're in control from the start, preferably early. This gives you a tremendous feeling of confidence and you are likely to get a lot more accomplished.

> THE ONE THING THAT SEPARATES WINNERS
> FROM LOSERS IS, WINNERS TAKE ACTION!
>
> —Anthony Robbins

A Is for Action

You'll notice the letter *A* is larger than all of the other letters in the **B-ALERT** acronym. This is no accident. When it comes to reviewing your results, the amount of action you put into your day will directly determine your score. Please notice, there is a major difference between being busy and taking specific, well-planned action. You can have a busy day with nothing to show for it. You didn't move closer to accomplishing your most important goals. The day just seemed to evaporate. Maybe you were dealing with little emergencies or you allowed yourself to be interrupted too many times. As we mentioned in chapter 3, Do You See The Big Picture?, it's better to invest your time in what you do best. Concentrate on the activities that produce the greatest results for you. Set limits on what you will and will not do. Delegate effectively, and be alert to stepping outside your boundaries.

In chapter 9, Taking Decisive Action, we'll show you some great strategies that will help you eliminate procrastination and become highly proactive.

One last comment: When you are on vacation or having a day off for fun, your action is simply to enjoy yourself. It's not necessary to review goals or do anything related to business. In fact, to properly re-energize, it's essential to relax 100 percent. Remember: You deserve time off, so take it.

THERE ARE ESSENTIALLY TWO THINGS THAT WILL
MAKE YOU WISER—THE BOOKS YOU READ
AND THE PEOPLE YOU MEET.

—Charles "Tremendous" Jones

L Is for Learning

Another feature of a well-balanced day is taking time to expand your knowledge. This doesn't require several hours of study. There are many ways to learn as the day unfolds. All that is required is that you be curious. Your level of curiosity about how life and business really work will go a long way towards helping you become wealthy. So let's look at some learning options. You can learn from books, tapes, videos and well-selected media. As mentioned earlier, develop the habit of reading at least twenty to thirty minutes in the morning. It's a great way to start your day.

What should you read? Anything that is stimulating, challenging, or gives you an edge in your industry or profession. There are lots to choose from, for example, reading a few short stories from our *Chicken Soup for the Soul* series only takes a few minutes as you eat breakfast. Biographies and autobiographies are particularly inspiring. Reading them will give you an extra boost of positive energy. Whatever you do, avoid digesting any negative portions of the newspapers. Loading up on wars, murders, riots and disasters will only drain your energy before the day has begun—not a good plan.

Thousands of books reveal the lives of interesting and successful people, from sports stars and celebrities to adventurers, entrepreneurs and great leaders. There is a wealth of ideas in these volumes waiting to be absorbed by anyone with a little curiosity and a desire to do better. You don't even have to pay for it. This vast storehouse of knowledge is available at most libraries across the country. And of course there's the Internet at your fingertips. Many of the best books can now be obtained in summary form. Instead of taking a week or a month to read, you can extract all the highlights and most important points. Of course, make sure that whoever is doing the summary is highly credible. (See the Resource Guide for our recommended reading list, plus some other great resources.)

One last comment on reading. Consider taking a good speed-reading course. It will dramatically reduce the amount of time you currently spend on reading. Like everything else, it takes practice to become proficient, but by now you already understand that.

Watch for special documentaries on TV, and ongoing series like *Biography* on A & E. The Learning Channel, Discovery Channel, the History Channel and PBS Television all offer excellent programming. You can even learn a lot from movies and powerful dramas that have an impact on you, not just intellectually but emotionally. When we're in touch with our emotions we acquire deeper insights and understanding. And remember, it's okay to shed a few tears now and then.

LEARNING FROM EVERY SOURCE

We mentioned this earlier but it's worth reinforcing. Did you know that you could gain the equivalent of a university diploma just by driving to and from work every day? Here's how: Instead of listening to some crazy disc jockey on the radio or a lot of negative news, turn your car into a learning center. Audiotapes are one of the most productive ways to expand your awareness. Tuning in for twenty minutes a day will give you over one hundred hours per year to learn more. And when you apply what you learn, you'll earn more.

There are thousands of tapes to choose from. Most bookstores sell cassette versions of the bestselling business and personal development books. You can also rent books on tape through specialty self-help stores, as well as excellent videos on a wide range of topics. These are often presented by some of the greatest speakers in the world. (See our Resource Guide for more details.)

Also learn from yourself. You can gain a lot from your everyday experiences. How did you overcome your last challenge? Every time you take a risk or move out of your comfort zone, you have a great opportunity to learn more about yourself and your capacity. More about this under the letter *T* in our **B-ALERT** system.

Learn from others. You can learn a lot more by observing and studying other people. What do wealthy people do? How did they become rich? Why do some people struggle throughout their lives? Why are only a small percentage of people financially independent? Why do some people have wonderful, loving relationships? Using other people's experience as a yardstick for learning will help you tremendously. All you need to do is keep your ears and eyes open, and ask a few questions.

JACK:
I recently conducted a sales motivation seminar for a California-based optical lens manufacturing company. There were about 200 salespeople in attendance. I asked members of the audience to raise their hands if they knew who the top two or three producers in the company were. Almost every hand went up. I then asked them to raise their hands if they had ever approached any of these two or three people to ask them what their secrets of success were. Not one hand went up. What a tragedy this is. We all know the people who are successful, but we are afraid to approach them and ask them for information, direction and guidance. Don't let the fear of rejection stop you from asking. The worst thing that could happen is they wouldn't tell you. You'd end up not knowing what they know. You already don't know what they know, so it can't get any worse, can it? So take the risk. Ask!

Make a habit of this. Here's another idea: Pluck up the courage and invite a successful person out to lunch every month—someone you really respect and admire. Drag the lunch out, the more courses the better. Ask questions. You'll uncover a gold mine of information, and buried in there may be some real nuggets of wisdom that can transform your business, financial affairs or personal life. Isn't that possible? Of course. But most people won't do this. They're much too busy to stop and learn from wiser, more experienced people. That just magnifies the opportunity for you.

JACK:
Early in his career my stepfather, who was one of NCR's top salespeople, made a habit of taking the top producers and managers out for a drink and asking them questions about how they got into the business, and for their advice on how he could do a better job. All this advice paid off. He eventually became president of NCR Brazil.

By the way, your daily learning doesn't need to be completely life-changing or on a mega-scale. It's often the little details that make a difference. Constant fine-tuning is the true path to wisdom, so learn a little every day.

MARK:
We were carrying our skis back to the car after enjoying a full day on the slopes. With a fair distance to walk, I was having difficulty supporting my skis. One of my friends pointed to the female ski instructor in front of us, effortlessly carrying her equipment. I noticed she had the center portion of her skis perched on her right shoulder, and her right hand was draped loosely over the front end, providing excellent balance. We copied her technique. What a difference! Hardly anyone else was using this simple method—they were all struggling as we had been.

The moral of the story is that life teaches you something every day if you just keep your eyes open and are conscious of what is going on around you.

Charles "Tremendous" Jones was right when he said, "There are essentially two things that will make you wiser, the books you read and the people you meet." Make sure you do both. In addition, the tapes you listen to and the personal coaching you receive will play a prominent role.

If you really want to rise to the top, invest one hour of your day to learn more about yourself and your industry. Developing this single habit can make you a world expert within five years. Remember, the use of knowledge is power. And powerful people attract great opportunities. This takes self-discipline, but won't the rewards be worth it?

> HAVING ALL THE MONEY IN THE WORLD ISN'T
> MUCH GOOD IF YOU CAN HARDLY GET OUT
> OF BED IN THE MORNING TO ENJOY IT.
>
> —Author Unknown

E Is for Exercise

Now don't heave a big sigh and say, "Oh no!" Please read through this section carefully. It will be extremely worthwhile. Most people don't like the thought of doing any form of regular exercise, and that's a big mistake. Here's the important question. Do you want to be rich in health? Again the answer is "Yes" or "No"—not, "I'll think about it."

Today the business of fitness and health is exploding. It's a multibillion-dollar industry. And the reason is that people are finally understanding there is a direct benefit to looking after their physical bodies. You will probably live longer. More importantly, you will enjoy greater vitality, and your quality of life will be substantially better. Let's face it, what's the point of earning a lot of money if you don't have optimum health to enjoy it in your later years? Wouldn't that be sad?

Creating an excellent balance in your life means you don't treat your health lightly. A little daily exercise is part of the prescription. Here's the good news. You don't need to run marathons or work out in the gym for three hours every day. About twenty minutes is all you need. And there are lots of ways to do it.

Do you remember George Burns, the famous comedian who lived a great life to the ripe old age of one hundred? In his nineties, George still enjoyed going out with women much younger than himself. A friend once asked him, "George, why don't you go out with women more your own age?" With a twinkle in his eye he quickly responded, "There aren't any!" George had a tremendous vitality for life. In a revealing interview with Barbara Walters, he was asked about his secret for longevity. He mentioned he'd always done a little stretching every day, usually about fifteen minutes. This was his long-term habit. There's a clue for you. The older we get the less flexible we become, especially if we stop exercising. There are lots of good stretching routines. Any chiropractor, physiotherapist or fitness facility will be able to help you; or you can pick up a book at the library. You will notice the difference in your mobility in a couple of weeks, especially if you are over forty years old.

One of the easiest ways to exercise is to enjoy a brisk walk. If you just take fifteen minutes and walk around the block a few times, your body will thank you. Note this: If you take a forty-five-minute walk four times a week, you can lose up to eighteen pounds over the course of a year, without dieting. Walking has other benefits. It gets you out in the fresh air and provides an opportunity to expand communications and relationships. Walk with your spouse, a family member or a friend. To achieve the best results, exercise for thirty minutes a day including stretching. Play a sport, do aerobics, jog, use an exercise bike or treadmill, join a fitness club or design your own routine.

Exercise does not need to be boring. There are a multitude of ways to create variety. If this is something new for you, understand one thing—like any habit, it will be difficult at the start. Set a thirty-day goal. Do whatever it takes to get through this critical time period. Have a no-exceptions policy, and give yourself a reward for not missing a single day. Here's the guarantee: You will feel much better at the end of thirty days. Remember, don't overdo it in these early stages. If you have a medical condition, check with your physician first.

If you are still not convinced, here's a list of eight specific benefits you will receive from a regular exercise program:

- Exercising improves your sleeping habits.
- Exercising increases your energy levels.
- Exercising relieves stress and anxiety.
- Exercising protects you against injury.
- Exercising promotes a healthy posture.
- Exercising relieves digestive disorders.
- Exercising enhances your self-image.
- Exercising expands your longevity.

With this multitude of benefits, why *wouldn't* you want to exercise?

LES:
Years ago I started a daily exercise routine. I like to do this first thing in the morning. It starts with five minutes of stretching, followed by a twenty-five-minute run, and another ten minutes of stretching. This is now ingrained as

a habit. It is just part of what I do every day. When I first started, my body would ache and I'd be gasping for breath, but gradually I have increased my capacity and now I genuinely enjoy getting out in the fresh air. Rafferty, our golden retriever, accompanies me, so I'm able to complete another of my duties at the same time. I also use this time mentally, to give thanks and reflect on my priorities for the day.

We have cold winters in Calgary. Sometimes the temperature drops lower than twenty degrees below zero. That's cold! Some people have asked, "You don't run in those temperatures, do you?" And the answer is, "Of course!" I derive so much benefit from my daily run that if I didn't go out, it would bother me psychologically for the rest of the day. It's easy to add a few extra layers of clothing to ensure that I stay warm. When I'm traveling I don't pack a lot in my suitcase. That gives me an excellent opportunity to be creative. Instead of running outside, I'll jog around the hallways in the hotel or use the underground parking lot if an exercise facility isn't available. There's always a way. The point is, if you discover something that improves your life, keep doing it. The rewards far outweigh the early discomfort. Stick with it until your new habit becomes part of your everyday behavior.

A couple of final thoughts on good health. Make it a study. Find out more about the unique metabolism you have and how to optimize the magnificent vehicle you have been given. Even people with so-called disabilities can enjoy a healthy physical dimension in their lives. Have you ever watched a one-legged skier come down the slopes, often more gracefully and as fast as those people with two legs? It's amazing. And of course these skiers don't regard themselves as handicapped. They just figured out another way to perform with the aid of a specially designed short ski. Also, study nutrition. There's a lot to learn. Your body responds best to certain food combinations. Enlist the help of an experienced nutritionist or naturopath. You'll increase your knowledge as well as your energy levels.

If you're struggling with the self-discipline to initiate a good exercise program, here's a way out. Hire a personal fitness trainer to make you accountable. As always, do your homework. Find out who the best person is in your area. Talk to a few different trainers and select the one who really understands your situation. This person can design a program just for you.

"We'll take you off the vitamins for a couple of days."

A good trainer will vary the type of exercises so you don't become bored. This is money well spent, and it costs a lot less than you may think. You will be taught the proper technique when you exercise, so that you derive maximum benefit. Most people who make up their own programs exercise incorrectly. Learning from a professional will accelerate your progress.

Your body is the physical vehicle you have been given to move around in. Don't neglect it, or it may grind to a halt like a car that's never been serviced. You could end up on the scrap heap of life as a burned-out observer, instead of enjoying the fun of being in the driver's seat. It's your choice. The message is simple. If you want to be rich in health, eat right and exercise.

By the way, in case you're wondering, we haven't forgotten the importance of mental and spiritual health. That's coming up in chapter 6, The Confidence Factor.

> OH, TO BE FREE FROM THE STIFLING PRESSURES
> OF LIFE—TO REST, A PEACEFUL SLUMBER
> THAT WILL REJUVENATE MY SOUL.
>
> —Les Hewitt

R Is for Relaxing

This is the time to recharge your batteries during the day. Years ago, people thought the computer would allow us to enjoy more time off for fun. We'd be on the golf course three days a week while all this new technology would handle the workload at the office. What a joke! In most cases people in business now work even longer hours than before. The workload is greater and because of downsizing, support has been significantly reduced.

Do you get physically tired during your average workday? If you do, is there a particular time that you seem to sag? If you are an early riser (5:30 A.M. to 6:30 A.M.), your sag-time is probably around 1:30 P.M. to 3 P.M. If you don't eat breakfast, it may hit you earlier. Some people fortify themselves with six or seven cups of coffee during the day to overcome the loss of energy. This may lead to caffeine addiction, hypertension and other side effects that certainly won't help you relax.

Here's an excellent way to preserve your energy so you can enjoy a productive day. Take a nap! We call it a TPM—that stands for Twenty-five Peaceful Minutes. In warm climates, a siesta is a normal part of the day. When you were a young child, your mother probably put you down for a nap after lunch. As an adult, why not do the same? It's good for you. And you won't be so cranky later in the day. Now in case you're thinking, "Are you nuts? I don't have enough time as it is without snoozing my afternoon away. And besides, where can I take twenty-five minutes with people all around me? I don't have a bed or a couch in the office. Do you expect me to lie on the floor?" Exactly!

LES:
Everyone in our office is entitled to take a TPM every day. I put a note on my office door that simply says TPM. This means Do Not Disturb. Then I switch the lights off, remove my shoes, and loosen my shirt and tie. I take a pillow that I keep in one of the cupboards and stretch out on the floor. Prior to that I unplug the phone and put on some relaxing background music. I set a timer for twenty-five minutes, take a couple of cleansing breaths, close my eyes and relax. There are no interruptions. My personal assistant knows the routine, as do the rest of my staff. It's wonderful. This mini-siesta rejuvenates my energy. I can stay focused and productive well into the evening, instead of collapsing on the sofa, never to stir again until bedtime. This extra energy allows me to enjoy real quality time with my family.

If you don't have an office, get creative. Relax in your car instead. If you're traveling on business, you may need to shift the time somewhat, but you can still find a way to grab those few minutes to rest. And if you own the business, don't be a dinosaur. The old, only-on-your-own-time routine is really outdated. The most progressive and profitable organizations realize that a highly productive workforce is not achieved by pushing people until they drop from exhaustion. This doesn't mean you need to lower your performance standards. It's simply recognizing that high productivity requires a lot of energy.

Another of our clients, Ralph Puertas, is president of Zep Manufacturing Company in Canada. He keeps a recliner in his office for self-rejuvenation, and encourages his other managers to take TPMs when necessary.

TPMs are a great way to boost your energy into overdrive. If you have a family, another important time to consider a TPM is the so-called cross-over time, when you arrive home from the office. Your mind is still buzzing with business and you haven't unwound from the tensions of the day, and suddenly the kids are unleashed on you. If you can plan a TPM for yourself before you switch roles, it will give you a chance to catch your breath, relax and be mentally ready to focus on the family. To enhance this, consider relaxing to your favorite music. Whatever method you choose, good communication is required to make this effective.

Looking at the bigger relaxation picture, how much time off do you take each week? And how many weeks per year do you schedule for fun? First let's define what time off is. If you plan to take one day off per week, make sure it's a full twenty-four hours. We call it fun-time. That means for the entire twenty-four-hour period you do absolutely nothing related to business. Not one phone call, or opening a single file for even a few minutes. Many businesspeople are confused about time off, especially entrepreneurs. To them a day off means packing their cellular phone around, answering incoming business calls and making a few of their own. "I must be available" is their passionate excuse. They have a fax machine or e-mail at home so they can monitor urgent messages, most of which, of course, aren't urgent at all.

Here's the point: If you have worked long, hard hours all week, you deserve a break to re-energize. Will you be more rejuvenated if you take a complete break for twenty-four hours versus grabbing an hour or two whenever you can? Unquestionably, a complete break serves you better. This is difficult for many businesspeople to grasp. They mentally tear themselves apart with guilt. For example, a father is taking his son to a swimming lesson on Saturday and he's thinking, "I should be at the office finishing that project." And when he's at the office on the weekend he feels guilty about neglecting his son, because he promised to take him to the football game. This ongoing cycle of guilt increases stress levels and frustration. When work wins the battle over enjoying fun-time with your family, relationships polarize. Other long-term consequences include burnout, divorce and health problems.

To avoid any potential rifts, schedule your family time every week. At the beginning of the year, decide when you want to take major breaks and reserve these on your calendar. You can select three- to seven-day getaways, or two- to three-week vacations—whatever works best for you. And if you're not in a position to do this right now, make sure you have at least one day off per week, and set a goal to increase your time off next year. The important thing is to develop the habit of creating real time for total relaxation. When you return from a week off, well-rested and refreshed, you will be more creative, better focused and more productive.

One of our colleagues has worked with thousands of highly successful entrepreneurs during the last twenty years. He has observed that the more time off these people take, the

TO MAXIMIZE YOUR PROGRESS

Take Regular Breaks To Re-Energize.

more money they make. He has proven this with the growth of his own company. Every month he takes one week off. As long as he gets out of the city, he doesn't really care where he goes. He doesn't make calls to the office, and he doesn't take calls either. Even though he takes three months annual vacation the business has achieved outstanding growth every year for the past eleven years.

We're not suggesting that you duplicate this strategy. Just make sure that you enjoy regular time off to replenish your energy and lower your level of stress. And please do it without guilt. Life's too short to constantly worry about everything. It really is okay to have some fun.

> IF YOU REALIZED HOW POWERFUL
> YOUR THOUGHTS ARE, YOU WOULD NEVER
> THINK A NEGATIVE THOUGHT.
>
> —Peace Pilgrim

T Is for Thinking

Yes, we know you are already thinking most of the day. However, this is a different kind of thinking. It's called reflective thinking. As mentioned before, if you want to have unusual clarity about what is working and what is not working in your life, schedule time for reflective thinking. This is the final part of your **B-ALERT** system that will help you create an excellent balance every day. Here's how it works. At the end of your workday, or just before you go to bed, take a few minutes to take a mental snapshot of the day. Regard each day as a mini-movie with you as the star. How did you do? Rerun the tape and take another look. What did you do well? Are there any adjustments you could have made to create a better result? Focus daily on the progress you made. Be alert to any shortcomings, but don't beat yourself up. Learn from your mistakes. After all, tomorrow is a new day, another opportunity to perform better. Make reflection a daily habit. It only takes a few minutes, and it will make you stronger and wiser in the weeks and months ahead.

At first, the **B-ALERT** system for optimum balance may appear overwhelming. One of our clients actually thought he had to do everything in sequence—start with the letter *B* and end with *T*. No, no, no! It's a lot more flexible than that. You will find that this unique system does not take a lot of extra time. In fact, creating a blueprint will save you time, because you have a clear picture of your priorities. By focusing on your most important activities during the day, you will be more productive and achieve greater results. Learning may

take thirty minutes if you choose to read or listen to a personal development tape. However, you can combine this with your exercise time. Be creative. On the other hand, experiential learning doesn't take any time at all. It's simply what you observe every day as you go about your business. This time to relax and reflect is an opportunity to replenish your energy and expand your clarity.

CONCLUSION

Consider this all-important question: Would you enjoy a better balance in your life if you had a clear blueprint for the day, were able to stay focused on your most important activities, maximized your energy and clarity with a little exercise and reflective thinking, and had some time off for fun? The answer is obvious. Of course you would!

So make the effort now. Use our **B-ALERT** checkpoint system. (See Action Steps.) This is a daily reminder that will keep you on track. Just photocopy it and attach it to each page of your planner. Or incorporate it into your computer or electronic organizer. And remember, excellent balance will greatly enrich your mind, body and spirit, not to mention your most important relationships and your bank account.

ACTION STEPS

The B-Alert Checkpoint System

The B-ALERT Checkpoint System

This is a simple way to monitor your progress. It only takes a minute to check. At the end of each day ask yourself if you completed all six parts of the **B-ALERT** system. For example, if you had your blueprint organized, put a check mark through the letter *B*. If you spent the greater part of the day working on your most important activities, check the letter *A*. Repeat this for the remaining letters. Be honest with your evaluation. You will notice patterns developing each week that will highlight what you are doing right, and what needs to be corrected. Use a red pen to circle the letters where your performance is lacking. For example, if you plan to do thirty minutes of exercise every day, and you notice the letter *E* has five red circles drawn around it in the first week, you need to make some changes! As always, ease into this new habit. Don't be too hard on yourself at the start. The more you practice, the better results you will have.

B-Alert:

A PROVEN SYSTEM FOR CREATING OPTIMUM BALANCE

Blueprint
My strategic plan for the day. Priorities, appointments, projects. Review the night before or early morning.

Action
Concentrate on the most important activities that will move you towards accomplishing your sixty-day goals.

Learning
Expand your knowledge through reading, cassettes, video, mentors, courses.

Exercise
Re-energize for thirty minutes.

Relaxation
Eliminate daily stress. Nap, meditate, listen to music, family time.

Think
Take time to reflect on the day. Review goals, visualize, develop new ideas, use a journal.

Track your progress every week. Set up your own simple recording chart, as in the example below. At the end of each day take a moment to record your score. Circle any area that you miss.

Mon	Tues	Wed	Thur	Fri	Sat	Sun
✓ B	✓ B	✓ B	✓ B	✓ B	✓ B	✓ B
✓ A	Ⓐ	✓ A	✓ A	✓ A	✓ A	✓ A
✓ L	✓ L	Ⓛ	✓ L	✓ L	✓ L	✓ L
Ⓔ	✓ E	Ⓔ	Ⓔ	✓ E	Ⓔ	✓ E
✓ R	✓ R	✓ R	✓ R	✓ R	✓ R	✓ R
✓ T	✓ T	✓ T	✓ T	✓ T	✓ T	✓ T

LIVING ON PURPOSE

TAKING DECISIVE ACTION

CONSISTENT PERSISTENCE

ASK FOR WHAT YOU WANT

THE CONFIDENCE FACTOR

BUILDING EXCELLENT RELATIONSHIPS

CREATING OPTIMUM BALANCE

DO YOU SEE THE BIG PICTURE?

IT'S NOT HOCUS-POCUS, IT'S ALL ABOUT FOCUS

YOUR HABITS WILL DETERMINE YOUR FUTURE

Almost halfway there—stay focused!

Building Excellent Relationships

"SOME PEOPLE ENTER OUR LIVES AND LEAVE
ALMOST INSTANTLY. OTHERS STAY, AND FORGE
SUCH AN IMPRESSION ON OUR HEART AND SOUL,
WE ARE CHANGED FOREVER."

—Author Unknown

LES:
At the time, my mother was eighty-five. She lived alone in Belfast, Northern Ireland, and had suffered a heart attack. My father had passed away sixteen years before, and being the only child in the family, I was concerned. My biggest fear was not knowing how serious the situation really was. And, living in Canada, it was not that easy for me to commute if her health deteriorated.

My good friend Denis, who worked at the local hospital in Belfast, kept me informed with regular phone calls. However, he and his family were leaving for a holiday in Cyprus in a few days, and they were excited about the trip.

The next phone call was one I will always remember. It was Denis. The good news was, my mother was being released from the hospital—but she was still very weak. He said, "I'm canceling our trip to Cyprus. Beenie (his wife, who is a registered nurse) and I would like to have your mum stay with us until she has fully recovered. Then you'll know she's getting proper care and attention." I felt a lump in my throat. Tears welled up in my eyes and I couldn't speak for a moment. He asked, "Are you all right?"

"Yes," I replied. "I don't know what to say—I'm overwhelmed." His closing comment was, "Think nothing of it. That's what friends are for, isn't it?"

Our relationship moved to another level after that. It's a wonderful feeling to have special people in your life who can enrich and nourish you in many different ways. In fact, when your time is almost up on this planet and you're doing a little reflection on how it all worked out, you'll probably remember the relationships you cultivated and the unique memories and experiences associated with those people, especially your family and friends. This is important stuff in life, versus burning yourself out at the office.

In this chapter, you'll discover several powerful strategies that will ensure that you enjoy outstanding relationships in both your personal and professional life. Building excellent relationships is a habit, and it produces wonderful rewards.

The Double
SPIRAL

Relationships can be very fragile. Many marriages don't survive, families are broken up and often kids are raised with only one parent to support them. What causes these relationships to fall apart when there is so much joy and love at the beginning?

It's helpful to look at your life as a spiral. Sometimes you are in an Upward Spiral. That's when things are going well, your confidence is high and life is rewarding. Your most important relationships are healthy and flourishing. The opposite is the

Downward Spiral. This is when things start to unravel, a lack of communication occurs, stress increases and life becomes a constant struggle. Relationships are polarized during the Downward Spiral.

Nature gives us dramatic versions of these spirals. A tornado is a powerful example. Spiraling down from the sky, these dark funnels hit the ground sucking up everything in their path with devastating results. The Michael Crichton/Steven Spielberg movie *Twister* provided a close-up view of these awesome spirals, and the incredible energy they contain.

Another example of a Downward Spiral is a whirlpool. On the outer edge of the whirlpool the water doesn't look too dangerous. If you are not aware of the powerful forces at the center, however, you can be pulled down very quickly.

UNDERSTANDING THE DOWNWARD SPIRAL

Let's look at how the Downward Spiral shows up in real life. To clearly understand the potential impact this can have on your current and future relationships, think of a relationship you have been involved in that didn't work out. You need to re-create in your mind all the steps that caused this relationship to fall apart. Visualize clearly what happened. Go back as far as you can and relive it. What was the first thing that happened? What happened after that? Then what happened? To understand the full impact of this, be sure to complete the Action Steps at the end of this chapter. Recording each individual step of your Downward Spiral all the way to the lowest point will help you understand the pattern.

For example, in a marriage the husband becomes self-centered and doesn't help around the house anymore. He spends more time at the office, leaving early in the morning before the kids are up and arriving home late in the evening. Communication is limited to business and finances. Maybe money is tight and there isn't enough to cover the mortgage, car payments, children's dance lessons and dental bills. Gradually the tension builds up, arguments occur more often and each partner blames the other for the situation they are in. The Downward Spiral is now gaining momentum, just like being drawn into the center of the whirlpool. Either, or both, may seek solace by drinking, going out with the boys (or girls), gambling, or, in the worst cases, abusing each other physically and mentally. At this point, the relationship has been sucked dry and the Downward Spiral is at its lowest point. Separation often occurs, ending in divorce, and another family is placed on the broken-home list, a statistic that seems to be growing annually.

When you carefully reflect on what causes relationships to fall apart, you can take steps to heal them. Even if the relationship is past saving, you'll be better prepared for the next one, and able to prevent the same pattern from materializing. Awareness is always the first step to progress. You can also use this spiral technique to review your most important business relationships. Here's a common scenario:

Two people form a partnership. They have a great idea for a new product or service and they pour a lot of time and energy into their exciting new venture. Because they're so busy making things happen, no legal partnership document was ever prepared or signed. They are good friends and they intend to do that down the road. Also, there are no clear job descriptions or methods for compensation and profit sharing.

Fast-forward this picture a few years. The partnership is now struggling because one person is a controller and won't allow his partner to make any decisions without his permission. Finances are tight and there's weekly bickering about the way revenues should be spent. One person wants to reinvest their earnings in the company so it can grow, whereas the other has a pay-me-first attitude. Gradually the rest of the staff are pulled into the conflict and two distinctive political camps emerge. A crisis develops and one partner wants out of the business, but there is no shotgun clause, and of course no agreement that would make this easy. The partners both dig their heels in and finally they set up their own legal teams. The battle is on. Often the attorneys end up with most of the money, the business collapses and two more people are heard to proclaim, "Partnerships never work!" Yes, the Downward Spiral can be equally devastating in the corporate world.

Here's a tip: If you are currently in a business arrangement with one or more partners, or are considering one in the future, always plan your exit strategy first, before you get too involved. Make sure it's in writing. And beware of emotional attachments. The undisputed fact that your new partner is a nice guy, or your best friend, is no reason to sidestep a written agreement. Lack of foresight and preparation ruins more businesses today than anything else.

Now that you've looked closely at how the Downward Spiral can show up in your life, learn from it. Because we are creatures of habit, there's a good chance that you will repeat the same behavior in your next important relationship. Really understand this. It's critically important for your future health and wealth. If you find yourself going into the same Downward Spiral, immediately take a mental time-out. Interrupt the pattern with clear thinking and decide to make positive adjustments. Changing your behavior is the only way you will get a different result. Here's how: Use a new template. That is, superimpose an Upward Spiral for excellent relationships on top of your Downward Spiral, the one that got you into so much trouble.

UNDERSTANDING THE UPWARD SPIRAL

Let's analyze how this Upward Spiral works so you can reap the rewards quickly. Repeat the process as before, except this time you are going to focus on a relationship that you gradually nourished, expanded and enriched, until it blossomed into a wonderful long-term friendship or business relationship. Go back in your mind and replay all the significant things that happened from the time you first met until the relationship fully matured. Most people don't do this, so you will enjoy a tremendous advantage in the marketplace when you develop an accurate blueprint that you can duplicate many times in the future. Powerful relationships ensure powerful results.

Here's a positive example to help you. . . . Dave owns an engineering business. He adapts ideas from clients and helps them create new products. Innovative design and efficient workmanship are Dave's areas of brilliance. Over the past twenty-two years he has honed these skills to a high level. Along the way, he's also learned how to treat people properly. He has a loyal customer base and pays attention to simple things like returning phone calls promptly and following through with his clients' requests.

When a new client approached him one day with an idea for a rubber extrusion product, he was happy to help. The young man had big visions. He dreamed of his own manufacturing facility that would supply some of the world's largest users of his unique product. Dave provided his expertise and made subtle changes to the prototype. These refinements made it less costly to make and more robust. This new alliance between the young entrepreneur and the experienced engineer blossomed over the next few years into an enjoyable, mutually rewarding friendship. Each in his own way helped the other to higher levels of creativity and productivity. Eventually the young entrepreneur's dream was realized. Because of his larger vision and persistence, he secured several exclusive multimillion dollar contracts. All along he stayed in touch with Dave for advice.

As his business grew, so did Dave's. One day, reflecting on his incredible success, he made an important phone call that would enrich their special relationship even further.

He offered Dave a percentage of all his future profits. It was his way of saying, "Thank you for believing in me, for helping me get started and for pushing me through the tough times."

All excellent relationships have a starting point. Often the first few interactions are not memorable. However, you soon develop a good feeling about the other person. Maybe it's his integrity, enthusiasm, positive attitude, or just that he does what he says he is going to do. A bond develops, and each new step strengthens the union further, making it more and more special.

Do you get the picture? When you review in detail how you developed your best relationships, it provides a unique process for creating bigger and better future relationships. Knowing what works and what doesn't work will help you avoid costly mistakes that create a Downward Spiral. The good news is, you can apply this template for excellent relationships to any area of your life. It works for personal and family relationships as well as for professional and business alliances.

Develop the habit of constantly reviewing your Double Spirals—use them to protect you from any negative downward pull, and to guide you into the positive world of truly special and loving relationships.

Say "No" to TOXIC People

Before we move on, please heed this important advice—**avoid toxic people!** Unfortunately, there are a few people out there who see the world as one big problem, and in their eyes you're part of it. You know the type. No matter how well things are going, they focus on the nitpicking little negative details. And they do it constantly. It's a habit that totally destroys relationships. One blast of negative energy from their lips can erase that smile on your face permanently. These people are poisonous to your health. You need a long-range antenna to keep them outside your boundaries at all times.

You may be thinking at this point, "Easier said than done. Do you mean if my friend, who I've known for years, is always complaining about his job and how awful things are financially, and nobody wants to help him out, that I should just turn and walk away when he talks like this?" No—run! As fast as you can, and as far as you can. His constant negativity will drain the life out of you.

Now please understand, we're not talking about someone who has a genuine challenge and needs real help. We're referring to those chronic whiners who take great pleasure in dumping all their negative garbage on your plate at every opportunity. They also inform you, with a not-so-subtle cynicism, that you can't do this and you can't do that, especially when you have a really great idea. They delight in bursting your positive bubble. It's the highlight of their day. Don't put up with it anymore.

Here's where the real power is: It's always your choice. You can choose the type of people you want in your life. And you can choose to pursue new opportunities. Maybe you just need to make some better choices. It's that simple. If it means letting a few people go, well, you'll get over it. In fact, take a close look now at your present relationships. If someone is dragging you down all the time, make a decision. Let go and move on.

JACK:
One of the first things my success mentor, W. Clement Stone, suggested I do was to make a list of my friends. Then he directed me to put the letter N next to each person who nourished me and encouraged me to be great—people who were positive, optimistic, solution-oriented, and had a can-do attitude. Next he asked me to put the letter T beside every person who was toxic—

people who were negative, whined, complained, put down other people and their dreams, and who were generally pessimistic in their outlook. Then he asked me to stop spending time with the people who had a *T* next to their names. This is one lesson you must learn—surround yourself with positive people. Mr. Stone taught me that you become like the people you hang out with. If you want to be successful, you must hang out with successful people.

The Three Big
QUESTIONS

Now that you've had a chance to understand your Double Spiral, and an opportunity to clean house regarding the negative people in your life, here's another great strategy that will benefit you immensely. It's called the Three Big Questions.

Business mogul Warren Buffet is one of the best-known and most successful investors in the world today. His company, Berkshire-Hathaway, has grown from a few private clients with modest holdings to a multibillion-dollar enterprise. Mr. Buffet is famous for careful analysis and for investing in long-term opportunities. He rarely sells his stock after making an investment. His intensive preparation includes a thorough analysis of the numbers, especially the company balance sheet. If these are to his liking, he spends considerable time meeting key people in the organization, getting to know how they run the business. He observes their philosophy and how they treat their staff, suppliers and clients. When this is completed, Buffet asks himself three questions concerning the key people: "Do I like them? Do I trust them? Do I respect them?"

If any one of these questions results in a "No," the deal is off. It doesn't matter how good the numbers look, or the potential for growth. These three simple, powerful questions are the foundation for Warren Buffet's relationships. Adopt them as your own. They will ultimately determine how rich you become.

A few years ago, Buffet was the wealthiest man in America. He recently relinquished this title to Bill Gates, founder of Microsoft. It's interesting to note that despite the age gap, these two phenomenally successful entrepreneurs are close friends. Who you hang around with *does* make a difference.

The next time you are about to enter into an important business or personal relationship with people you don't know very well, do your homework first. Look for clues that demonstrate their integrity, honesty and experience. Watch how they treat other people. Little details will offer big insights: Are they in the habit of saying "Please" and "Thank you," especially to people in service positions, such as waiters and waitresses, bellhops and cab drivers? Are they down-to-earth with others, or do they have a need to impress people? Take sufficient time to digest their overall behavior before you make a commitment. And always refer to the Three Big Questions. Pay attention to your intuition. That gut feeling will guide you. Don't let your heart rule your head. When we are too emotionally involved, we often make bad decisions. Give yourself time to think before rushing into any relationship. Look at this another way: Why would you choose to build relationships with people you don't trust, don't respect or don't like? Going ahead when your instinct is telling you not to is a formula for disappointment or even disaster.

There are lots of excellent people out there to enjoy your valuable time with. So whether it's marriage, a business partner or hiring a sales team, choosing the right people is critically important to your future health and wealth. Choose carefully.

Core Clients and
THE DOUBLE WIN

The next step in developing the habit of Excellent Relationships is learning to nourish your most valuable relationships in a win-win atmosphere. A lot has been written and spoken about the philosophy of win-win. In our experience, most of it is just surface talk. Win-win is essentially a philosophy of how you live your life. In business, win-win means having a genuine concern for the other person; that they win as much as you do, whether it's a sale, employee contract, negotiation or strategic alliance.

Sadly, the attitude of many people in business has been to grind every last cent out of every situation. These so-called guerrilla tactics cause a lack of trust, cynicism, questionable ethics and a high level of anxiety in the marketplace. The result is win-lose. On the other hand, win-win doesn't mean giving the farm away every time you make a deal. That's lose-win, with the other person receiving too much, which would eventually put you out of business.

There's also another category called lose-lose. This happens when both parties are too stubborn or too egotistical to create a winning solution. A common example is contract negotiations between management and unions. If a stalemate occurs, the result may be a long, drawn-out strike where nobody really wins.

In your personal life, win-win is the foundation for warm, loving relationships. It's a husband wanting to create a win for his wife and family. He's willing to pitch in and do an equal share of household duties and help with the children's extracurricular activities, especially when his wife is also working full time. Win-win is a wife giving solid support to her husband as he strives to build a new business or start a new career, and is willing to accept a few sacrifices along the way. Win-win is giving to your community, being an outstanding neighbor and being less self-centered. For win-win to really work, you must practice it every day. This takes time, and challenges you to make a serious commitment to building these important alliances.

Now let's look at another crucial element in growing your business—building excellent **Core Client Relationships.**

Your core clients are people at the heart of your business. They buy from you consistently and are a main source of revenue. They are also happy to provide excellent referrals for new business, because they genuinely love your products and service.

Amazingly, many people today don't even know who their core clients are. Core clients are your passport to future growth. Unfortunately, these important relationships are often taken for granted. The attitude is, "He always orders two thousand units every month. We need to focus on new business."

NOT EVERY DEAL IS WORTH SAVING

New business is important. Staying in touch with your best clients is more important. It's a lot more difficult to find new customers than it is to keep and serve your old customers.

Also, be aware of the time you spend on people who are peripheral clients. The word *peripheral* is worth noting. It means at the outer edge, unimportant or not worth mentioning. Another term is dispensable. Do you have any peripheral clients in your business? If you're not sure, here's how you can spot them. They commonly take a lot of your time and energy and give you very little business in return. Sometimes they give you no business at all. But they will question you on every little detail, and they'll place unreasonable demands on your time. Of course, you may not want to turn any business away from your door. But what is it costing you in time and energy to dabble in minor results? Some deals just aren't worth the effort.

Let's look back to your core clients. There's one critical element you need to understand about these people. You don't ever want to lose them. Here's the big question. How much real time do you spend with your most important core clients?

This is worth studying. Our research indicates that very little time is allocated to core clients. Consequently, these relationships never mature to their full potential. On the bottom line, that means a lot of money is squandered.

Now that you know who these important people are, pay more attention to them. The long-term rewards are well worth the effort. Your business will increase, and you'll also minimize the likelihood of losing any of these top clients to your competitors.

Lori Greer is the national sales director for a successful organization called Company's Coming that specializes in selling cookbooks. To date, Company's Coming has sold fourteen million books. One of Lori's core clients places an order annually for one million dollars worth of books. To service this client, Lori and her account representative meet the client at least once a year. In one of our coaching workshops, she was challenged to expand this relationship to

a new level. Accepting the challenge, she brought her in-house team together and held a special brainstorming session that lasted five hours. The sole purpose of this meeting was to come up with ideas that would be helpful for their core client.

When they made their next sales presentation, many of these new ideas were included. To further enrich their relationship, Lori spent extra time with the client to socialize instead of rushing back to her office. The result? An order for 20 percent more cookbooks. More importantly, a new level of appreciation and trust was established that will ensure a long-term, win-win relationship. More than anything, this will keep predatory competitors at bay.

Now let's take a look at your most important personal relationships. These include family and friends, mentors, spiritual advisers and anyone who is special in your life outside the business world. Again, think carefully about who qualifies to be on this unique list of core people. Then write down their names. If you are tempted to skip over this exercise, stop! Procrastination is your greatest enemy. Don't put off your better future. Do each step as soon as you finish reading this chapter. Remember, this book is a work in progress. By the time you finish it you will have kick-started many of these exciting new habits. Your life will be richer and eminently more satisfying.

Take a close look at this list and review the amount of time you spend with these people. Is it sufficient? Do you enjoy quality time, or just a few seconds on the telephone? Who else do you spend your personal time with? Are they robbing you of time that would be better spent developing your core relationships? If you answered "Yes" to this last question, what are you going to do about it? Maybe it's time to say "No" to those people who distract you every day. They're not on your most-important-people list, so why are they stealing your time? From now on, protect your family time and personal time. Be polite but firm.

We briefly mentioned win-win as it relates to the people in your life. It's important to really understand what this means. Bestselling author Stephen Covey provides a good analogy. He says you should treat your most important relationships like a bank account. For example, the more deposits you make in your core relationships' bank account, the stronger these associations become. In the process you become more valuable to these people.

Normally, money is what you deposit at the bank. However, with your core relationships you can make a variety of deposits. With your core clients in business, you will probably offer special services and all those little extras that define you as unique. These may include golf outings, dinners or special trips. Other healthy deposits include allocating time to share ideas or advising how to handle certain challenges. Maybe you consistently provide good referrals to expand their business. Sometimes it's making them aware of a great book, or faxing an article about their favorite pastime or hobby. You could also connect them to people who have a unique service or product. The more you know about the people on your core client list and core personal list, the more you can help them. And the true spirit of win-win means that you make these deposits unconditionally. In other words, don't give to get something back. Just experience the sheer joy of giving.

If you don't already have one, create an information file for every one of your core clients and core personal relationships. Find out everything you can about these individuals. Include their likes and dislikes, favorite restaurants, birthdays, anniversaries, kids' names, favorite hobbies, sports and pastimes.

Business guru Harvey MacKay, owner of the MacKay Envelope Corporation in Minnesota, calls his information file the MacKay 66, because there are sixty-six questions that his sales team asks to gain an in-depth knowledge of every important client. Most people don't keep files like this because they are not really serious about win-win. It takes considerable time and effort to cultivate highly successful relationships. It means that you will often be required to go the extra mile. This way of living gradually becomes your new normal behavior. You do it without thinking. When win-win behavior becomes truly embedded in your everyday life, the floodgates of opportunity will open up for you like never before. You will indeed be richer for it, and we don't just mean financially.

LES:
Here's a humorous story about win-win. Two Irish laborers, Big Paddy and Wee Jimmy, had just won the lottery. They were rich to the tune of five million dollars each. Having cashed their winnings the previous day, they were eager to celebrate. The happy pair were strolling downtown, still amazed at their good fortune, when they saw a fish-and-chip shop. Big Paddy said, "I'm famished—let's have a lovely fish supper and a big drink to wash it down." So in they went, Big Paddy wearing his green duncer cap and Wee Jimmy still in his black rubber work boots. By their appearance, people would never have guessed they had millions in the bank. Big Paddy paid for the fish and chips and they both savored every last bite.

Their appetites satisfied, they continued walking and a few minutes later came across a Rolls Royce dealership. Wee Jimmy gasped when he saw the luxurious automobiles. "I've always fantasized about owning a Rolls," he whispered.

"Let's take a look," laughed Big Paddy, holding the showroom door open for his long-time friend. Inside, Wee Jimmy's gaze fixed on a beautiful silver-gray car that gleamed from front to rear.

"Paddy, wouldn't you love to have a car like this?" he exclaimed.

"That would be grand," Paddy agreed.

Wee Jimmy turned to the immaculately-attired sales manager and asked, "Sir, how much is this beautiful car?" The six-figure answer didn't deter him for a moment.

"Okay," he grinned. "I'll take two—one for me, and one for my friend here." Then he turned to Big Paddy and said, "Put your wallet away, Paddy, I'll get the cars. You paid for the fish and chips!"

. . . And Then SOME

Yes, win-win is a great way to live, and true friendships are hard to come by. Value the ones you have and do whatever it takes to make them even richer. Here's a powerful strategy that will make it easy. It's called the And Then Some technique.

Let's say you want to expand an important personal relationship with your husband or wife. If you are not married, you can apply this technique to almost any meaningful relationship, so adapt it accordingly. In fact, pick someone you'd like to enjoy a deeper level of friendship with. To show you how it works, we'll use the husband and wife example.

Imagine it's the end of the week, and David the good husband has arrived home from work. His equally good wife Dianne has dinner ready, and they both enjoy an excellent meal. David compliments her and then poses the following question: "Dianne, on a scale of one to ten (one being pathetic and ten being wonderful), how would you rate my performance as a husband during the last week?" This is a serious question. Dianne reflects for a moment and says, "I'd give you an eight."

David accepts the answer without comment, and asks the And Then Some question: "What would I have needed to do to make it a ten?"

Dianne answers, "Well, I would have really appreciated you helping John with his homework on Wednesday. I was under pressure to be at my computer class by 7 P.M., and I felt guilty leaving without him being looked after properly. Also, you promised to repair the tap in the bathroom this week. It's still dripping. I'd really like it fixed, please." David simply says, "Thank you, I'll be more attentive next time."

Then the roles are reversed. When Dianne asks David to give her a score out of ten, David awards her a nine. Now it's her opportunity to ask the And Then Some question. "How could I have scored a ten?"

David gives her sincere feedback. "You were great, but there was one little thing. Remember you promised to tape the football game for me when I was away Monday and Tuesday? I know it just slipped your mind, but I was looking forward to watching the highlights when I got home. I was really disappointed." Dianne listens, offers an apology and makes a commitment to record requests like this in her daily planner.

Before you say, "That sounds great, but it would never work for me," stop and think. You're right, very few people use the And Then Some technique, and even fewer do it on a weekly basis. The most common excuses are, "I'm too busy," "That's silly," or "Get real, my husband (or wife, or friend) would never agree to that."

BE TOTALLY OPEN TO FEEDBACK

Here's what these well-worn excuses are really saying: "My partner and I are not open to feedback, because our relationship has not matured to that level." Regularly giving and receiving honest feedback is one of the best ways to enrich your marriage, friendship or business relationships. It's the hallmark of human beings who have a high level of awareness and a unique sensitivity to the needs of others. Because of this maturity they enjoy honest, open and fulfilling alliances with the most important people in their lives. You can also use this technique with your children and other family members. Your kids will tell you the real story—they don't pull any punches!

By asking a few simple questions every week, you can learn more about yourself from people who care enough to give you honest feedback. Instead of becoming defensive like most people, accept the information as a gift. It will help you become more genuine and trustworthy.

And Then Some means you are willing to learn more, do more, and put more into the relationship because it's important to you. In the process, both parties are rewarded and strengthened. Consider the benefits of applying the And Then Some technique in your professional life. If you own the company, you could ask your key people, "On a scale of one to ten, how do you rate me as a boss? What can I do to become better—to rate a ten?" Managers could do the same with their sales or administrative teams. What about your core clients? Here's a great opportunity to understand the strengths and weaknesses of your business, and how to improve those areas that are not performing well. Remember, your core clients may also include suppliers, or your outside support team.

If this technique is new to you, the first few attempts may be awkward or uncomfortable. That's normal. Any new habit takes a lot of practice and perseverance before it finally clicks. Hearing the truth from people you respect and love also takes some getting used to. Sometimes the truth hurts; you may need to swallow your pride a few times in order to enjoy the future benefits. One other note here——if you are giving critical feedback, always do this in private. On the other hand, give praise in public. People need and enjoy well-deserved recognition of any kind. Simply stated, criticize in private; praise in public.

REMEMBER, FOR THINGS TO CHANGE

You've Got To Change.

How to Find Great
MENTORS

Surrounding yourself with well-chosen mentors can dramatically change your life. A mentor is someone with vast experience or unique talents, who is willing to share ideas with you on a regular basis. You, as the *mentee*, the recipient of this great information, have a responsibility to use it wisely by furthering your career and financial status or by enhancing your personal or family life. It's like a teacher-student relationship, except that you have the benefit of one-on-one tutoring. And the big bonus is that you normally don't pay for the lessons. What a deal!

Here's a proven three-step method to help you enjoy the considerable advantages of mentorship:

1. Identify the target.
Select one specific area of your life that you want to improve. There may be several, but for the purpose of getting started, choose only one. Here are a few ideas—growing your business, sales, marketing, hiring excellent people, preparing financial statements, learning new technology, investment strategies, accumulating wealth, eliminating debt, eating and exercising for optimum health, being an excellent parent, or doing effective presentations.

2. Select your mentor candidates.
Think about someone who is exceptionally experienced or talented in the area you have selected for improvement. It could be someone you know personally, or it could be a leader in your industry. Maybe it's someone who is recognized as a top authority on this topic—a well-known writer, speaker or celebrity. Whoever it is, make sure he or she has a proven track record and is truly successful.

3. Create your strategic plan.

If you don't already know the whereabouts of your proposed mentor, how are you going to locate this unique individual; and when you do, how will you make contact? The first thing to realize is that you are probably never more than six people away from anyone you want to meet, including your new mentor. That's exciting to know—treat it like a game. There may be six doors you need to open before you have all the information you need. Who could open the first door for you? Proceed from there, and keep asking. You'll be surprised how quickly the other doors open up once you put the word out.

You may be looking at the name of your proposed mentor and second-guessing yourself with thoughts like, "I don't even know this person and she certainly doesn't know me. And if she did, she probably wouldn't give me any of her valuable time." Stop right there! The following story is big proof that finding and contacting mentors is well within your capabilities.

LES:
One of our core clients is a young man who owns a small trucking business, and he was keen to expand. After attending our Achievers workshop on mentorship, he selected one of the major players in the trucking industry to be his new mentor. This man had started and built a huge business over the years, and was widely respected by his peers and competitors.

Our client, Neil, located the head office in Texas. He made several phone calls and eventually was connected to this successful businessman. (We'll tell you what to say when you make a call like this in a few minutes, so be patient.) Neil was a little nervous, but he summoned up the courage to ask. The successful businessman agreed to spend twenty minutes every month with Neil on the telephone, sharing his experience and best ideas. True to his word, this arrangement was carried out, and one day Neil received an interesting offer. His new-found mentor invited him down to Texas for five days to study every aspect of his business. He could be a fly on the wall, talk to the staff, and observe firsthand why the company had prospered.

Of course Neil didn't hesitate. The result? Not only was he able to expand his business in many profitable ways, his relationship matured to another level. Instead of a mentor-mentee association, a growing friendship developed. In addition, he was able to share some of his own successful strategies that were not being practiced by his mentor. Over time, a true win-win relationship formed, and Neil's confidence grew along with his profits.

It all started with that one phone call. So let's analyze how you can enjoy similar success. The most important thing is to be sincere. Sincerity goes a long way in helping you get what you want in life. Here's what Neil said when he first got through on the telephone, "Hello, Mr. Johnston (not actual name), my name is Neil. We haven't met yet. And I know you're a busy man, so I'll be brief. I own a small trucking business. Over the years you have done a fantastic job, building your business into one of the largest companies in our industry. I'm sure you had some real challenges when you were first starting out. Well, I'm still in those early stages, trying to figure everything out. Mr. Johnston, I would really appreciate it if you would consider being my mentor. All that would mean is spending ten minutes on the phone with me once a month, so I could ask you a few questions. I'd really appreciate it. Would you be open to that?"

When you ask that closing question, the answer will usually be "Yes" or "No." If it's "Yes," control your excitement and ask another question. "When would be a good time to call you in the next few weeks?" Then confirm a specific time for your first mentor meeting. Follow up with a handwritten "thank you" note right away.

If the answer is "No," politely thank the person for his time. Depending on how firm the refusal was, you could ask if it would be okay to call back at a more convenient time to reconsider your request. Otherwise move to plan B—call the next person on your list.

Let's review the key elements in the phone call. First, get right to the point. Busy people appreciate this. Don't socialize. Stick to a well-prepared script using a relaxed conversational tone. It only takes a minute. Also, it is important to control the conversation. Say what you want to say, ask the closing question and then shut up. At this point, you allow your potential new mentor to speak. If you follow this sequence, your success ratio will be high. Here's why: First of all, when you ask someone to be a mentor, it is the ultimate compliment. Second, they are rarely asked. And if you do it with total sincerity, having reminded them of their own earlier challenges, you will often receive a positive response.

Before you make the call, it's useful to have as much information as possible. Ask the company to send you any promotional material they have, including the most recent annual report.

Remember, you can have several mentors. You can select people for any area of your life that you want to improve. They may live in another city or country, or they may be half an hour's drive away. So get started and have fun. These unique relationships can dramatically accelerate your progress. Trial and error is one way to gain experience, but it's hard work figuring everything out on your own. Tapping into other people's successful formulas and adapting their ideas is a lot smarter. It's usually who you know that opens up the doors for bigger and better opportunities. Treat it like a "connect-the-dots" game. Successful people are well-connected. Simply follow their moves. To help you further, you will find a step-by-step Action Plan for Developing Mentor Relationships at the end of this chapter.

Mentor relationships are one-on-one, similar to that of a tutor and student. Another unique way to accelerate your growth is to set up a Mastermind Group alliance. Like mentoring, it will add a whole new dimension to your life that will be a powerful source of support and strength.

MASTERMIND Groups

A Mastermind Group, as the name implies, requires a meeting of the minds. The origins go back a long way. Ancient Greek philosophers, such as Socrates, enjoyed lively debate and an opportunity to share their ideas and insights. Our concept of a Mastermind Group is ideally made up of five or six people who want to develop excellent long-term relationships. The primary purpose of the group is to establish support for each other emotionally, personally and professionally. It also provides a unique forum for sharing ideas and information, as well as discussing meaningful topics and everyday challenges. If you select the right people, this wonderful support system can be enjoyed for many years.

There are four main action steps that will help turn this concept into a reality for you.

1. Select the right people.
For best interaction, you should limit your group to six people; five others and yourself. You don't need to select everyone at the same time. You may start with one or two and gradually build up to a full complement. Remember, the first team member may be the hardest to find. But don't let that stop you. Whom should you choose? That's the big question. Here are a few guidelines to help you. Choose people who are likely to create synergy—ambitious, open-minded, goal-oriented individuals who have a positive outlook and bring a

healthy, positive energy to each discussion. You don't want a bunch of whiners who are looking for a regular opportunity to dump all of their negative garbage.

It's also beneficial to include people who have real experience and success in business, or who have overcome challenging personal situations. In your selection process, decide if it's important to have people from different industries or not. For example, you may not want five salespeople in the group. A blend of different experiences and backgrounds will add depth and variety to your meetings.

Consider whether you want a mixed group, or an all-male or all-female group. Also, what age group do you prefer? A broader age group with men and women included adds a different perspective and a wider range of opinion. If you'd rather have a narrower focus, then select people of the same gender close to your own age. It's entirely up to you. But do give this selection process serious thought. It's vitally important to the success of your group.

2. Everyone must make a commitment.

A Mastermind Group is designed as a long-term support system. It's not for people who are casual. You know the type. They show up when they feel like it or there's nothing else on their schedule that day. Explain this clearly to each candidate. You also want agreement at the start on a termination policy. If one person isn't fitting in, for whatever reason, it's important for you to have a process that handles this. You don't want to end up with the "bad apple in the barrel" syndrome, where one controlling or negative individual dominates the entire group process. A democratic vote within ninety days of your opening meeting is an easy way to avoid any early disruption. You can also implement this course of action at any future date.

The level of commitment will determine how successful your Mastermind Group becomes. Commitment requires regular attendance, a willingness to participate each time you meet, and an agreement to keep confidential anything that is shared in the group. This code of confidentiality is extremely important. In our experience it takes several months before people really emerge in a setting like this, especially men. There's all that macho image stuff to get over. Women are generally much more open to sharing their true thoughts and feelings.

The real benefits occur only when there is a high level of trust within the entire group. The environment you create should be a safe place, where absolutely anything can be shared with no concern about indiscretion.

3. Decide when, where, how often and for how long you want to meet.

Two to three hours every month is a good rule of thumb, or you can meet more frequently if you want. Some people prefer an early-morning breakfast in a relaxing, well-appointed location. Others would rather meet in the evening when the business day is over. Again, it's up to you. Some key points are: Choose a location where you will not be interrupted by phones, faxes or other people. Make it a rule to turn off cellular phones when you are together. Don't treat your Mastermind Group like a typical office meeting. This is special time with special people, so maximize the opportunity to focus on the issues at hand.

4. What will you talk about?

Good question! What you don't want is a couple of hours chit-chatting about the local news and weather. High-energy achievers won't waste their time in this fashion. Here are a few suggestions: Elect a chairperson whose main role is to keep the conversation flowing, and to allow everyone equal time. Start each meeting with a brief comment from everyone about the best thing that happened since the last meeting. This will get things off to a positive start. Then ask two questions: "What's happening in your business life (or job)," and "What's happening in your personal life?" Go around the table one person at a time. This process alone might take up the entire meeting. And that's okay. It gives you an opportunity to learn more about each other. Another good question is, "What's your greatest challenge at this time?" Also, discuss and support each other's individual goals. Inspire everyone to achieve what they want. Encourage them to think big and introduce them to people who can accelerate their progress.

Sometimes you may want to have a special topic on the agenda. It's also a good idea to reserve time for someone who has a particular need—a financial crisis or health problem that needs to be addressed. These situations are what really bonds your Mastermind Group. Take the opportunity to help in whatever way you can to resolve the issue. If an urgent situation arises, you can always call a special meeting to handle it quickly.

LES:
Our Mastermind Group is made up of five people. Each person owns his own business, encompassing five different industries. As of this writing, the group has been meeting for fourteen years. We don't socialize a lot outside of the monthly meetings. During our association everyone has faced a variety of difficulties and enjoyed significant achievements. Subjects for discussion have covered a wide range of topics including current business challenges and opportunities; how to create high-impact presentations; where to find venture capital, and how to fire a key employee. We have also faced marriage difficulties, problems with teenage children, health issues, financial crises and major career changes. Several of our meetings have been emotional, with tears shed openly. We now enjoy a wonderful bond and the richness of knowing that when anyone needs help, four people will be ready and willing to provide immediate assistance. That's a very powerful position to be in. It was definitely worth all the time and effort.

MAKING YOURSELF BULLETPROOF

Now we want to share with you another important building-block in developing the habit of Excellent Relationships. It's called Building Your Own Fortress. Mentors and Mastermind Groups provide a terrific foundation. The definition of a fortress is a structure that is impregnable, a sanctuary or a place of refuge. Within a fortress you are protected from the storms of business and life. Here's how you can build one.

It's like building a championship football or hockey team. Each player has a role to play, and the team is only as good as its weakest member. The team is molded by the coach. He or

THE FORTRESS

Your Unique
Total Support
System

Use the following categories to guide you in the building of your Fortress. These are not ranked in any specific order of importance.

1. The Family Unit.

2. Specific Mentors and Coaches.

3. Health and Fitness Team.

4. Business Support Team (Interior).
   (e.g., Administrative Staff, Sales and Management Team.)

5. Business Support Team (Exterior).
   (e.g., Banker, Lawyer, Suppliers.)

6. Core Clients.

7. Personal Mastermind Group.

8. Personal Development Library.

9. Spiritual Adviser.

10. Other Strategic Alliances.
    (e.g., Networking Groups, Passive Income Pipelines.)

11. The Sanctuary. (Your own personal retreat, or getaway location.)

© 1976 JIM UNGER

"I found him working in the stockroom, J.D. He's perfect!"

she is at the center of the action. The combination of uniquely gifted team players and a coach who can create and implement a successful game plan produces triumphant winners.

Consider yourself as the coach. Two major questions you need to address at this point in your life are, "Who is on my team?" and "Do they perform at the level I require to achieve my dreams and goals?" Make sure you do the Action Steps. They will help you discover who deserves to stay on your team and who you need to replace. This is all about setting very high standards so that you can enjoy a lifestyle that gives you total freedom, ongoing prosperity and a unique sense of worth. When you need help, you'll have the best people to assist you. This is an ongoing process, not a quick fix.

Here's how it works: Take a close look at your important relationships—the people who support and help you throughout the year. Separate them into two main categories: business/career and personal. Make a list of these important people. In your business/career list, examples would include your banker, lawyer, accountant, bookkeeper, tax specialist, suppliers, financial adviser, management staff, sales team, administrative staff, personal assistant and secretary/receptionist. In the personal category, the range is much broader: doctor, chiropractor, medical specialist, massage/physiotherapist, personal fitness trainer, nutritionist, dentist, dermatologist, financial consultant, hairstylist, dry cleaner, plumber, electrician, travel agent, realtor, insurance agent, car dealer, tailor, gardener, home help, babysitter and anyone else whose expertise you might need.

Obviously you don't interact with all of these people every week. The question is, when you do require their help, do they consistently do a brilliant job for you? Sometimes the person you select doesn't do a very good job. To avoid this, take time to check the person's history. Brilliant people do brilliant work. They do it on time and they do it consistently. They make you feel good in the process, and they charge a fair price. These are people you can always rely on to get the job done right.

How many don't deserve to be on your team because their performance is not good enough? Be totally honest. How many gaps are there on your team? This is easy to determine. These are the times you rush to the Yellow Pages hoping to find someone at the last minute. Often the person you select doesn't do a very good job because you didn't have time to check his background.

From now on, don't make decisions "on the run." And don't tolerate sloppy workmanship, tardiness, exorbitant pricing and any sort of hassle that creates more stress in your life. You don't need that. Ask your friends for references. Do your homework. Do the research. Be patient, and gradually surround yourself with a first-class team of people who will make your life joyful and rich beyond measure. Start right away. You'll be amazed at how this will transform your relationships.

CONCLUSION

Alan Hobson and Jamie Clarke are two exciting young "adventurepreneurs." They coined this name to describe their love for combining adventure and business. One of their shared goals was to climb Mount Everest, the highest mountain in the world. In 1991, their team's first attempt to reach the summit failed. In 1994 they went back again. This time the team was smaller. One member, John McIsaac, reached 28,500 feet but couldn't continue because he developed severe pulmonary edema. Only 641 feet short of the summit, he had to turn back. A major rescue was required to bring him down the mountain safely, as he didn't have the strength to descend on his own. This required a total team effort with everyone contributing their unique talents. Other mountaineers were recruited from different teams on the mountain to assist.

Finally in 1997, having learned from their previous two experiences, Alan and Jamie took on Everest for the third time. They both made the summit, a truly magnificent achievement. They said, "It was relationships that made our experiences on Everest what they were. Even if you didn't summit, you still had the good times, you still had the good feelings, despite the hardships.

You come out of it alive, looking to do more with those people. On an expedition, we share our lives together. We pretty much know everything there is to know about each other."

One of the reasons Alan and Jamie finally achieved victory was that they surrounded themselves with brilliant teams of people. These teams included a professional expedition organizer, a fund-raising team, a support team, a route-fixing team and a summit team. Without this unique "Fortress," the expedition would not have succeeded. But with these teams supporting them, Alan and Jamie were able to focus totally on preparing themselves physically and mentally for the climb.

Make a decision today to build a fortress around you. Select only the best people. There are many to choose from. Remember, life is all about building and enjoying great relationships. You deserve your fair share! It takes confidence to assert yourself and seek out excellent people. You'll learn all about this important habit in the next chapter.

PROSPERITY IN LIFE IS DERIVED MORE FROM WHO YOU KNOW, NOT WHAT YOU KNOW.

ACTION STEPS

The Double Spiral

Building Your Fortress

Developing Mentor Relationships

Make sure you complete these exercises. If you skip over them, you're probably not serious about developing excellent relationships. Don't sell yourself short. Make the effort now to learn about yourself and the impact you have on other people.

1. The Double Spiral

FAILED RELATIONSHIPS—Mentally revisit a significant relationship that didn't work out. Starting at number one, identify each step in the process that caused the relationship to fall apart. Be specific.

1. _____

2. _____

3. _____

4. _____

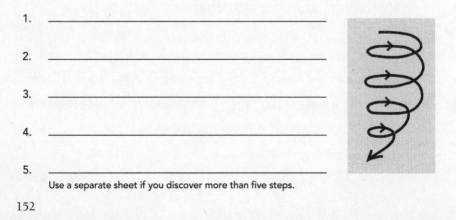

5. _____

Use a separate sheet if you discover more than five steps.

EXCELLENT RELATIONSHIPS—Mentally revisit one of your greatest relationships. Starting at number one, identify each step in the process that caused this excellent relationship to expand.

5. _____

4. _____

3. _____

2. _____

1. _____

Use a separate sheet if you discover more than five steps.

2. Identifying Core Clients

Write down the names of your ten most important business relationships. These are the people who bring you most of your sales and income. They love your products and service. They give you repeat business and are happy to refer you. (Note: if you are a manager or supervisor, the team of people you look after would be part of your core client list.) Please take sufficient time to think about this. These people are the building blocks to your better future. Treat them well! The most important people are your core clients. The word core means at the center, the heart or essence of anything valuable.

Now record how much time you spend with each of these people in a typical month. What does this tell you? What adjustments do you need to make?

1. _____   6. _____

2. _____   7. _____

3. _____   8. _____

4. _____   9. _____

5. _____   10. _____

BUILDING YOUR FORTRESS—Analyzing strengths and weaknesses

This is an example of how to define and evaluate your Business Support Team (Interior/Exterior) and what will be required to boost it to the next level. Use this model to create the other areas of your Fortress.

Business Support Team	Names	*Grade	Changes Required	Action Steps	Investment Required
A	Administrative (receptionist, secretarial)				
B	Marketing and Promotion				
C	Sales				
D	Management				
E	Suppliers				
F	Financial (bankers, investors, shareholders)				
G	Accountant				

Business Support Team	Names	*Grade	Changes Required	Action Steps	Investment Required
H Bookkeeper					
I Tax Specialist					
J Legal Consultant (lawyer, negotiator)					
K Staffing (hiring, training, coordination)					
L Personal Assistant/ Project Person					
OTHER For example: advisers, mentors, coaches.					
OTHER					

*Grade: This is evaluated as follows: Suitability for the position, skill level, ability to synchronize with other team members and overall performance. Also consider how much you trust, like and respect these individuals. Be honest!

B = Brilliant   G = Good   A = Above Average   U = Underachiever   N/A = Not Applicable   O = Position Open

Create and implement a specific plan to constantly upgrade your support team. Fill any positions that are open.

155

DEVELOPING MENTOR RELATIONSHIPS

What specific areas of expertise do you want to improve?

1. Check the most important

- ☐ Expanding My Business
- ☐ Sales and Marketing
- ☐ Health and Fitness
- ☐ Hiring Excellent People
- ☐ Balanced Lifestyle
- ☐ Financial Strategies
- ☐ Communication Skills

- ☐ Developing Strategic Alliances
- ☐ Eliminating Debt
- ☐ New Technology
- ☐ Parenting
- ☐ Other _____
- ☐ Other _____

2. List the top three areas of expertise you want to improve, and name two possible mentors for each.

1. _____   _____
                               _____

2. _____   _____
                               _____

3. _____   _____
                               _____

3. From the list above, select the most important area you want to work on right away, and your number-one preferred mentor.

_____

4. Take a blank sheet of paper and, using the example on page 141, create your own script for your first contact. Practice on the phone with a friend. Rework this until it begins to flow.

Now Pick a Time and Date and Make the Call.

If you are not able to speak to the person right away, keep calling until you do connect. Persistence really pays off. Remember, just one excellent mentor relationship can help you jump to a whole new level of confidence and awareness.

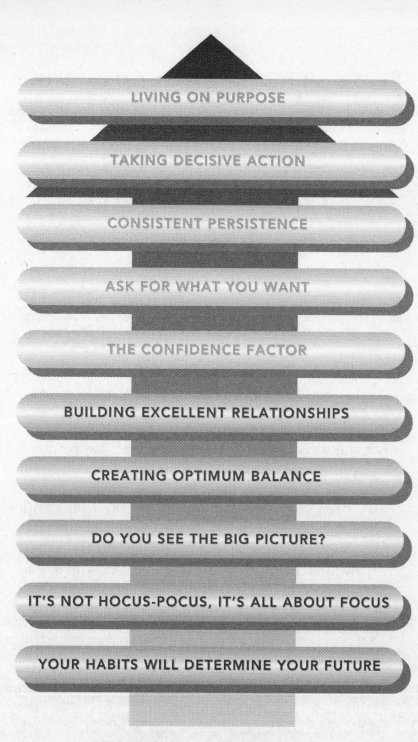

LIVING ON PURPOSE

TAKING DECISIVE ACTION

CONSISTENT PERSISTENCE

ASK FOR WHAT YOU WANT

THE CONFIDENCE FACTOR

BUILDING EXCELLENT RELATIONSHIPS

CREATING OPTIMUM BALANCE

DO YOU SEE THE BIG PICTURE?

IT'S NOT HOCUS-POCUS, IT'S ALL ABOUT FOCUS

YOUR HABITS WILL DETERMINE YOUR FUTURE

You made it—now keep going!

The Confidence Factor

"EXPERIENCE TELLS YOU WHAT TO DO;
CONFIDENCE ALLOWS YOU TO DO IT."

—Stan Smith

In 1999, South African President Nelson Mandela celebrated his eightieth birthday.
For almost twenty-six of those years, he was confined to a prison cell because of his outspoken views about apartheid. During this time, Mandela's confidence must have been severely tested. It is a tribute to his faith and conviction that he ultimately triumphed and went on to be elected to his country's highest office.

Confidence is a habit that can be honed and strengthened every day. During this process you will be challenged by fear, worry and uncertainty. These elements constitute the ebb and flow of life. It's a constant struggle, a mental battlefield that must be won if your life is to be filled with abundance. To start, carefully read the words spoken by Nelson Mandela at his inaugural speech. This is a man who accepted the challenge and won. Digest each sentence slowly. Use them as a foundation for your next level of achievement.

Our deepest fear is not that we are inadequate.

Our deepest fear is that we are powerful beyond measure.
It is our light, not our darkness that frightens us.

We ask ourselves, who am I to be brilliant, gorgeous,
talented and fabulous?

Actually, who are we not to be?

You are a child of God.

Your playing small doesn't serve the world.

There's nothing enlightened about shrinking so that
other people won't feel insecure around you.

We were born to make manifest the glory of God
that is within us.

It's not just in some of us, it's in everyone.

And as we let our own light shine, we unconsciously
give other people permission to do the same.

As we are liberated from our own fears,
our presence automatically liberates others.

SOURCE: A *Return to Love* by Marianne Williamson
(as quoted by Nelson Mandela in his inaugural speech, 1994)

This chapter contains many practical strategies that will boost your confidence to an all-time high. It is important that you utilize these on a daily basis. Confidence is the all-important factor you need to protect yourself from the slings and arrows of negativity. In the absence of confidence, fear and worry take control. Progress is held in check and momentum grinds to a halt.

So let's tackle this essential habit with gusto and a commitment to stamp out the negative forces once and for all. First, you need to clean up any unfinished business that's holding you back. Make that your starting point.

Resolving Unfinished
BUSINESS

Unfinished business is a term describing all of the messes in your life that you haven't dealt with. You may be struggling with legal, financial, relationship, organizational, health or career messes, to name just a few. When you allow these to build up, they can overwhelm you. The reason many people won't deal with this unfinished business is fear. Fear breeds doubt, and doubt leads to a loss of confidence. It's a vicious cycle. If left unchecked, a downward spiral begins and is soon gaining momentum. Suddenly life is out of control. This excess baggage is like a dead weight around your neck. It can bring you to a standstill.

The result is a tremendous drain on your energy. Some people have accumulated so much unfinished business over the years, it feels like they're pulling an elephant along behind them. There are three ways to handle this:

1. You can play the denial game.
Some people pretend it's not really happening. For example, a man worrying about his debt-load refuses to look at the real numbers in the hope that they will somehow disappear. Rather than change bad habits, such as spending more than he makes, he finds it easier to live in a fantasy world. Denial usually results in major consequences of the variety you won't like.

2. You can go into limbo.
Life sort of stops and you tread water. You don't fall back, but you don't make any progress either. It's frustrating, and of course the unfinished business is still there waiting to be dealt with later. Being in limbo keeps you stuck.

3. You can confront the issue head on.

This seems like the obvious course of action, yet many people choose the previous two options. Why? We usually don't like confrontation—it's uncomfortable and there's a certain amount of risk involved. Sometimes it can be painful, and may not work out the way you want it to. Here's a phrase that will help you: **Step into your fear.**

Most of the time fear only exists in our mind. Our imagination is powerful. Small issues often get blown out of proportion, and we create mental pictures that are ridiculous when compared to the facts. A friend in Arizona, George Addair, told us about a firefighter who attended one of his self-knowledge workshops. He said, "Firefighters deal with fear every time they prepare to enter a burning building. Just before they go into action they experience it—the uncertainty of not knowing if they'll survive or not. An incredible transformation takes place as soon as they go inside the building. They literally step into the fear, and because they do, the fear disappears. They are 100 percent in the present moment. They are then able to concentrate on fighting the fire, evacuating people and doing all the things they were trained to do. By confronting their fear, they can focus on the immediate situation and get the job done."

Another important factor is the energy you consume when you live in fear. You can't afford to have all that vitality bottled up. It restricts your capacity. If you want to gain confidence, accelerate your progress and restore your energy to maximum levels, you must confront your fears. Make a decision now to deal with your unfinished business once and for all. Give it your best shot. Put it behind you, and move on.

Make this a habit. Be aware that unfinished business is an ongoing reality. Every week something will happen that needs to be resolved. Don't allow these things to fester. Handle them promptly, with confidence. Your life will become refreshingly simple and uncluttered when you do.

The Road to Freedom
PARADIGM

We just mentioned Arizona businessman George Addair, who has created unique personal development training programs for more than twenty years. One of the strongest components in these workshops is The Road to Freedom Paradigm. Addair's philosophy is: Everything you want is on the other side of fear. To overcome fear you must have faith in the outcome. In fact, it usually takes a leap of faith to bridge the gap between fear and confidence. Someone who understands the significance of this is Dr. Robert H. Schuller, pastor of the Crystal Cathedral in Garden Grove, California. He says—

> *Faith is often called a "leap."*
> *Faith is leaping across the gaps*
> *between the known and the unknown,*
> *the proven and the unproven,*
> *the actual and the possible,*
> *the grasp and the reach.*
>
> *There is always a chasm between where you*
> *are and where you are going—by faith make*
> *the leap forward!*
>
> *What lies ahead? Tomorrow? Next week?*
> *Next month? Next year? Beyond this life?*
>
> *Believe in faith! Believe in God!*
>
> *Believe in tomorrow! Take the leap of faith!*
>
> SOURCE: *Putting Your Faith into Action Today!*

So how can *you* overcome these fears and uncertainties and start developing the habit of confidence? There are two initial steps: resolve your unfinished business and identify your deeper fears. Look at The Road to Freedom Paradigm graphic on page 164. Notice the big garbage can full of your unfinished business. Our Action Step called Resolving Unfinished Business, will show you how to get rid of it. This important exercise will help you create a practical solution that will bring your unfinished business to closure. Make a commitment to follow through, so you can experience that wonderful positive energy and sense of relief. Just releasing the guilt is well worth the effort.

Now take another look at the Wall of Fear below. In order to break through this major obstacle, you need to clearly identify your fears. Here are a couple of suggestions. Schedule some quiet time to think. It's important that you are not interrupted. Ask yourself this fundamental question: What do I really fear?

THE ROAD TO FREEDOM PARADIGM

Reprinted with permission from George Addair.

Keep repeating this question to yourself, varying it if you wish. What do I fear most? What do I fear in the future? What do I fear right now? Write down your answers. Keep adding to your list and be open to whatever comes up. The most meaningful answers may not surface right away. You may gain more insights from this exercise by having a trusted friend ask you the questions. He or she can record them while you sit quietly thinking, with your eyes closed.

Before you discount this activity as hokey or silly, take a moment to consider the benefits. The best way to really understand how and why you sabotage your results is to know yourself better. Reflective thinking gives you clarity. It's a wise choice. Don't be like the majority of people who sidestep the real issues and end up later feeling desperate and unfulfilled.

Once you have clearly identified your fears, you have a tremendous advantage. Now you can design strategies to topple them whenever they show up. Address each fear with the question, *What can I do to overcome this?* By doing so, you are preparing yourself in advance, just like professional speakers prepare a speech, by creating an outline of the key points. When you have a strategic plan to counteract your fear, you sow the seeds of confidence and certainty.

Self-knowledge is the key. Make it a habit to learn more about yourself; how you think, feel, react and behave. Below you will find a list of common fears and specific strategies to overcome them. Make a note of the ones you relate to most.

Common fears	Strategic plan to counteract fear
Poor health	Learn more about good health habits, nutrition, exercise and your genetics.
Losing your job	Become so valuable that you can't be fired. And if you are, your special skills will open up new opportunities. Keep refining your strengths. Focus on your brilliance; develop excellent connections.
Loneliness	Surround yourself with positive, supportive people. Be a giver. To attract friends, become a friend.
Uncertainty about the future	Most of the jobs in the future haven't even been invented yet. Focus on developing your greatest talents. Design exciting goals.
Dying	It happens to all of us. Have faith. Live every day to the fullest. Explore spiritual truths.

Common fears	Strategic plan to counteract fear
Failure	The spiritual side of you proves there is a bigger plan. God gave you talent. Seek it out. Surround yourself with winners. "Failure" is an opportunity to learn. Making mistakes is essential for long-term success.
Making major decisions	Think on paper—plan ahead—seek good advice. (See chapter 9, Taking Decisive Action).
Rejection	Don't take it personally, especially if you're in sales. We all experience some form of rejection every week. Become thick-skinned.
Conflict	Step into the fear. Look for a win-win solution. Accept that conflict is a part of life. Take a course in conflict resolution.
Ignorance/Lack of knowledge	Practice the habit of learning something every day. Read, study, become more conscious. Remember: The use of knowledge is your greatest power. Learn more. Become an expert in what you do best.
Losing your family	Continually nourish your most important relationships. Build a lifetime of positive memories you can cherish forever.
Public speaking	Join Toastmasters, take a Dale Carnegie course, join the National Speakers Association (see Resource Guide for details), choose a great mentor, write out a ten-minute speech on your favorite subject. Practice. Accept opportunities to speak when asked. Hire a speech coach.
Poverty	Learn about money and how it works. Check your belief system. Find an excellent financial coach. Set specific goals to save and invest a portion of everything you earn. (See chapter 10, Living On Purpose.)
Success	Embrace the fact that success comes from study, hard work, good planning and taking risks. You deserve it if you do all of this.

© The Achievers Coaching Program.

One of our clients has a goal to be a professional singer. She has a wonderful voice and specializes in country-and-western music. Until recently, she had only performed for friends and local community groups. Then one day a real opportunity arrived. Diane was offered a ten-minute spot in a major concert that was coming to town.

When the big night arrived, she stood backstage, trembling at the thought of singing in front of ten thousand people. Her heart was pounding, and she was imagining everything that could go wrong. Maybe she would forget the words, or her mouth would be so dry she couldn't sing at all.

Finally, a few minutes before her curtain call, she steadied herself. Quietly she repeated these words over and over again. "I can do this, I can do this, I can do this!" By focusing on the belief that she would perform well, and by eliminating her negative fear thoughts, the fear melted away. Upon finishing, she received a thunderous ovation, proof that her initial fears were totally unjustified.

Confidence is required at the height of your fear. It's one of life's greatest challenges. Accept it with a new resolve to do well, no matter what situation you are facing.

The Twenty-Five-Cent
CHALLENGE

Our friend Wayne Teskey has a Mastermind Group consisting of four other business friends. They are a dynamic bunch of entrepreneurs who meet monthly to share ideas and offer support to each other. At one meeting they agreed that life had lost some of its challenge. Their businesses were doing well, but they needed a new stimulus. They came up with an idea that would test their confidence and cause them to stretch out of their all-too-familiar comfort zones.

The plan was to fly from Edmonton, their home city, to Toronto, more than three thousand miles away, on a one-way ticket with only twenty-five cents in their pockets. Upon landing they each had to figure out how to get back home with no credit cards, no checks and no friends to help them out. To make it more interesting, they agreed to use at least three modes of transport. In other words, if one person was able to arrange a flight home, part of the journey had to include two other forms of transportation—train, bus, car, bicycle or on foot. Also, they could not tell anyone the nature of their challenge.

Picture yourself in this situation. What would you do?

It would obviously require creativity, innovation, courage and a strong belief in your ability, as well as money, to successfully make the trip back home.

Unknown to this madcap group, a friend had alerted the local media in Edmonton as well as major radio stations and newspapers. Upon arrival in Toronto, they were met at the airport by several photographers and reporters, all intrigued by this unique adventure. Now there was real pressure to perform!

It took most of the group about a week to get home, and everyone accomplished his goal. There were some interesting stories. One person took the long route by hitching rides. Stopovers included Minneapolis, where he worked as a croupier in a casino. He came back with more than seven hundred dollars. Two of the other members talked their way into staying at one of Toronto's finest hotels at no charge. Others found odd jobs.

EVERYTHING YOU WANT IS ON THE OTHER SIDE OF FEAR.

Wayne had fun on the street asking well-heeled businessmen, "Do you have any money that you don't plan on spending today?" If the answer was "Yes," he'd continue with a big smile, "Can I have some of it, please?" Some people actually paid up!

Back in Edmonton, the story gained front-page coverage. In fact, the group created more publicity than many expensive advertising campaigns. The "Masterminds," as they were now affectionately known, unanimously agreed that the trip was one of their all-time greatest learning experiences. They discovered that no matter how little they had, it was possible to not only survive, but to prosper. Confidence levels soared and their twenty-five-cent challenge created bigger and better business opportunities in the months that followed.

Forgive and FORGET

You have an incredible capacity and ability to overcome life's greatest challenges. Embrace this reality, and use it the next time a crisis occurs. In fact, celebrate the opportunity to perform at a higher level. When you break through the wall of fear, the rewards are many. You will enjoy peace of mind and the ability to dream and design an exciting future without being shackled by worry and guilt. When you continually clean up your unfinished business, life becomes simple and uncluttered. This gives you a surge of new energy.

All of this breeds confidence. It's critical that you understand one thing—confidence grows by doing, not by thinking. Only action produces results. As Sheryl Crow sings, "A change will do you good." To produce a different result, you need to change something. It all starts with you. Until *you* change, nothing else will change. Procrastination is a one-way ticket to staying stuck. It's an excuse not to perform.

Here's a big point about unfinished business. You really need to grasp this, so stay focused. To release yourself totally from the baggage of the past, you must learn to *forgive*. Read it again: **You must learn to forgive**. There are two sides to this. First, you need to forgive the people who obstructed you in the past—parents, friends, relatives or teachers. In fact, anyone who undermined or abused your confidence verbally, physically or mentally. No matter how traumatic the experience, to be free you must forgive them. This may not be easy, but it's essential if you want to have peace of mind and a happier future.

How do you do this? Write a letter, make a phone call, have a face-to-face conversation, whatever it takes, but it is of paramount importance that you settle the issue within yourself. Just let it go, and move on.

Second, forgive yourself. Silence forever those negative thoughts of guilt. The past is history. You will never be able to change it. Instead, accept the fact that whatever you did, your choices were based on your level of knowledge and awareness at the time. The same goes for your parents. Don't blame them for your upbringing—they did what they did based on their circumstances, belief systems and parenting ability.

Look at the word *forgiveness*. In the center are four letters, *give*. There's the clue. You must give to be free. The biggest gift you have to offer is love. Remember, you can't give what you don't already have. If you don't have love within you, how can you give it? It starts with forgiving yourself. You must move past the "It's not my fault," and the "Poor me" syndromes, or you'll never enjoy real love in your heart. This takes a special type of awareness. It's living at a higher level. To do this effectively requires detaching yourself from the past events of your life, so you can be free to give without conditions.

Too many people never let the real person within them come alive. Consequently, they live a dormant and unfulfilled existence. Instead of gloriously stretching and challenging themselves to be all they can be, they flounder in the everyday stuff of life. You can be different! Make a decision now to remove yourself from this futility and explore the unique talents you've been given. They are within you, just waiting to be let loose.

Release your fears. Forgive those who need to be forgiven, and be confident in the knowledge that you can have what you want by taking one step at a time, making one decision at a time and accomplishing one result at a time.

One of the most wonderful stories about forgiveness and love started many years ago in the Vietnam War. Journalist Patricia Chisholm recalls the story in *Maclean's* magazine: Nine-year-old Phan Thi Kim Phuc was fleeing her village when American bombs intended for military installations started exploding all around her. She recalls, "Right away, I know my clothes are burning, everything, and I saw my hand, my arm burning." But then she started to run, desperate to escape the circle of fire. There was, she says, "No more thinking." Just overwhelming fear, and later a searing heat. She had terrible injuries to her back, where great swaths of skin were destroyed by the napalm, a thickener that turns gasoline into a jelly-like concoction that sticks to surfaces, including skin, as it burns. At the scene, photographer Nick Ut rushed her to a nearby hospital, where she stayed for fourteen months, enduring many operations. Nick's dramatic photograph, which won him a Pulitzer Prize, captures the agony of the moment.

Now living in Canada after years of rehabilitation and adjustment to Western life, Kim has displayed a remarkable capacity to forgive. In the fall of 1996, she participated in a Veteran's Day ceremony at the Vietnam War Memorial in Washington D.C. There, she had an unanticipated and emotional meeting with Capt. John Plummer, the man who ordered South Vietnamese pilots to make the fateful air strike on her village. As the two sat side by side, smiling and holding hands, it was clear that Kim bore him nothing but goodwill. In this respect Kim is rare. Many people would live with resentment and hate that would consume them for years. She has chosen to avoid reflecting on the war. "I never do sorrow like that," she says. "To feel a trace of bitterness, even deep inside, is too tiring, too heavy." Instead, Kim decided to move forward. She is now happily married and has a young son to nurture. Undoubtedly, her ability to love and forgive has accelerated her progress.

The terror of war—Phan Thi Kim Phuc (left) flees from bombing raid.

Usually we don't think about confidence as a habit. Often we look at other people who seem to be enjoying life to the fullest, and wish we had been born with the same genes. While it's true that certain individuals seem to be more outgoing than others, confidence can be developed. And having confidence doesn't mean that you need to be jumping up and down every single day with off-the-scale positive energy. Some of the most confident and successful people we know have a quiet inner strength that is rarely expressed in gregarious fashion. Essentially, confidence evolves from combining a positive attitude with positive action. Both of these involve the power of choice. Every day you can make a conscious choice to think more positively. And you can also choose to take positive action or not. There is a direct link between your attitude and the choices you ultimately make.

A Winning ATTITUDE

Attitude has a lot to do with your success and your ability to get what you want. As you are probably aware, attitude can change quickly. In fact, every day your attitude is severely tested. One of the greatest examples of losing confidence occurred at the 1996 Masters Golf Tournament in Augusta, Georgia. Australian Greg Norman, a premier golfer and one of the favorites to win the championship, had performed brilliantly. At the end of the third day, he was six strokes ahead of his nearest rival, and with only one more round remaining, Norman seemed a cast-iron certainty to wear the famous green jacket presented to the winner on Sunday afternoon. All he needed was an average performance to secure the win. Inexplicably, however, his game collapsed during the final round. Within twenty-four hours his six-stroke lead evaporated, and he ended up losing by five strokes to Nick Faldo, who had quietly chipped away at Norman's seemingly insurmountable lead. Indeed, it was Faldo's persistence and confidence that eventually caused the upset. In fact, Faldo has made a habit of coming from behind to win, having won back-to-back Masters (1989–90) in similar fashion.

As the final round progressed, Greg Norman's attitude noticeably deteriorated. The confident stride seen the day before changed to slumped shoulders, and a blank expression appeared in his eyes as he saw his long-time dream to become Master's champion disappearing. His plummeting downward spiral was a poignant reminder of how fickle confidence can be. Strong and positive one day, in total disarray the next. To combat this, let's look at some practical strategies that will help boost your confidence.

Six Confidence-Building
STRATEGIES

1. Every day remind yourself that you did some things well.
Instead of dwelling on what didn't work or the tasks you didn't finish, focus on what you did accomplish. Don't minimize these. Use your **B-ALERT** daily habit to clarify this. Give yourself a mental pep talk at the beginning and end of the day. Coach yourself, just like you would help someone else to overcome a challenge.

2. Read inspiring biographies and autobiographies.
We want to reinforce this one more time. Read books, articles and magazines. Build a file of those stories that inspire you most. Record special TV documentaries. Listen to tapes or watch videos. Go to the movies—there are a lot of great stories out there. Find out about people who started with nothing, or who had devastating setbacks, and still found a way to win. Remember, your capacity far exceeds your current level of performance. Life without challenges is an illusion. Accept the fact that you will have ups and downs, just like

everyone else. Your confidence grows when you actively take on the challenges of life. You won't win them all, but with the right attitude you'll win more than enough.

3. Be thankful.

No matter how bad your circumstances may be, there's probably someone worse off than you. If you doubt this, volunteer your time in an acute-care burns ward at the children's hospital. Put things into perspective. Think of all the things (and people) you take for granted that are not available in other countries. Most of your problems will pale in comparison when you take a mental snapshot of all the benefits you enjoy every day.

175

4. Build excellent support around you.

If you need a boost, refresh your memory by reviewing chapter 5, Building Excellent Relationships.

5. Push yourself to accomplish short-term goals.

There's no greater way to build confidence than getting things done. Create an environment of accomplishment every week. Focus on your three most important targets. Every day do something that moves you closer to finishing a project, closing a sale or expanding a relationship. Don't allow yourself to be distracted or interrupted. By doing so you'll eliminate the feelings of guilt and failure. Take one small step at a time.

Make sure your goals are realistic. Self-rejection can shatter your confidence, so don't beat yourself up when everything doesn't come together as planned. Be flexible. And when others say "No" to you, don't take it personally. Accept the fact that you need to lose sometimes before you can win.

6. Do something for yourself every week.

Find a way to celebrate your weekly accomplishments. Don't you deserve it? If you said "No," go back to step one and start again.

THE ROAD TO CONFIDENCE IS PAVED WITH WEEKLY VICTORIES

Learn To Applaud Them.

Check Out Your
FAITH FACTOR

Recent studies show that happiness is clearly related to our level of confidence. Many people are also finding solace and unreserved joy in a strong spiritual connection. George Gallup, whose family pioneered surveys probing people's attitudes, has focused his work increasingly on religion. "I've always wanted to see surveys that probe beneath the surface of life," Gallup said. "We've learned a great deal about the breadth of religion, but not about the depth of religion. We're now trying to explore that more."

He said initial studies of this "depth dimension" have discovered that the most committed (13 percent of believers) are among the happiest, most charitable, tolerant and ethical people. "They're a breed apart from the rest of the population. A third of the population now operates in a variety of small, shared-interest groups, 60 percent church-related. That's quite a phenomenal finding. It's very important in our fragmented society."

According to Gallup, in such small, intimate groups, people are finding themselves, finding each other and finding God. Gallup said modern times have confronted people with a "bewildering array of problems," including disappointment with materialism as a measure of success. "It's a failure of the American dream, if you will. It's not only discouragement at the failure of the material world, but disenchantment with lifestyles. Loneliness is a factor. We're acutely lonely. We're searching for meaningful relationships."

What to Do If You
HIT A SLUMP

1. Recognize you are in one.

Take time out to rethink, re-energize and refocus. Talk to the people who support you best—your mentors, friends and family.

2. Remind yourself of a major accomplishment.

Select a notable victory that made you feel great. Replay it vividly in your mind. Talk about it. Look at photos, achievement plaques or thank-you letters. Keep a Success Log, a scrapbook of your most positive memories. Understand that you have talent. You've proved it before, and you can do so again.

"He was very romantic when we first got married, but you know how they change."

© 1986 JIM UNGER

3. Get back to basics.

One of the main reasons for a stoppage in results is that you're not practicing the fundamentals. Do a mini reality check. Are you doing the easy things instead of activities that guarantee you results? Take a break if you're physically or mentally drained. Recapture your energy before you start up again. Understand that you can work your way out of it. Life is full of cycles. They don't last forever, so take it one day at a time. Remind yourself, "This too will pass." Gradually the sun will start shining again.

As we stated before, famous adventurer and explorer John Goddard is one of the world's greatest goal-setters. He has accomplished more in his own lifetime than twenty people would have achieved collectively. When questioned about how he overcomes roadblocks, he replied, "When I get stuck, I restart myself by focusing on one goal I can finish in the next seven days—something simple. I don't think about anything else—that usually starts my momentum again."

WHEN YOU THINK YOU CAN'T...

Revisit A Former Triumph.

CONCLUSION

The habit of confidence is a vital component in your everyday quest to enjoy continuous success. Like the other important pieces of the puzzle, it is invisible. Love, faith, honesty and integrity are all invisible when you attempt to define them individually. So is confidence. Here's an example. . . .

At the time of this writing, Elvis Stoijko was already a three-time men's world figure-skating champion, and an Olympic silver medalist. In his early twenties, he had reached the pinnacle of a sport that is not only demanding, but laced with controversial politics. Usually you must wait your turn before being accepted into the upper ranks. Elvis is unique. He skates a different program, one that incorporates his martial arts expertise on the ice.

He is a refreshing talent. Like every other top athlete, he trains hard and practices relentlessly. When asked what the number-one reason for his outstanding success was, he paused for a moment to think, and then simply said, "I believe in myself. Yes, that's it, I believe in myself."

Confidence—it's the glue that holds everything together, a habit forged from many sources. You now have a multitude of ways to increase your level of faith in yourself. Relish the challenge. Review these strategies carefully. Make sure you complete all of the Action Steps that follow, then start putting them into use, one at a time. Practice. Make it a daily habit. When you do, it won't be long before you are creating your own list of outstanding successes.

ACTION STEPS

Resolving Unfinished Business

Make a list of the issues that you want resolved. Write down at least three. Then write down a specific way to resolve each one. What's your action plan? Define it clearly. Finally, decide on the date you are going to have this completed. Then get started.

Unfinished business I currently want to bring to closure.

Relationship issues, financial, legal, business, health, physical organization (office, home, garage, etc.).

1. _____

2. _____

3. _____

4. _____

5. _____

Specific benefit for resolving this unfinished business. Describe how you will feel.

1. _____

2. _____

3. _____

4. _____

5. _____

Action plan for closure. What specifically are you going to do?

1. _____

2. _____

3. _____

4. _____

5. _____

Date for completion.

1. _____

2. _____

3. _____

4. _____

5. _____

LIVING ON PURPOSE

TAKING DECISIVE ACTION

CONSISTENT PERSISTENCE

ASK FOR WHAT YOU WANT

THE CONFIDENCE FACTOR

BUILDING EXCELLENT RELATIONSHIPS

CREATING OPTIMUM BALANCE

DO YOU SEE THE BIG PICTURE?

IT'S NOT HOCUS-POCUS, IT'S ALL ABOUT FOCUS

YOUR HABITS WILL DETERMINE YOUR FUTURE

We're confident you'll finish the last four—go for it!

Ask For What You Want

> "IF THERE IS SOMETHING TO GAIN AND NOTHING TO LOSE BY ASKING, BY ALL MEANS ASK."
>
> —W. Clement Stone

Jonathan is eleven years old, and loves music.
He is exceptionally talented on soprano saxophone and also likes to compose. One day, maybe he'll play in a famous philharmonic orchestra and eventually become the conductor. Awesome!

Right now, Jonathan's biggest goal is to earn enough money to buy a new saxophone and a keyboard to compose on. When you're eleven it's hard to find a good-paying job, especially when school takes up most of the week. Jonathan, however, is determined. He really wants the new instruments. Every Saturday he goes down to the local food market and stands near one of the main entrance doors. He sets up a music stand and takes a clarinet from an old case. In front of him he places a hand-written sign, and then he starts to play. His sign reads:

MY NAME IS JONATHAN AND I'M ELEVEN YEARS OLD. I'M EARNING MONEY TO BUY A SOPRANO SAXOPHONE AND A KEYBOARD. CAN YOU HELP? THANK YOU VERY MUCH!

Beside the sign is a plastic container and a personal requests list. Jonathan has discovered a magic formula. It's called *asking,* and he's doing what most people won't do—he's taking action.

As Jonathan skillfully plays a selection of well-known tunes, the money rolls in. A dollar from a passing businessman, fifty cents from a young girl, five dollars from a well-dressed grandmother. At this rate it won't be long before Jonathan's goal becomes reality. By using a little creativity and summoning up the courage to ask for help, he's found a unique way to get what he wants. With this type of gutsy determination, who would bet on him not achieving his greater musical ambitions? Not us, that's for sure.

Ask and
RECEIVE

It's been around for a long, long time, this gift called asking. In fact, one of life's fundamental truths states, *Ask and you shall receive.* Isn't that simple? Of course it is. And kids are the masters. Their formula is usually to ask until they get what they want. As adults, we seem to lose our ability to ask. We come up with all sorts of excuses and reasons to avoid any possibility of rejection. Kids haven't been programmed like that. They really believe they can have anything they ask for, whether it's a fifty-foot swimming pool or a chocolate ice cream cone.

Here's what you need to understand: The world responds to those who ask. If you are not moving closer to what you want, you probably aren't doing enough asking. Fortunately, to create future abundance there are many ways to ask. In the next few pages you will learn a variety of asking strategies that will guarantee you tremendous success. These are powerful for business as well as your own personal life.

Here's a useful acronym to remind you about asking:

ALWAYS

SEEKING

KNOWLEDGE

Some people say knowledge is power. Not true! The use of knowledge is power. That's something to imprint in your mind forever. When you ask, you can receive all sorts of information, ideas, strategies, names of people with influence and, yes, even money. There are many good reasons to ask, and the rewards are substantial. So why do people stumble when they have an opportunity to ask? Essentially there are three reasons.

1. They have a belief system that says it's not right to ask.

2. They lack confidence.

3. They fear rejection.

(For an in-depth look at how to overcome personal barriers to asking, read *The Aladdin Factor*. See Resource Guide.)

Old, deep-seated belief systems can paralyze you. The Bible says, "Ask and you shall receive, seek and you shall find, knock and it shall be opened unto you." That comes from a pretty high authority, one that has far more power than some outdated belief system you may have inherited years ago as a child. If this describes you, then you'll need to do some analysis of your limiting belief systems. Get help. Talk to a trusted friend, adviser or counselor. Work through it. Realize there are other ways to view life and circumstances. Make a change in how you see things and what you really value. Let go of all that old stuff. It's clogging up your future and strangling your ability to ask.

Remember the second reason? Yes, it's that self-defeating old confidence trait we discussed in the last chapter. Lack of confidence will definitely stunt your desire to ask. Again, it's all about breaking old barriers. Trust yourself. Take a step forward. Ask anyway. The worst you'll hear is "No," which brings up the third reason—rejection. When you get a negative response, are you any worse off? Not really, unless you take it personally—which is the number-one reason people fear rejection. Some people can't handle their emotions, even though the word "no" was never intended as a personal put-down.

So how do you rate in the asking stakes? Are any of these three negative forces playing havoc with your opportunity to get ahead? If they are, this is where you must start. It's called taking the leap of faith. And that means releasing old beliefs, feeling good about yourself and understanding that life isn't perfect—it's normal to experience a lot of roadblocks along the way.

Seven Ways to Boost
Your Business,
SIMPLY BY ASKING

Here are seven big ways to ensure that your business becomes more profitable. Do these, and your revenues will soar. To assist you with this, do the Action Steps called Seven Ways to Boost Your Business.

1. Ask for information.

To win potential new clients, you first need to know what their current challenges are, what they want to accomplish and how they plan to do it. Only then can you proceed to demonstrate the advantages of your unique product or service. It's amazing how so many people get this simple process screwed up. Salespeople are notorious for ignoring this essential part of the presentation. They often have dollar signs in their eyes, illustrating that their main focus is on lightening your wallet.

We call them dinosaurs. Here's a better way: First, suspend your own self-interest. This is critical. Focus on sincerely helping the person with whom you are meeting. Ask questions, starting with the words *who, why, what, where, when* and *how,* to obtain all the information you need. This is called the discovery process. Trial lawyers are experts at this. In discovery, they are allowed to ask virtually any question that will help them prepare their case. They don't rely on guesswork. Only when they are armed with the facts of the case can they make a compelling defense or prosecution in court.

It's the same in business. Only when you truly understand and appreciate the needs of the people you meet can you offer a solution. And if everything fits, the solution for them will be your product or service.

There are two important questions to ask in the discovery process. First, "What is your single biggest challenge at this time?" We have found this question is a great way to develop rapport. Here's the key: You must show genuine interest when you ask. If you sound like a cliché out of some ancient sales manual, you will experience resistance. When the person answers, listen carefully and ask another question, one that will give you more information. Repeat this process until you have explored this topic as fully as you need to. We call it peeling the onion. Each time you ask a new question, you peel away another layer. Removing more layers eventually leads you to the core of the issue. Often that's where the most important information lies, but it takes skillful questioning to uncover it. A good marriage counselor or psychotherapist uses the same technique to discover what lies behind a dysfunctional relationship, or acute depression. So practice asking simple, direct questions. Be attentive. Listen well, and learn to read between the lines. Remember, the real issues are usually below the surface.

The second important question to open up the conversation is, "What are some of your most important goals and objectives in the next few years?" If you think people won't answer a question like that, think again. If you have developed good rapport in the first ten minutes, suspended your desire to make a sale, and demonstrated a sincere interest in their business, people will tell you a lot more than you think.

LES:
It's amazing—ten minutes after meeting a business owner or manager for the first time, when I ask the goals question they often stand up and say, "Let me close my door." Then they open their hearts. It's like they were waiting for someone to come along who was willing to listen, so they could unload some of the heavy burdens of their business and personal life. Never underestimate the power of well-chosen questions and an ability to listen.

One other tip when you are asking for information. Don't interrogate people with a constant barrage of bottom-line questions. In between your questions make a few comments, share an idea or offer a helpful suggestion. Relate to what the other person is saying, and then gently ask your next question. The more you can relate, the more comfortable and relaxed your prospect will become. This develops that magic ingredient called trust. When you establish trust, the door of opportunity swings wide open and you are welcomed in with open arms. Eventually this leads to big checks. You can also practice this type of asking in your personal life, with family and friends. The rewards are equally substantial.

"You hit him up for a million bucks.
I'll ask him for five bucks and he'll think
he's getting a deal."

2. Ask for business.

Here's an amazing statistic: After doing a complete presentation about the benefits of their product or service, more than 60 percent of the time salespeople never ask for the order. That's a bad habit, one that could ultimately put you on the business scrap heap.

If you need help with this, kids are your best role models. As young Jonathan demonstrated, they are naturally gifted salespeople. Here's more proof: We're playing golf on a hot, sunny July afternoon. The tee-off area at the sixth hole is close to a perimeter fence. On the other side of the wire mesh a six-year-old girl is sitting at a small wooden table. On the table are two big plastic jugs, one filled with iced tea, the other with lemonade. As our foursome waits for the players ahead to finish the hole, the little girl asks, "Would you like a nice cool drink while you're waiting?" She stands there holding a plastic cup in one hand and wearing a great big smile. Her name is Melanie.

It's hot and we're all thirsty, so we walk over to the fence. "Would you prefer iced tea or lemonade?" she asks. After we make our selections, she pours the drinks, holds out her hand and says, "That's fifty-five cents each, please." We pass four one-dollar bills through the wire mesh. When she has the cash carefully tucked away in a little money pouch, she passes the drinks through a hole in the fence and says, "Have a nice day." None of us receives any change! And who's going to complain? After all, she's worth the 45 percent tip with a presentation like that.

ALWAYS ASK FOR BUSINESS,

Always.

How often do you think she asks? You're right. Every time someone shows up at the sixth tee. This little entrepreneur didn't have a ten-week sales training course—she did it naturally. Consider her brilliant strategy—a lesson in business we can all benefit from. First, she picked an excellent location. She also provided a valuable service on a hot day. "Would you prefer iced tea or lemonade?" proves she knew the importance of choice. And her confidence factor was so high that she felt it wasn't necessary to give change.

Like Melanie, you must always ask a closing question to secure the business. Don't waffle, or talk around it, or even worse, wait for your prospect to ask you. Here are a few examples that have worked well for us.

"Would you like to give it a try?" This is a no-pressure, non-threatening type of question. If you have given an effective presentation loaded with value and benefits, most people will think, "What have I got to lose? I might as well try it." When selling our coaching programs and seminars, we ask directly, "Would you like to attend the next program?" Another direct way of asking is to say sincerely, "May I please have your business?" Well-known consultant Barney Zick adds a touch of humor. He suggests if you're really stuck, just say, "Do you wanna buy one?" The point is, just ask. Also, note that your closing question is designed to produce a "Yes" or "No" answer, unlike your earlier questions in the discovery process, where you simply want more information. If successful speakers and writers can do this, why can't you? It obviously works.

3. Ask for written endorsements.

Well-written, results-oriented testimonials from highly respected people are powerful. They solidify the quality of your work and leverage you as a person who has integrity, is trustworthy and who gets the job done on time.

Here's what's fascinating—most people in business don't do this. That gives you a great opportunity to jump ahead of your competition. All you need to do is ask. When is the best time?

Right after you have provided excellent service, completed a major project under budget, gone the extra mile to help out, or any other time you've made your customer really happy. Under these circumstances, people will be glad to praise your efforts. Here's how to do it:

Simply ask if your customer would be willing to give you a testimonial about the value of your product or service, plus any other helpful comments. To make it easy, we suggest that you ask a few questions on the phone, and take good notes. Ask your client to clearly describe the benefits. Probe for specific results that were achieved because of your work.

For example, a sales trainer who has just completed a three-month program with the entire sales organization of a rapidly growing company could ask, "What results have you noticed in the last sixty days?" The sales manager might reply, "Since you shared your ideas with us, our total sales volume has jumped 35 percent compared to the previous few months."

This is an excellent, specific, measurable result. Stay away from general statements like, "It was a very good program—everyone really enjoyed it." This type of statement has little impact on the reader. But if you have a sales team that needs help and you read about a 35 percent increase in sales, you're more likely to think, "That's what we're looking for. If it works for them, it could work for us, too—how do I contact this sales trainer?"

When you have finished your mini interview on the phone, offer to write the testimonial yourself. This will save your client's time. This is important for two reasons. First, it removes any pressure from your client. He or she may not be very skilled at writing powerful testimonials, and it's time-consuming. Second, you have an opportunity to craft the letter in a way that produces maximum impact. If you are not great at writing, hire a professional—it's well worth it. When you have completed this, fax the testimonial back to your client for approval. Then have it typed on their letterhead and signed.

Make a habit of collecting great testimonials. Put them in a three-ring binder and leave it on a coffee table in the reception area of your office, or frame the best ones and hang them on a wall where everyone can read them. Use a highlighter pen to draw attention to the most important comments. All of your promotional literature should have at least three excellent testimonials prominently featured.

Another good option is to take the most powerful sentences from ten different testimonials and place these on one page along with the names of your clients. Even better, include a small head-and-shoulders photograph of each client. If your product is easy to photograph, like a car or furniture, create an action photograph. For example, your new customer sitting in the car or showing off their beautiful dining room table. Visuals have great impact.

ENLIST HIGHLY CREDIBLE PEOPLE

If you have a few comments from local well-known people, chances are, your prospects will recognize them and be impressed.

Here's another important aspect of written endorsements: Include a few people who are peers in your industry. The more established they are, the better. For example, the first few pages of this book contain comments from superstars in the training industry and top business achievers. Didn't they influence you just a little?

You can also group your testimonials into specific categories. If your product or service has several benefits, place each of these under separate headings such as excellent service, price, quality, product knowledge and on-time delivery. If a prospect is concerned about one area in particular, you can show several testimonials that prove you are wonderful in that capacity.

These are simple strategies that will bring you a lot more business. So take advantage, and from now on make a commitment to ask for high-impact testimonials.

4. Ask for top-quality referrals.

Just about everyone in business knows the importance of referrals. Simply put, it's the easiest, least-expensive way of ensuring your growth and success in the marketplace. However, here's the reality: In our experience, only one out of ten companies has a system for gathering referrals. How do you explain that?

Well, it's the same old story—bad habits, plus that recurring theme you've been reading about—fear of rejection. In chapter 5, Building Excellent Relationships, we talked about the importance of developing core clients. These are the people who will gladly give you referrals because you treat them so well. So why aren't you asking all of them for referrals? Maybe you don't believe the benefits yet. Here's an example that will persuade you to think again:

Helen is an expert financial planner. In fact, she is consistently in the top 5 percent of the two thousand representatives who make up her company's sales team. Over the years, Helen has built a foundation of core clients. Her target market is people in the fifty- to sixty-year-old age group who have at least two hundred thousand dollars in their investment portfolios. Here's one way she boosted her business recently: She invited her core clients to attend a Saturday morning breakfast at a nearby hotel. The invitation informed them that they would hear some important information about new government regulations, which could affect their future prosperity. Included in the invitation was a request for each core client to bring three or four friends who were similarly qualified.

The result? A total of ninety-two people showed up for breakfast, many of whom were guests. The breakfast cost eight dollars per person, which Helen was happy to pay. After her forty-five-minute talk, many of these guests requested more information. This turned into ten new clients, and twenty-two thousand dollars in commissions for Helen. Not a bad morning's work!

As all top businesspeople know, asking for qualified referrals is an important part of an overall marketing strategy. It's a habit that will dramatically increase your income. Like any other habit, it requires that you do it often. Then eventually it becomes easy.

Obtaining good referrals is not limited to your core clients, although they provide the distinct advantage of opening doors for you that otherwise might remain closed. Opportunities exist every day. When you meet a new prospect who doesn't need or want your product or service, you can still ask if he might know someone who does. What have you got to lose? The worst thing that can happen is that he may say "No." You really aren't any worse off. And often he'll say, "As a matter of fact, I do know someone who might be interested in this."

> LES:
> I had an appointment with the owner of a real estate development company. He listened to my presentation and indicated he was not interested in our services. However, when I asked him if he could suggest anyone else, he sat down and carefully went through his Rolodex file and gave me twenty-seven names of top-quality people.

By the way, make sure you describe in detail what your definition of a good prospect is. The last thing you want is a bunch of names that are unsuitable. This will only waste your time as well as theirs. When someone gives you a referral, always double-check. Ask questions about the person until you are confident that they really do qualify.

Another smart thing our friend Barney Zick does is to ask for referrals up front. In fact, consider making asking for referrals a condition of every sale. Most people never do this, so you have a wonderful opportunity to capitalize on their oversight. For example, you might say, "One reason we can offer you such a great price is that we also ask for three excellent referrals. I'm sure you know the value of referrals. In return, we promise to give you the best of service, so you'll be happy with your decision to do business with us."

At this point you can reinforce your comments by sharing wonderful testimonials from other happy customers. Another way Barney asks is, "Would you please introduce me to a few people of equal quality to you?" In this way you extend a genuine compliment, and that makes your client feel good.

A question we are often asked is, "Should I pay people for giving me referrals?" This is entirely up to you, although most people, especially your core clients, will be happy to refer you without an inducement. On the other hand, if a referral fee, say 10 percent, will stimulate someone to provide good leads every month, then do it.

You can also develop creative ways of saying "Thank you" to consistent referral givers. Find out what they like and surprise them with an unexpected gift. This could be a couple of movie passes, a unique coffee mug (with your logo on it), a specialty foods basket or a dinner for two at their favorite restaurant. Recognition of their help is more important than the size of the gift. And if their referrals lead to a substantial increase in revenue, you can upgrade the reward accordingly.

Another way to ensure that you receive referrals is to give your own clients referrals first. Also, consider offering a free consultation or trial offer in return for some good references. This works well when you are just launching a new venture, or don't know a lot of people in the marketplace.

As you can see, there are many opportunities for you to create new business by linking yourself to core clients, and others who are well-connected to people you'd like to meet. Make an effort to do something different compared to your normal networking procedures. Plan to talk to a higher caliber of client or ask for referrals more often to increase your business. Remember, continually harvesting excellent referrals can make you wealthy. One last point: Use the word "introductions" instead of referrals. It's less intimidating. Some people may have had a negative experience because a pushy salesperson pressured them into giving referrals.

5. Ask for more business.

Many people lose thousands of dollars in sales every year because they have nothing more to offer after the initial sale. Look for other products or services to add to your portfolio. Also, develop a system to determine when your clients will require more of your own product or service. People buy in cycles, and you need to know when those cycles are most likely to occur. The simplest way to determine this is to ask your customers when you should contact them to reorder. It's often easier to sell your existing clients more of what you have than it is to go out looking for new clients.

> LES:
> Keith and his partner Bill own an electrical contracting company. For fifteen years they have steadily built their business on top-quality workmanship and excellent relations within their industry. They have a major client who used to split the electrical contracting work between their company and another much larger competitor. This arrangement had been in place for several years. Keith would have liked to capture the other half of the business, but his competitor always seemed to have the edge. However, every year when the bids were tendered, Keith submitted a complete and detailed proposal, knowing that there was little chance of succeeding. But he kept on asking.
>
> One year a new buyer was appointed to look at the two bids. The competitor, assuming they would win the contract as usual, drafted a one-page proposal. On the

other hand, Keith submitted his normal detailed script outlining the benefits and cost-effective advantages of using their organization. When the new buyer considered the two proposals, he gave Keith the business because he had taken the time to ask properly. As Keith remarked afterwards, "We didn't really win the contract. Our competitor dropped the ball." If you are persistent in your asking and do it with integrity, eventually the tide may turn your way. The bonus for Keith was that once the word got out that they had secured all of the business from this major international client, the floodgates opened, and inquiries from other major players began pouring in.

Remember this: Business grinds to a halt when you stop asking. Asking for more business helps you gain momentum.

Years ago McDonald's, the hamburger people, came up with a unique way to ask for more. They trained their staff to ask one more question when someone ordered a hamburger and a drink. This single question added more than twenty million dollars to their bottom line. The question was, "Would you like fries with that?" Obviously a lot of people said, "Sure, why not." Here's what's worth noting: How often do they ask that question? Every single time! This requires good communication, and training all staff to be alert with each customer. It obviously pays big dividends.

This is commonly known as the "upsell." In the car industry, once you've purchased a new vehicle, you will probably be asked to buy an extended warranty for a few hundred dollars more, or a perma-coat finish that will give you years of protection from rust and stone chips.

What else could you be asking for when you do business? Adding one more question at the end of the sale could significantly increase your income. Remember: If you don't ask, someone else will!

6. Ask to renegotiate.

Regular business activities include negotiation and the opportunity to renegotiate. Many people get stuck because they aren't very good at this. It's another form of asking that can save you a lot of time and money.

For example, if the mortgage on your home is coming up for renewal and the interest rate is currently at 7 percent, you can say, "That's a pretty good rate; I'll just sign on for another three years." But what if you met with your banker and said, "I'm looking at my renewal options. There are other banks who would like my business. I'd be happy to stay with you if you can give me a 6 percent rate." You'd be surprised how often the bank will agree to this, because they know the competition is fierce for this type of lending. That extra percentage point can save you a significant amount of money, and it only took one question to secure it.

Other opportunities to renegotiate include stretching payments over a longer period of time. If you have a cash-flow crunch, an extra thirty days at no interest (you might as well ask for that, too) can help stabilize your finances.

All sorts of contracts can be renegotiated simply by asking. As long as you do it ethically and in the spirit of win-win, you can enjoy a lot of flexibility. Nothing is ever cast in stone. If your situation requires change, ask for it.

> LES:
> One morning I was flying to another city to conduct an Achievers workshop for a group of entrepreneurs. The biggest snowstorm of the year had delayed my departure by more than an hour. By the time we were ready to land at the international airport on the outskirts of the city it was 8:30 A.M. My workshop started at 9 A.M. The captain then informed us we couldn't land because of fog, so we would continue on to the municipal airport downtown. I thought, "Great, that's closer to where I want to go," and

started preparing to disembark. Upon landing, the captain announced, "We have no baggage-handling facilities here so we are going to refuel, wait until the fog lifts at the international airport and fly back there." Then he added, "Until the fog lifts I guess you are trapped in the aircraft." Interesting choice of words!

This provided me with another great opportunity to ask. I summoned the flight attendant, and explained that I only had carry-on luggage, and that my meeting was due to start in fifteen minutes. She agreed to ask the captain if he would make an exception and allow me to leave the plane. She came back smiling a few minutes later, opened the door and lowered the stairway. Until then no one on the plane had moved. As I glanced back, several other businesspeople were making similar requests. It never occurred to them that to change their predicament they just had to ask.

7. Ask for feedback.

Another important component of asking is often overlooked. How do you really know if your product or service is meeting the needs of your customer? Ask them, "How are we doing? What can we do to improve our service to you? Tell us what you like about our products and what you don't like." Set up regular customer surveys that ask good questions, and include the tough questions. Consider a monthly focus group where you can meet your customers face-to-face. Buy them lunch and ask them lots of questions. It's a great way to fine-tune your business.

If you supervise a team of people or run a large organization, ask the people you work with for ideas. They are often the most knowledgeable when it comes to practical, everyday activities that make the business run smoothly. Also talk to your suppliers. There may be ways to improve efficiency with better distribution, or to reduce costs using just-in-time inventory policies. No matter what type of industry you work in, you are surrounded by people who can give you valuable feedback. All you need to do is ask. As we mentioned earlier, there is a valuable workshop at the end of this chapter that will help you create an action plan to implement these seven ways to ask.

DILBERT *reprinted by permission of United Feature Syndicate, Inc.*

How to ASK

Some people don't enjoy the fruits of asking because they don't ask effectively. If you use vague, unspecific language you will not be understood. Here are five ways to ensure that your asking gets results.

1. Ask clearly.
Be precise. Think clearly about your request. Take time to prepare. Use a notepad to design words that have the greatest impact. This is extremely important. Words are powerful, so choose them carefully. Being incoherent won't serve you well. If you need to, find people who are great at asking, and pick their brains. Ask for help.

2. Ask with confidence.
People who ask confidently get more out of life than those who are hesitant and uncertain. Now that you've figured out what you want to ask for, do it with certainty, boldness

and confidence. This does not mean being brash, arrogant or conceited. Confidence can be a quiet strength, but to the people you are asking, it's visible. The only negative thing that can happen is that your request may be denied. Does this put you in a worse position than before? Of course not. It just means that this particular route to getting results is closed. So look for another one.

3. Ask consistently.

Some people fold up their tent after making one timid request. They quit too soon. If you want to unearth the true riches in life, you'll need to do a lot of asking. Treat it like a game, keep on asking until you find the answers. Ask consistently. In sales, there are usually four or five "No"s before you get a "Yes." The top producers understand this. It's normal. And when you find a way to ask that works, keep on doing it. For example, some companies use the same advertising campaign for several years. Why? Because it works.

4. Ask creatively.

In this age of intense global competition, your asking may get lost in the crowd, unheard by the decision-makers you are hoping to reach. There's a simple way around this. In his book, *Don't Worry, Make Money,* bestselling author Richard Carlson describes the technique as "purple snowflakes." This is a strategy to help you stand out in the crowd. For example, if you want someone's attention don't just send an ordinary letter. Use your creativity to dream up a high-impact introduction. Here's a good example from *The Best of Bits and Pieces*:

The chief buyer for a thriving company was particularly inaccessible to salespeople. You didn't call *him*, he called *you*. On several occasions when salespeople managed to get into his office, they were summarily tossed out.

One saleswoman finally broke through his defenses. She sent him a homing pigeon with her card attached to one leg. On the card she had written, "If you want to know more about our product, just throw our representative out the window!"

This is a good example of a "purple snowflake." What could you do to create a powerful impact with your most important prospects? Make it fun. Brainstorm with your Mastermind Group. Schedule time every month for "purple snowflaking," and don't be surprised when those impenetrable doors swing wide open and welcome you in.

5. Ask sincerely.

When you really need help, people will respond. Sincerity requires being real. It means dropping the image facade and showing a willingness to be vulnerable. Tell it the way it is, lumps and all. Don't worry if your presentation isn't perfect; ask from your heart. Keep it simple and people will open up to you.

Also, your request will be favored if you can clearly show that you have already put in a lot of effort. For example, if a charitable youth organization needed only $50 to achieve its target of $1,000, and the youngsters demonstrated all the things they had done to earn the first $950—car washes, bake sales, garbage clean-ups and bottle drives—you might donate the remainder, especially if they had a specific deadline, and there were only a few hours left.

When you've exhausted all avenues to get what you want, people are more likely to give you a helping hand when you ask for support. People who ask for a free ride all the time rarely succeed.

THERE ARE MANY WAYS TO ASK

Learn All Of Them!

CONCLUSION

The Habit of Asking has changed the world. There are many examples of great leaders who knew how to ask well. And they did it with commitment and passion. Jesus asked his disciples to follow him. They did, and Christianity was born. Martin Luther King Jr. had a dream of equality for all people. He asked, and changed the course of history, giving his life in the process. Mother Teresa asked for help to assist the poor and dying and the Missionaries of Charity was created, involving thousands of supporters around the world. During World War II, Winston Churchill asked the people of the United Kingdom to, "Never, never, never, never, give up," and Great Britain was saved from invasion. It's important to note that each of these leaders had a powerful vision and total commitment to accomplishing their goals. For them, asking was the natural way to make continuous progress.

Every day presents numerous opportunities to ask for what you want. Be conscious of those moments. Step forward boldly and make your requests known. These are the seeds of your future prosperity. Plant them now so you can enjoy the harvest later.

Well, we're down to the final three chapters. You're on the last lap. Congratulations for sticking with it to this point. These final three strategies will put you into overdrive, as far as results go. It will require a big effort on your part. So stay focused as we introduce you to consistent persistence, taking decisive action and learning to live on purpose.

ASK YOURSELF:

Am I Now Ready To Make Some Changes?

ACTION STEPS

Asking for What
You Want

To help you increase your productivity and income right away, take a few minutes to complete this Action Plan for asking. Successfully implementing these strategies can increase your revenue by at least 50 percent. Start now!

1. Ask for information.
What single improvement can you make in the way you ask for information?

_____

_____

2. Ask for business.
Is your closing question for business bringing you the level of success you want? If not, create at least two new ways of asking for business. Keep them simple and specific.

A. _____

B. _____

3. Ask for written endorsements.

Write the names of five people who can give you excellent testimonial letters. Set a time to call these people and follow through.

1. _____   4. _____

2. _____   5. _____

3. _____

4. Ask for top-quality introductions.

Outline a specific system for continually bringing new people into your business. Remember, the key word is *continually*—that means you do it every week.

_____

_____

_____

5. Ask for more business.

Name five clients you will approach for more business. Create a good reason for them to buy more—special discounts, a new product launch or a free draw for a special prize.

1. _____   4. _____

2. _____   5. _____

3. _____

6. Ask to renegotiate.

Name one situation that you want to renegotiate in the next month. Consider interest rates, lines of credit, time off, salary, job description, etc.

_____

_____

_____

7. Ask for feedback.

List two ways you can improve your feedback from customers. Consider telemarketing, customer focus groups, questionnaires, etc.

A. _____

_____

B. _____

_____

In addition to these seven strategies, continually check to see if there's anything you have stopped asking for.

Make a list now of three things you have stopped asking for that you would like more of.

A. _____

_____

B. _____

_____

C. _____

_____

LIVING ON PURPOSE

TAKING DECISIVE ACTION

CONSISTENT PERSISTENCE

ASK FOR WHAT YOU WANT

THE CONFIDENCE FACTOR

BUILDING EXCELLENT RELATIONSHIPS

CREATING OPTIMUM BALANCE

DO YOU SEE THE BIG PICTURE?

IT'S NOT HOCUS-POCUS, IT'S ALL ABOUT FOCUS

YOUR HABITS WILL DETERMINE YOUR FUTURE

Only three strategies left—good job!

Consistent Persistence

> "THE MIRACLE POWER THAT ELEVATES THE FEW
> IS TO BE FOUND IN THEIR INDUSTRY, APPLICATION
> AND PERSEVERANCE, UNDER THE PROMPTINGS OF
> A BRAVE DETERMINED SPIRIT."
>
> —Mark Twain

If you take a close look at people who are truly successful in life, you will find one character trait in abundance.

We call it Consistent Persistence. At first glance, the words consistent and persistence may seem similar. That's true, they are. We have double-barreled them to emphasize the importance of this habit. In case you feel like skipping over this without due thought and consideration, here's an important statement to digest and store forever in the deepest recesses of your brain: **You will never achieve big results in your life without consistent and persistent action.**

In this chapter, you will discover how to make consistently good choices so that your dreams and goals turn into exciting reality. You will also learn what a higher level of consistency means, and how you can implement this daily. In addition, we'll show you how to build your mental toughness so you can endure hard times and unexpected challenges when they arise.

Lack of consistency.

Many organizations struggle because their leaders put up with a high level of inconsistency. Well, we have news for you. The business world today is a lot different than it was ten years ago. The performance bar has been raised to a new level. Ineptitude will not be tolerated. For example: You call a team meeting for 9 A.M. Monday. Each one of your twenty sales representatives is asked to attend. At 9:15 A.M. only fourteen people have shown up. Two more eventually stroll in at 9:25 A.M. and the rest never appear. And it's like that almost every week.

This lack of consistency will wreck your team unity. Usually a few prima donnas are the root cause. Sometimes they show up, sometimes they don't. It's really frustrating. In today's world the answer is simple—lock them out! That's right, at 9:00 A.M. sharp, lock the doors of the meeting room. The message will soon be understood: "If you want to play on our team, be consistent."

213

The Benefits of
CONSISTENCY

First, to give you a taste of what we're referring to, let's look at a wonderful role model. He's known as Mr. Consistency: Cal Ripken Jr.

In case you are not a baseball fan, Cal Ripken Jr. plays for the Baltimore Orioles. The reason he is a legend in the sport is his incredible consistency. On September 6, 1995, Cal played his 2,131st consecutive major league baseball game. In doing so, he broke the record of 2,130 games set by Lou Gehrig, a record that had remained unbeaten for more than fifty-six years.

Let's put this into perspective: To equal Cal Ripken Jr.'s consistency, an employee working an average eight hours a day, five days a week, would need to work eight years, one month and twenty days and never call in sick! No wonder he's called the Iron Man of Baseball. He played in every single game for more than thirteen years. (On the night he broke the record, the closest person to him in consecutive starts was Frank Thomas of the Chicago White Sox, who had played a mere 235 games.)

Ripken's ability to show up for every game translated into a remarkable list of successes. During the streak he was the winner of two Most Valuable Player awards, in 1983 and in 1991. He also played in twelve consecutive All-Star games, and hit more home runs than any other major-league shortstop. Financially he is set for life, but more than the money, he has a tremendous feeling of accomplishment.

His philosophy about work is refreshingly simple. All he ever wanted was to play baseball, preferably for Baltimore, and to do his best in every game.

This demonstrates a keen sense of responsibility and a work ethic that is all too rare today. By simply showing up consistently and playing his best, the rewards eventually materialized. And through it all, Ripken maintained a humble unassuming attitude.

It's interesting that Cal Ripken Jr. has also developed the same consistency in his family life. His wife and children are important to him, and it shows. Compare this to the weekly ritual of scandals and contract demands now rampant in the world of professional sports, perpetuated by individuals of lesser maturity and weakness of character.

One last footnote to the story, and a point worth remembering. When you stand for something and do a remarkable job of it, you attract the top people and create huge rewards for yourself. On his record-breaking night, Cal Ripken Jr. was feted by world-famous celebrities, multinational corporations and even the president of the United States. He was showered with gifts and received numerous standing ovations. Imagine! All for showing up every day and doing what he loves to do.

JACK AND MARK:
One of the main reasons we have enjoyed considerable success with our *Chicken Soup for the Soul* series of books is the consistency in setting weekly, monthly and yearly targets. These are well-defined and challenge us to the max. Our goals inspire us because we are not exactly sure how we will accomplish them. This stirs our creative juices. With the help of our Mastermind Group partners, we always find solutions. Currently we have twenty-nine *Chicken Soup* titles in print.

In our first year of publication, we sold 135,000 books. In year two, that figure grew to 1.35 million, and in year five (1998), our total book sales were 13.8 million. We also discovered that when you have consistent persistence and a proactive game plan, you build momentum that becomes unstoppable. Like Cal Ripken Jr., you develop a winning streak.

Now put yourself under the microscope for a moment. What sort of a streak do you have going right now? Does your consistency show up in real terms every day? Or are you bouncing around all over the place, dabbling here and there with the opportunities of life? If you are doing pretty well, we applaud you. But let's move your abilities to another level, that rarefied atmosphere where the challenges are greater and the rewards are even more lucrative.

Embrace Your Greatest POWER

In previous chapters we positioned all of the Action Step exercises at the end so you could focus better and take as much time as you want. That's about to change. **In fact we want you to stop right now, get mentally prepared and do the following two-part exercise before continuing. If you decide to keep on reading, you will completely miss the impact of this powerful lesson.**

Using the following worksheet, make a list of six things you absolutely have to get done in the next three months. These are activities that must be completed, for whatever reason. They may include some of the short-term goals you established earlier. Keep your statements brief. Opposite each activity that you have to do, write one word that describes your feelings about it.

Things I have to do in the next three months.

EXAMPLES

1. Reorganize and clean my office.
2. Pay my taxes.
3. Have a heart-to-heart talk with my sixteen-year-old son.

Think of how you honestly feel when you visualize each task. To help you, here are a few examples of "feeling" words: angry, sad, happy, excited, upset, worried, frustrated, joyful, loving, thankful. These are all words that directly relate to emotions. Choose your own word to describe how you feel about each item on your Have-To list. It is really important that you complete this exercise *immediately* to gain the most benefit. In our Achievers Coaching Program this has been one of the biggest breakthrough activities for our clients.

HAVE-TO'S

Things I have to do in the next three months,

i.e., no later than _____ date

FEELINGS

What word best describes your feelings about having to do these activities?

HAVE-TO'S	FEELINGS
1. _____	_____
2. _____	_____
3. _____	_____
4. _____	_____
5. _____	_____
6. _____	_____

Well done! Now let's review your list. Take a look at each item and, one at a time, put a line through each task. **That's right, cross it off your list.**

Here's why: You don't **have to** do any of these things. No, you really don't! Now, you may be protesting that some of these things really must be done. They can't be avoided— taxes must be paid, you say. No, you don't have to pay taxes. You may end up in jail or pay a fine, but you don't have to pay taxes. These are just the consequences if you don't pay— but you don't have to. In case you are a little confused by this, let's make a simple defining statement:

IN LIFE, YOU DON'T HAVE TO DO ANYTHING.

That includes paying taxes, working seventy hours a week, or staying in a job, business or relationship you don't enjoy.

Now look at your list again—will your world really come to an end if you do not complete these tasks in the next three months? Of course not. You may not be happy if you don't complete them, and there may be real consequences if you don't. We understand that. The big point we are making is that **you don't have to.**

Let's switch gears for a minute. (If you are still confused, bear with us. Everything will become crystal-clear shortly.) Notice the words you selected to describe your feelings. Based on years of experience, we'd guess a lot of those words are negative, especially if the task is something you have been putting off for a while or are not looking forward to. It's normal to feel anxious, concerned, or frustrated in these situations. Take another look at the words you used. What sort of energy do these "feeling" words bring out in you—

negative or positive? You're right! If the feeling is negative, you automatically create a negative energy that drains your capacity to perform at a high level.

Okay, let's move on to the second part of the exercise, using the worksheet that follows. Make a list of at least six things you want to do, or choose to do in the next three months. This is a different list. What are you really looking forward to doing? Again, choose a word to describe how you feel about completing each item on your list. Review the following examples first.

To get the full benefit of this it's important that you sit down and complete this activity now.

CHOOSE-TO'S

Things I choose to do in the next three months. (e.g., plan a special anniversary, launch a new product, start guitar lessons)

i.e., no later than _____ date

FEELINGS

What word best describes your feelings about wanting to complete these activities?

CHOOSE-TO'S	FEELINGS
1. _____	_____
2. _____	_____
3. _____	_____
4. _____	_____
5. _____	_____
6. _____	_____

Now look at those feeling words. They are probably much more positive than the ones on your Have-To list. If your activities are producing positive energy, then you will have a greater capacity and desire to complete them. Isn't it better to be feeling happy and excited instead of worried and frustrated?

At this point you may be thinking, "Well, it's easy to feel good about the things I want to do, but life isn't always like that. There are a lot of things I don't like to do, but I have to do them anyway. That's just the way it is."

No, it isn't. Here's the mega-point:

EVERYTHING IN LIFE IS A CHOICE

Absolutely Everything.

A Star is Born—The mother and daughter who believed in making better choices.

On June 23, 1940, Wilma Rudolph was born prematurely, weighing only 4.5 pounds. She was born into a poor black family who, like many others, were almost destitute because of the Great Depression. Her mother spent the next several years nursing Wilma through one illness after another: measles, mumps, scarlet fever, chicken pox and double pneumonia. However, Wilma had to be taken to the doctor when it was discovered that her left leg and foot were becoming weak and deformed. She was told she had polio, a crippling disease that had no cure. But Mrs. Rudolph would not give up on her daughter. As Wilma later recalled: "The doctor said I'd never walk again. My mother said I would. I believed my mother!" Mrs. Rudolph discovered that Wilma could be treated at Meharry Hospital, the black medical college of Fisk University in Nashville. Even though it was fifty miles away, Wilma's mother took her there twice a week for two years, until she was able to walk with the aid of a metal leg brace. Then the doctors taught Mrs. Rudolph how to do the physical therapy exercises at home. All of her brothers and sisters helped too, and they did everything to encourage her to be strong and work hard at getting well. Finally, by age twelve, she could walk normally, without the crutches, brace or corrective shoes. Mrs. Rudolph initially made a choice—that her daughter would get well and be able to walk. Her consistent persistence in the face of rejection and extreme hardship finally paid off. Then Wilma herself made an all-important choice. She decided to become an athlete. That turned out to be an inspired choice.

In high school, she became a basketball star, setting state records for scoring and leading her team to a state championship. Then she became a track star, going to her first Olympic Games in 1956 at the age of sixteen. She won a bronze medal in the 4 x 4 relay. But this was only the start.

On September 7, 1960, in Rome, Wilma became the first American woman to win three gold medals in the Olympics. She won the 100-meter dash, the 200-meter dash, and ran the anchor on the 400-meter relay team.

This achievement led her to become one of the most celebrated female athletes of all time. In addition, her celebrity caused gender barriers to be broken in previously all-male track and field events.

Among the many awards she collected during and after her athletic career, she was the first woman to receive the James E. Sullivan Award for Good Sportsmanship, the European Sportswriters' Sportsman of the Year Award, and the Christopher Columbus Award for Most Outstanding International Sports Personality.

Despite her early physical struggles, Wilma Rudolph chose to live and perform on a much bigger stage. In doing so, she became a tremendous role model for disadvantaged children everywhere. In 1997, three years after her death from brain cancer, Governor Don Sundquist proclaimed June 23 as Wilma Rudolph Day in Tennessee.

By now we hope you are convinced that life is all about choices. Look at the evidence surrounding you every day. Have you noticed that some people choose to lead lives of mediocrity? Sadly, some people even make the ultimate choice —they choose to take their own lives.

In contrast, others arise from the most difficult setbacks and choose to create better circumstances for themselves. And they often do it magnificently. Libraries are full of biographies and autobiographies about men and women who developed the habit of Consistent Persistence to turn their lives around. The trigger point came when they realized they could choose a different future.

Please understand this. It's vital. All of the results you are currently experiencing in your life are absolutely perfect for you. This includes your career, personal relationships and financial status. How could it be otherwise? The reason you are where you are in life, is simply a result of all the choices you have made to this point. In other words, the consistency of your positive choices, or the lack of them, has given you the lifestyle you now own. When you accept total responsibility for this fact, you are well on your way to enjoying peace of mind. Many people endure a life filled with frustration because they are stuck in Have-To's.

When you say things like, "She made me angry," the truth is that you *chose* to be angry. You didn't have to be angry. You responded with anger instead of making a different choice.

Other popular commentaries you'll hear are, "I'm stuck in this relationship." In other words, I have to stay stuck. Or, "I hate this job, I'll never make enough money to enjoy real freedom," which really means, "I have to stay in this low-paying job forever." How sad!

Have-to's put you in a position of pressure, whereas choose-to's put you in a position of power.

Choose wisely!

When you constantly live your life in Have-To land, you put yourself in a position of pressure. This causes resistance and resentment, and drains your life of energy.

When you live each day from a position of Choose-To, you are in a position of power. You feel in charge, in control of your life.

This takes a conscious effort to consistently think about your everyday decisions—even simple tasks like washing the dishes. Say to yourself, "I'm choosing to wash the dishes now, and I'll do the best job possible." This is much better than, "Oh no, I have to do the dishes, what a drag." If you really detest doing mundane tasks, choose now to create a lifestyle where you won't be required to do those things. Delegate them to someone else, or hire the work out.

It's also worth noting that the resistance caused by your Have-To jobs often leads to chronic procrastination, and you know how unproductive that can be. Decide now to shift your focus. Make every activity a conscious choice. No more Have-To lists. Starting today, eliminate those words from your vocabulary. Regain your power. Expand your energy and enjoy the freedom that consistent choosing adds to your life.

Here's a good example: One of our clients, a man in his early fifties, was frustrated about his inability to stop smoking. In one of our Achievers workshops he stood up, and in a voice filled with emotion said, "I have to quit smoking or I'm going to die, and I don't want to die yet!" He felt totally frustrated and was obviously anxious about his future.

We asked him to reframe his situation to one of choice, instead of Have-To. He came up with this very powerful statement: "Today, I choose to win the battle over smoking."

Being competitive, he decided to treat his smoking like an adversary. It was a battle, and he was going to win it. He used this affirmation every day, and within two months he quit smoking for good. By putting himself in charge through choosing to, and acting on his new choice, it was no contest. That victory spurred him on to make other lifestyle changes, including a regular exercise program and better eating habits. As you can see, consciously making better choices creates an exciting chain of events.

When you consistently make better choices you create better habits. These better habits produce better character. When you have better character, you add more value to the world. When you become more valuable, you attract bigger and better opportunities. This allows you to make more of a contribution in your life. This in turn leads to bigger and better results. Some people have really figured this out. They stand out in society as people of strength and power.

Another of our clients, a sprightly seventy-three-year-old lady, was given the Have-To list in one of our workshops. When confronted with this, she folded her arms and in a loud voice declared, "I don't have to do anything!" She simply refused to participate. We later found out that she had a long history of successful enterprises and had obviously learned this important lesson many years ago.

Remember, your dominant thoughts usually win out when it comes to everyday decisions. Make sure your conscious choices are moving you closer to the completion of your most important goals. It's also important to understand that choosing not to do something is a valid position. If someone asks you to join a committee that will require you to give up two evenings every week, you can always decline if it's not in your best interest. Choosing to say "No" is often the best strategy to keep your life well-balanced, and in control.

The Consistency CIRCLE

YOUR CONSISTENCY OF PERFORMANCE AUTOMATICALLY CREATES YOUR BETTER FUTURE. IT'S AN ENDLESS CIRCLE.

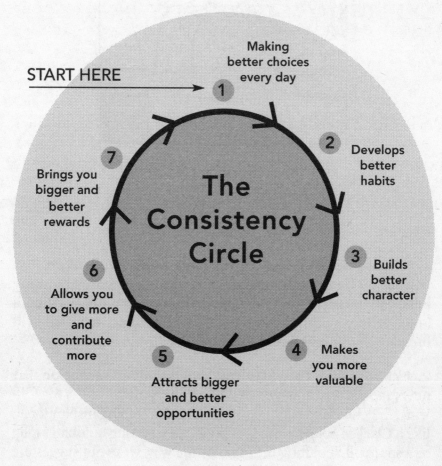

Author's Note: This cartoon has no particular significance in this chapter—we just thought it was too good to leave out!

"Well, that's it for reading!"

Here are a few more examples for you to consider:

1. I choose not to watch TV for three hours every night.
Instead, I choose to invest one hour learning more about my business, financial independence, public speaking, writing a book or any number of other interesting activities that will broaden my knowledge and awareness.

2. I choose not to waste my time reading sensationalist newspapers and trashy magazines every day.
Instead, I choose to start my day reading something inspirational, like a *Chicken Soup for the Soul* book, an inspiring autobiography or a spiritually uplifting message. By the way, we're not suggesting

you stop reading relevant newspapers. In business it's important to keep up with current events. Just avoid the tabloid nonsense.

3. I choose not to become a workaholic.
Instead, I choose to schedule personal time off every week with my family and friends, as well as special time for myself, to be enjoyed guilt free.

Are you starting to get the picture? Do you see how powerful you can become by owning your choices every day? From now on, when the words, "I have to" jump into your head, yell, "Cancel, cancel—I choose not to suffer any more Have-To's in my life." It's exhilarating. In the early stages you will need to be on guard at the doorstep of your mind to prevent those nasty little Have-To's from sneaking inside. Be absolutely ruthless in this respect. Stamp them out persistently until your new Choose-To habit is firmly entrenched.

> "IF I'M EVER ON A LIFE-SUPPORT SYSTEM I CHOOSE TO BE UNPLUGGED, BUT NOT UNTIL I'M DOWN TO A SIZE EIGHT!"
>
> —Henriette Montel

The Double-A
FORMULA

Now that we've sorted out the importance of choices, get ready for one of the single-most-important strategies you will find in this entire book. You'll need total consciousness to fully grasp this one. If you need to stretch, or take a quick energy break, do it now so you'll be alert. Here's our guarantee: If you adopt 100 percent of what you learn in the rest of this chapter, your business and personal life will leap to a whole new level of performance. In our experience, very few people utilize this strategy consistently. As a result, their lives are like a roller coaster, often having more downs than ups.

The Double-A formula is all about you. It stands for: **Agreements and Accountability.**

Here's a vacation story to introduce this all-important formula, and to illustrate our point:

LES:
We were holidaying in a popular Central American resort, strolling through town one afternoon. A young woman approached us and asked if we would like to have our hair braided. She showed us photographs of other people who had transformed their appearances, and pointed out the beautiful beads used in the braiding process. Intrigued, my wife and daughter asked, "How much?"

"Only fifteen dollars," was the reply.

"That's all?" they queried.

"Yes, that's all, no more than fifteen."

"How long will it take?"

"No more than thirty minutes," the young woman assured them.

We had planned a few sightseeing activities later that afternoon, but we decided to adjust our schedule for half an hour. At the last minute my teenage son also decided braids were cool, so I agreed to pick them all up at the hair salon in thirty-five minutes.

I dutifully arrived at the salon on time, but to my dismay the braiding was not nearly finished. It was a busy place, with every chair taken and nine "braiding personnel" chatting and casually going about their work. To cut a long story short, the braiding for the Hewitt family took more than three hours. Needless to say, our afternoon plans were shattered. The second surprise came at the end. Instead of being fifteen dollars maximum per person, the real price was seventy-five dollars. Our salesperson had neglected to inform us that there was an extra charge for every single bead. My daughter needed 120 beads to keep her braids together.

We paid the inflated prices and left feeling conned, although the new look certainly gave us a few laughs. Would they get our business a second time? No chance!

Have you ever gone into an agreement thinking you knew what the deal was, and then the tables were turned unexpectedly? How did you feel when that happened? Probably upset, frustrated, angry and disappointed, maybe even blaming yourself for not being smarter. Here's the first big point we want to impress upon you:

ALL BROKEN RELATIONSHIPS CAN BE TRACED BACK TO BROKEN AGREEMENTS.

This includes business deals, marriages, family situations, your banker, friends, partnerships and any other flawed relationship between two or more people.

Have you noticed how Western society in particular is having more difficulty keeping agreements these days? If you need proof of this, just look at the thousands of lawyers required to sort out all the messes. Fear of being sued today is stunting growth in many industries, particularly the medical profession. That's crazy. Here's the good news. You have an incredible opportunity to stand out, simply by maintaining your integrity. You may be thinking, "But how do I maintain my integrity consistently?" Thanks for asking that all-important question. Here's the all-important answer:

TRUE INTEGRITY IS BASED ON KEEPING YOUR AGREEMENTS.

Really digest that sentence. If you seriously want to live on higher ground and reap bigger rewards, your consistency will be tested frequently. Consider this: Every day you make agreements. And every day you are judged by others on the way you act after those decisions have been made. What does your scorecard for keeping agreements look like on an average day? Here's a clue: There is no such thing as a small agreement.

One of our clients made that remark, and it's a profound statement. For example, a salesperson calls and invites you to lunch tomorrow at 12:15 P.M. You arrive on time and he shows up twenty-five minutes late, with no excuse and no apology. Assuming that you waited for him, how do you feel? Is this acceptable? If there is a reasonable excuse, like heavy traffic or a mini-crisis at the office, you might let it pass. But what if it happens a second or a third time? Now we have a series of broken agreements. You are always on time, but the other person is chronically late. In today's competitive marketplace this will not be tolerated.

When you break an agreement once, you will probably be given a second opportunity. When you repeatedly break agreements, your stock and value in the marketplace rapidly diminishes—people go elsewhere. When you develop the habit of consistently keeping your little agreements, the big ones will look after themselves. Make this a philosophy for how you choose to live your life. When you do, you will be blessed beyond measure. It's been that way for centuries.

Here's another example. This one's for the married men, although if you are a woman you'll probably relate to the situation. Your wife asks you to replace the burned-out light bulb in the hall at home. You reply, "Okay, I'll do it before lunch." By supper it's still not fixed. Your wife asks again, politely but firmly. Two days later there's still no light in the hallway. Frustrated, she eventually does the job herself. You may delight in getting out of that little diversion and not think any more about it, but here's the point: If you consistently avoid doing what you say you will do, your reputation becomes tarnished. The relationship gradually deteriorates, because bigger commitments are not being kept too, and in many cases the marriage eventually collapses. If this happens you may end up with the letters DD—Duly Divorced—after your name. That's a pretty serious consequence, and one you may regret for a very long time.

In contrast, when you consistently do what you say you will do, the names attached to you are *reliable* and *trustworthy*. When you practice this every day, your rewards are numerous. They include loyal clients, increased profits, loving relationships and maybe most important, a sense of well-being in the knowledge that you are a person of high integrity. That's a badge you can be proud to wear. It will serve you very well indeed.

In remote parts of Ireland, farmers have a traditional way of sealing an agreement. After the sale of a few cattle they spit on their hands, rub them together and seal the deal with a firm handshake. Their word is their bond—and there isn't a lawyer anywhere in sight. It's that strength of character that breeds trust and respect.

There is one situation where it is okay to break your agreement. It's called Intelligent Disobedience. Let's say you have a value system that strongly believes it is wrong to physically injure anyone. One day you arrive home and hear a scream. You quietly open the door to your living room and see a man with a gun, threatening your family. It's a potentially explosive situation. You intervene by smacking the intruder with a golf club behind the knees, disarming him and defusing the situation. Now you know why it's called Intelligent Disobedience!

One other point. Remember, in normal circumstances if you have difficulty keeping an agreement, it is possible to renegotiate. Always use this option to maintain your integrity. It only takes a moment to call and say, "I'm running fifteen minutes late, is that okay with you?" When you develop the habit of being accountable for your actions, you will stand out as a unique individual. Eventually, when the book is written about your life, you will be remembered for what you did, not what you said. So be accountable for your performance. Make your actions measurable. As film director Woody Allen says, "A big part of life is just showing up!"

Andre Agassi is one of the top tennis players in the world. Known for his flamboyance and unique clothing, he has won several major tournaments including Wimbledon and the U.S. Open. However, as often happens, the success cycle can suddenly turn upside down. For Andre, it happened in 1997. He had a disastrous year, ending up ranked 122 on the tour, a mediocre position compared to his first-place status a few years earlier. It got so bad, Agassi considered quitting the game.

In 1998 he roared back into contention and in 1999 won the U.S. and French Open titles and reached the finals at Wimbledon. Because of this he regained his number-one world ranking. What caused this dramatic turnaround? Agassi made these observations in an interview with journalist Brian Hutchinson. "It was very frustrating for me. I suffered a severe lack of confidence after eight years of top-ten consistency. I realized I had to go back to square one. I had to get back into shape and start over again. I had fallen so far in the rankings I didn't know what was realistic or what wasn't. I didn't have any goals beyond just wanting to get better, day by day."

He no longer harbors any thoughts of retirement. "I'm just out there working now, and at the end of the match I look around and see a lot of happy people, and it makes me feel good," he says. It's another great example of consistency, accountability and personal integrity—the fundamentals for consistent success.

The Integrity
FACTOR

This is a three-part formula to help you live with the utmost integrity. It's simple and effective. We challenge you to start using it every day.

1. **When you always tell the truth, people trust you.**

2. **When you do what you say, as promised, people respect you.**

3. **When you make others feel special, people like you.**

The words "as promised" in part two are significant. Use these in your regular correspondence. It will reinforce the fact that you really do follow through. If a client requests you to fax specific information within the next twenty-four hours, always start the correspondence with, "As promised." For example, "As promised, here is the quote you requested yesterday." When you do this, it is a subtle reminder that you really do keep your commitments, as you promised you would.

Do you remember the Three Big Questions we referred to in chapter 5, Building Excellent Relationships? *Do you like them? Do you trust them? Do you respect them?* The Integrity Factor couples these with the principles of being accountable and keeping your agreements. It's a powerful formula. Learn to live it. Decide now to set a new standard in the way you operate every day. It will put you in the top 3 percent of achievers. You'll attract more and bigger opportunities than you ever thought possible. When you practice the Integrity Factor, your clients will be more than happy to refer you. And that goes straight to the bottom line.

INTEGRITY

Don't Leave Home Without It.

CONCLUSION

To finish, here's another inspirational story, one that incorporates everything we've talked about in this chapter—consistent persistence, agreements and accountability, and of course, The Integrity Factor.

Ken Hitchcock is a big man in many ways, not the least of which is physical. Several years ago Ken weighed in at more than 450 pounds. His huge size did not deter him from pursuing his love and passion —coaching hockey. He became a great coach, leading a junior club to division championships in five out of six seasons, a truly remarkable record.

But Ken's real ambition was to coach in the National Hockey League. As a strategist, he knew just about everything there was to know about the game. He also knew how to inspire players to consistently turn in top performances. His weight, however, was a factor. He was told that he probably wouldn't be selected for a big-league coaching position because of his size.

One day at the end of a practice with his junior club, he slipped and fell on the ice. To his embarrassment and frustration, he could not get back on his feet again, and required assistance from his players to make it to the bench. This was a defining moment for Ken. He realized with absolute certainty that his ambitions would never be realized unless he tackled his weight problem. So he made a choice to take charge of his future, by choosing to win the battle over obesity.

With the support of a close friend, he started an arduous weight-loss program that included training every day and eating a carefully balanced diet. With consistent persistence and a commitment to succeed, he lost an amazing 250 pounds in less than two years. Ken had decided to become accountable for his results. He made an agreement with himself that he would do whatever it took to compete for a coaching position in the National Hockey League.

In 1997 his dream was realized when he became coach of the Dallas Stars. In his first full season, he expertly guided the team to the top of the regular-season standings, another remarkable achievement. Two years later he achieved every coach's dream in the NHL—winning the Stanley Cup. It was the first-ever championship for the Dallas Stars.

If Ken Hitchcock could do it, why couldn't you do something outstanding? We'll repeat it one more time . . . true integrity is making good choices consistently, keeping agreements with yourself, persisting through the tough times and being 100 percent accountable for your results. It's a winning formula. It takes courage and a desire to be the best you can be. And once you make the decision, there's no turning back. Unless you prefer the guilt of knowing that you never really gave it your best shot.

KEEP GOING—SUCCESS IS OFTEN JUST AROUND THE CORNER

For Those Who Won't Quit.

ACTION STEPS

▼

**The Integrity
Factor**

Answer these questions honestly. They will help you plot a new course of action. They will also clearly demonstrate your current level of integrity and accountability.

1. In what areas of my life do I not consistently keep agreements?

_____

_____

_____

_____

2. What will this cost me if I don't change? Consider the long-term consequences.

_____

_____

_____

_____

_____

3. What specifically do I need to change to enjoy The Integrity Factor lifestyle?

_____

_____

_____

_____

4. What specific rewards and benefits will I receive by making these adjustments?

_____

_____

_____

_____

Understanding the importance of integrity in your life is one thing; living it is an entirely different challenge. The next chapter will show you how.

LIVING ON PURPOSE

TAKING DECISIVE ACTION

CONSISTENT PERSISTENCE

ASK FOR WHAT YOU WANT

THE CONFIDENCE FACTOR

BUILDING EXCELLENT RELATIONSHIPS

CREATING OPTIMUM BALANCE

DO YOU SEE THE BIG PICTURE?

IT'S NOT HOCUS-POCUS, IT'S ALL ABOUT FOCUS

YOUR HABITS WILL DETERMINE YOUR FUTURE

You're in the home stretch...
persistence will pull you through.

Taking Decisive Action

"FOR THINGS TO CHANGE YOU'VE GOT TO CHANGE.
OTHERWISE, NOTHING MUCH WILL CHANGE."

—Jim Rohn

Are you in the habit of putting things off?
For example, you need to complete a report by the end of the month, but instead of planning to do it in three simple stages, you leave everything until the last couple of days and it becomes a panic. Other people get pulled into your mess, creating even more turmoil and anxiety. Somehow you manage to get it done, vowing, "Never again—that's the last time I'm letting things go like that —it's not worth the stress." But you do repeat the same behavior again and again, don't you? Why? Because it's your habit. Go on, admit it. You're a procrastinator.

If it's any comfort, you're not the only one. Just about everyone procrastinates. Sometimes that's good, but mostly it's an insidious, chronic malaise that will cripple your future.

In this chapter we'll help you get rid of this nasty habit once and for all. Of all the strategies we've discussed, Taking Decisive Action is easy to measure. It's black and white. You won't be able to hide from the consequences with this one. It separates the weak from the strong, the timid from the courageous, and the talkers from the doers.

Decisiveness is your greatest ally as you chart your path through life. Procrastination is a thief, waiting in disguise to rob you of your hopes and dreams. If you want proof, take a closer look.

There is another word hidden inside the word procrastinate that will alert you to the perils of not taking action. Can you see it?

What a cunning word procrastinate is. It disguises the real word, castrate, which also means, to impoverish or render ineffective. Do you get the picture? When you procrastinate, you are actually impoverishing your future, cutting it off. "Y-E-E-A-A-O-W-W . . . that's painful!" You're right, it's very painful. From now on, every time you go into procrastination mode, sear this painful image of castration into your mind so that it shocks you into action.

Ed Foreman, president of Dallas-based Executive Development Systems, is a man who enjoys taking action. At the age of twenty-six he had already made his first million. He then went on to create many successful businesses including oil and gas, ready-made cement, sand and gravel, and cattle ranching. Ed even found time to get elected to the United States Congress on two different occasions, from two different states—Texas and New Mexico—the only person to do so in the twentieth century.

Now he spends most of his time sharing positive action strategies with corporate executives from all over the world. He has a contagious energy and enthusiasm for life, and no time for people who sit back whining and complaining about what they don't have. He calls their malaise the Someday Syndrome. It was written especially for procrastinators, and is also known as the Procrastinator's Creed.

"Someday when I grow up, finish school and
get a job, I'll start living my life the way I want....
someday after the mortgage is paid off, the finances are
on track and the kids are grown up, I'll drive that new
car and take exciting trips abroad.... someday, now that
I'm about to retire, I'll buy that beautiful motor home
and travel across this great country,
and see all there is to see.... someday."

—Ed Foreman

One day, after a lifetime of someday-thinking and someday-regrets, these procrastinators come to the end of their lives. The one sentence that fills their thoughts as they prepare to pass on is, "If only I'd done the things I really wanted to do, my life would have been so different." They sadly reflect on all the missed opportunities. "If only I'd invested 10 percent of my income every month." "If only I'd taken care of my health." "If only I'd bought that one-hundred-dollar stock when it was selling for a dollar." "If only I'd taken a chance and started my own business." Alas, now it's too late. And another procrastinator makes his or her exit, consumed with feelings of remorse, guilt and a lack of fulfillment.

Beware, dear reader, the Someday Syndrome is a fatal trap. Life is too short not to enjoy it to the fullest. Indecision and uncertainty will confine you to a world of "if only." That's not what you want, is it? Okay, so let's put together a powerful plan of attack that will guarantee you a life full of positive action and unique memorable experiences.

"He's terrible at making decisions."

Six Good REASONS

First we'll take a look at why people procrastinate. Then we'll show you how to get this annoying monkey off your back. If you are not a procrastinator, please read the rest of this chapter anyway, just in case you get the urge later. You'll learn some excellent techniques that will make you even more decisive than you are now.

There are six good reasons you may be procrastinating:

1. You're bored.

It's a fact of life. We all feel less than enthusiastic from time to time. Sometimes our work becomes routine, and we end up just going through the motions. As we mentioned earlier, entrepreneurs are famous for this. After the initial thrill of launching a new business wears off, they need a new challenge, something that keeps the adrenaline pumping.

How do you combat inertia? Here are a few suggestions: First, recognize that you are bored. Be conscious of your feelings, your falling energy levels and your lack of desire to finish projects. You may feel tired and yet not be doing much physical activity. (If you are unusually tired, check things out with your doctor. There might be a medical reason for your sluggishness.)

Ask yourself a few questions and be totally honest with your answers. Am I bored with what I'm doing? (The answer to that is "Yes" or "No.") Why am I bored? What would give me more energy?

Successful entrepreneurs maintain their excitement by constantly going after new projects and bigger opportunities. They keep raising their level of expectation and are never satisfied with routine business that requires no challenge or ingenuity. They thrive on taking new risks and the possibility that they might hit a massive home run. And the uncertainty makes it even more appealing!

One way to get your juices flowing again is to think about creating bigger deals and what it would take to produce that kind of revenue. There are two possibilities. You could sell more of your product or service to your existing clients. Or you could go fishing for bigger clients. Imagine closing deals two or three times larger than any you've ever had before. Start expanding your vision.

This of course requires a whole new set of contacts and connections. You also need to be more creative and innovative. Creativity produces energy, and innovation starts the adrenaline pumping. Suddenly you are developing much bigger goals and a new excitement starts to permeate the office.

Be careful, this can be extremely contagious! Pretty soon everyone on your team is charging forward with a whole new set of incentives and initiatives. Suddenly life is fun again and you are on a roll. Good-bye boredom, hello bigger targets and even bigger rewards.

2. You are overwhelmed with work.

Often people procrastinate because they let things pile up, instead of handling one task at a time and taking each task to completion. This may start with one little thing that doesn't get done because the time wasn't right, or you just didn't feel like doing it.

Then something else comes along, and you postpone that, too. Now you have two things to do. Individually, neither one seems too big to accomplish, but together they create resistance. You end up postponing them both. After a while a growing list of half a dozen items has been put off and procrastination has reared its ugly head. It begins controlling you. Soon there are so many things to do you feel overwhelmed at the thought of even starting, so you don't. If this describes you, take heart. There are ways to help you break through the roadblocks. We'll show you how before the end of this chapter.

3. Your confidence has slipped.

This is where fear and doubt join forces to hold you back by painting vivid negative pictures in your mind. Here's what you need to learn: Most of the things you fear will never happen. If fear is one of the prime reasons that you are not moving forward, please reread chapter 6, The Confidence Factor.

Procrastination equals your level of doubt. Don't allow doubt and uncertainty to take away your power. Remember, it's more mentally tiring to think about what has to be done, and all the things that might go wrong, than it is to physically do the job.

People who are decisive, and who move quickly from one task to the next, do so because the thought of having to do it later creates even more pressure and stress. As we mentioned before, fear can also be a great motivator. Successful football coach Dan Matthews explains it this way: "What has always driven me is that the fear and disappointment of losing always outweighs the joy and satisfaction of winning. If that ever changes, then it's time for me to get out of coaching."

4. You have a low self-worth.

This is entirely different from a temporary lull in your level of confidence. People with poor self-esteem often develop the habit of sabotaging any potential success because, in their minds, they don't deserve it. This may involve old negative belief systems and a traumatic past.

One way to kill an opportunity is to avoid taking it. Individuals with low self-esteem can come up with all sorts of excuses to avoid taking the first step to a better future. And sometimes they will actually move forward and be doing well. Their goal is within easy reach and suddenly they drop the ball for no apparent reason. If this is something you do (or someone close to you), we suggest taking real time to investigate the source. *The Tomorrow Trap*, an excellent book by Karen Peterson, discusses this particular challenge in depth. You'll find it very helpful.

5. You are doing work you don't really enjoy.

There are two sides to this dilemma. First, all of us are required to do certain things we don't enjoy. That's one of the rules of the game if you want to become more successful. You may not like it but that's the way it is. For example, you may not like to do mundane things like paperwork or book-keeping, but it's hard to completely avoid these tasks even if you are a really good delegator. Our friend Ed Foreman did some major research on this issue. Here's what he found: Successful people do the things that unsuccessful people don't like to do. They don't enjoy doing some of these things either, but they go ahead and do them anyway. This is a fundamental point, one that you need to fully understand.

The other side of the coin is that you may be stuck in a mediocre job or career that doesn't allow you to use your greatest abilities. If that's true, then look for an opportunity to expand your talents. Life is too short to be stuck in work you don't enjoy. Most of the time the type of work you do should stimulate you and give you energy. Why stay in something that drains your energy and is not fulfilling?

Many people don't shift because they have a need for security, or the thought of doing something different scares them. Change is out of their comfort zone and is intimidating. Well, here's the reality: The biggest rewards in life are found outside your comfort zone. Live with it. Fear and risk are prerequisites if you want to enjoy a life of success and adventure.

6. You are easily distracted, or just downright lazy!
There's not much to talk about here. Let's be blunt. If you avoid taking action because you'd rather put your feet up every night and watch movie reruns on TV, there's little chance you'll be enjoying an abundant lifestyle any time soon. The bottom line? Success takes effort and consistent, focused activity. Laziness is not part of the equation. It's a banned substance.

Active
DECISION-MAKING

Generally speaking, lack of motivation is usually at the root of your procrastination. It's easier to put things off than it is to act decisively. Being conscious that you are going into a downward spiral of inactivity is important. When you are aware of this, have a little chat with yourself and focus on finding a way to work things out.

There are primarily two ways to motivate yourself: You can fear the consequences of not taking action; or you can get excited about the rewards and benefits of being proactive.

You must keep these two pictures front and center, one negative and one positive. Ask yourself, "What do I really want —a future where I'm always struggling to make ends meet, or a lifestyle of prosperity, joy and fulfillment?" The more vivid these two pictures are, the more decisive you will become. Don't allow yourself to be lulled into a false sense of security. When you hear that destructive little voice whispering inside your head, "Leave it until tomorrow, next week, next month or next year," immediately flash those two pictures on your mental TV screen. What's the picture look like if you don't get started? Do you want to look back on your life with a big list of If Only's? Of course not! Clearly understand this and feel the pain of your castration. (No, that's not a misprint!)

Now flip the switch and take a look at the other picture. This time see all of the rewards and benefits that happened just because you took action and didn't hold back. Feast on this picture. Imprint it into your mind. Sense the feeling of accomplishment. Feel good about challenging yourself to a higher level of performance. Here's a good example of what we're talking about.

In the mid-1970s, Susan Brooks, a schoolteacher in Florida, enjoyed collecting old family recipes. What attracted her most were the ones for home-baked cookies, so she made lots. Her friends loved these traditional goodies so much that the word spread and cookie production in the Brooks's household dramatically increased. It wasn't too long before she left Florida and moved to Georgia, along with her best friends who soon became partners in their first retail cookie store. In the next four years, thirteen franchises were established and a lot of cookies were sold.

However, in 1981 the cookie bubble abruptly burst, the partnership cratered and so did the integrity of the franchise operation. Susan was left holding an empty "cookie jar," consisting of a few furnishings and two industrial ovens. Says Susan, "This was my Cookie University phase—I learned on the front line what it takes to run a business!"

This is where many people would quit. But not Susan and her family. Everything they owned was loaded up into two U-Haul trucks. Along with her husband Barry, and two young children, they headed west for a fresh start in Tempe, Arizona.

Learning from the past, Susan made an important strategic decision—this time, instead of retail stores, she decided to create a mail-order catalogue to sell her cookies and other assorted items. From then on she was in the gift business, not the cookie business. This willingness to take decisive action and go in a new direction really paid off. Cookies From Home (*www.cookiesfromhome.com*) now operates out of an 18,000 square-foot facility, serving corporate and mail-order accounts from coast to coast. The customer base has mushroomed from 3,000 to 75,000. In fact, Susan's cookies have shown up in many interesting places, including Canada, Mexico, England, France and Saudi Arabia.

Susan used decisive action to push through the tough times. She is not in the habit of putting things off just because a few obstacles show up along the way. A favorite picture on her office wall shows a small boat being tossed about in a rough sea. The caption underneath reads, "Anyone can hold the helm when the sea is calm."

Susan says the biggest lessons she has learned are: "I know what I don't know, so I surround myself with people who do. That allows me to focus on what I do best. Also, I *choose* to go to work every day." Susan Brooks was determined to see her vision become a reality. Her consistent persistence ensured that she would succeed.

The message is clear: Whether you're working on a small project or a major goal, stick with it so you can celebrate its completion. Make sure you are not one of those frustrated individuals who goes through life with the label, Does Not Complete. As Jim Rohn so eloquently says, "The pain of discipline weighs ounces whereas the pain of regret weighs tons."

To ensure that you have absolutely no excuses for being indecisive, we are now going to reveal two proven formulas that will help you resolve any future situation that requires you to take action. The first one, the TA-DA formula, is a mini-formula that you can use effectively every day. The second one, the Problem Solver, is more comprehensive.

The TA-DA
FORMULA

This will help you stay alert as you head into the uncharted waters of the future. Before you make any major decisions, we highly recommend that you use this acronym to guide you as outlined below.

1. Think.
As we discussed earlier, time for reflection is essential. Reflective thinking allows you to pause so you can consider all of your options. "Will this help me accomplish my major goals more effectively?" "Why do I want to do this?" "What specific benefit will I gain from taking this course of action?" "What is the downside if it doesn't work?" "How much time will this really take?" The more conscious you are when going into a major decision, the less likely you are to screw things up. Take time to think. Like an airplane pilot, create a foolproof checklist to guide you every time.

2. Ask.

Ask good focusing questions. Find out everything you need to know to make an intelligent, informed decision. Ask other people, your mentors or people who have specific knowledge and experience in this area. The more important the decision, the more time you should take to check everything out. This doesn't mean analyze it to death. Only when you have gathered sufficient information from a variety of sources are you ready for the next step in the formula.

3. Decide.

Use the Double Spiral technique to increase your decisiveness. Visualize the negative consequences if you don't make a decision. Compare these with the positive benefits of moving forward.

Then make a firm decision about what you are going to do. Making the decision is half the battle. Chronic procrastinators lead lives of discontent because they won't make the decision to go forward. After awhile, sitting on the fence becomes very uncomfortable. If you're not careful, you'll stay stuck, unable to get off.

4. Act.

Now that you have done some reflective thinking, asked around for more information and finally made your decision, it's time to act. This is the most important part of the TA-DA formula. Many people live their lives in ready-steady mode, instead of ready steady GO! You must go. Kickstart yourself into focused action. Just take the first step. Gradually you will build momentum. Like the proverbial snowball rolling downhill, you won't be able to stop after you make that early push. Remember, the big rewards in life only materialize when you start doing.

W. Clement Stone, one of America's greatest success stories and the coauthor of *Success Through a Positive Mental Attitude*, had a unique way of pushing himself to take action.

He would stand in front of a mirror and with great vigor smash his hands together, exclaiming loudly as he did so, "Do it now!" He would repeat this action three times. This anchored him for the tasks ahead. It must have worked. At age sixteen he was selling life insurance like there was no tomorrow. When he was twenty-one the Great Depression had set in, and many people said it was impossible to survive. Undaunted, young Stone started his own company, called Combined Insurance, hired 1,000 salespeople, and built it into one of the largest enterprises in North America. Remember, it's little habits like the mirror exercise that are often the catalyst to get you started.

DILBERT *reprinted by permission of United Feature Syndicate, Inc.*

The Problem
SOLVER

Our second formula for active decision making is called the Problem Solver. This is a series of ten steps that will help you solve any major problem or challenge you may experience in the years ahead. It's powerful. Make this a priority when you don't know which direction to turn. It's all laid out in our Action Steps at the end of this chapter.

These two excellent strategies will support you in all of your decision-making situations. Develop the habit of using both of them. This is an essential part of your armor and will help ward off the daily negative assaults as you stride towards a happier, healthier lifestyle. Be diligent. Stay on guard. Learn to observe what you do well and what needs your attention. Good decision-making requires practice and a high level of awareness. You now have the tools to master this part of your success plan.

Let's Talk About MONEY

Hitting your financial targets with certainty every year is obviously very important, especially if you live in a society where the price of almost everything keeps going up. If you have a growing family that includes teenagers, you'll know what we mean!

A complete in-depth analysis of money and investment strategies is way beyond the scope of this book. However, as your income is closely tied to the amount of time off you have, and enjoyment of a well-balanced lifestyle, we thought it would be a good idea to share some basic essentials from our perspective. It's all part of your education in the field of taking decisive action.

What does money mean to you?
Everyone forms beliefs about money. Contrary to what some people think, money is not the root of all evil. If that were true, just about every nonprofit organization, charity and church would cease to exist. However, the total love of money to the exclusion of everything else causes all sorts of anxiety.

There are basically three things in life that can ruin you:

1. Power—observe the dictators and megalomaniacs of this world.

2. Sex—usually with too many people, the number-one example being politicians, of course.

3. Greed—the unhealthy pursuit of too much money, often at the cost of someone else.

To understand how you really feel about money, ask yourself a few simple questions. For example: Is it okay to have a lot of money? What money habits have shown up in my life so far? Do I joyfully earn and accumulate money, or do I sabotage myself when things go well unexpectedly?

We've included an excellent Money Quiz at the end of this chapter that will really help you identify your financial realities. Make sure you complete it.

Here are a few other thoughts about belief systems around money. Some people were brought up in a very thrifty environment, so penny-pinching was a natural way of life. Others were told by parents and various authority figures that money was "dirty." Did you ever hear this one? "Don't put that money in your mouth, it's dirty!"

Some people were more fortunate and were brought up in an environment where a good work ethic was valued and money was spent and invested wisely. There was also an element of fun without being too frugal.

Money flows to those who attract it.
In our opinion, money is simply a reward for services rendered. If you provide excellent service and create significant value for the people around you, the money will show up. Therefore, to attract more money, you must be attractive, in the sense that people will want and prefer your products or service over those of your competitor. The bottom line is always

to focus on creating more value. Do whatever it takes to make whatever you offer in the marketplace the absolute best.

If you are struggling financially or would like to significantly boost your net worth, understand this: Your money habits are primarily the cause of your current financial status. So if you've never been in the habit of saving or investing, you may be experiencing some consequences right now. If you constantly spend more than you earn, you will definitely experience major consequences at some point. People who earn $50,000 per year have $50,000 habits. People who earn $500,000 have $500,000 habits. And that's an absolute take-it-to-the-bank fact.

To change your habits you must first accept your present financial reality. Denying the obvious won't work! The next step, if you want to be financially independent, is to make it a study. Do your homework. Learn how money flows, how it expands and grows and most of all, who is really good at attracting it.

Undoubtedly there are people in your neighborhood or city who have earned a lot of money. Find out how they did it. Be creative. Be courageous. Be so bold as to set up an appointment to meet with them. In addition, you must have a brilliant financial coach or team of advisers to help and support you. Ask around. Find out who is the best. Again, do your homework. Focus. Most people won't make this type of effort. It's probably easier to sit in front of the TV every night instead of creating a strong financial future that their families would relish in later years.

Basic rules for creating wealth.
We are now going to introduce you to two wealthy individuals —Sir John Templeton and Art Linkletter—and share their specific Top-10 lists on how to create unlimited prosperity. We selected these individuals because of their integrity and ability to accumulate money. You may be surprised at the

simplicity of their findings. Study each one carefully. Their insights can shave years off your wealth curve.

First, Sir John Templeton. The founder of the Templeton Group, Sir John Templeton is a legendary mutual fund manager. His genius for financial management has created wealth for thousands of investors all around the world. The following ten principles are the heart and soul of his incredible success.

1. To achieve success, be neither an optimist nor a pessimist, but a realist with a hopeful nature.

2. Count your blessings to enrich yourself and your neighbors, first spiritually, and then, perhaps, financially.

3. Debt, whether personal or collective, should not keep you from investing in your future. Strive to be debt free.

4. Invest in many different places—there is safety in numbers.

5. Money should do far more than simply reproduce itself.

6. Remember that patience is a virtue.

7. If you want to prosper, investigate before you invest.

8. Never forget: The secret of creating riches for oneself is to create them for others.

9. Looking out for Number One doesn't make you Number One.

10. Make success with a single word—*Love.*

SOURCE: *Ten Golden Rules for Financial Success*

Art Linkletter is probably best known as an entertainer and show business personality. As a baby, he was abandoned and then adopted by a church minister, in the small community of Moosejaw, Saskatchewan, Canada. His famous show, *House Party* on CBS, was one of the longest-running programs on television. Art Linkletter is also a very astute businessman with direct involvement in dozens of successful enterprises. Here are Art's most important insights for creating wealth and success.

1. I'm going to do the work I enjoy. You only live once, so do what you love.

2. There will always be difficulties, failures and challenges along the way.

3. The margin between mediocrity and success is very small when related to time and effort, over and above what is expected.

4. I will use pull whenever I can to open the doors to opportunity, but I will make sure to work when the door is opened for me.

5. I will recognize and be alert to my own weaknesses, and find people who excel in the things where I falter.

6. I will consider an opportunity to advance more important than the immediate money and fringe benefits of the situation.

7. I will always stretch my abilities and goals a little further than my comfort zone, within reason.

8. I will learn from my failures and then put them behind me.

9. I will follow the Golden Rule. I will not do a deal where someone else is short-changed, cheated or taken advantage of.

10. I will use other people's money provided I feel certain the money itself can grow at a faster rate than the interest charges. I will not be greedy.

To wrap this up, we'll throw our hats into the ring as well. These are the most important strategies we focus on.

JACK:
- Do what you love with passion and excellence and the money will follow.

- Read all you can, attend seminars, listen to tapes and put what you learn into action.

- Make a study of the universal laws of success, prosperity and abundance.

- Tithe a percentage of your income to your church and favorite charities.

- Always strive for constant and never-ending improvement in everything you do.

MARK:
- Make the decision to be financially independent and your subconscious will make a provision. Write it into a plan, "I will earn . . ."

- Carry a 3" x 5" card that says, "I am so happy I am . . ." (On schedule to be a millionaire; growing 50 percent annually; meeting one new prospect or client per day; selling X amount of Y daily; or whatever your particular goal is.) Read this card at breakfast, lunch, dinner and just prior to sleep, so you become one with the idea, and eventually it will become reality.

- Love your job or right livelihood, and let it love you. I love speaking, writing, creating, thinking, promoting and marketing and because I love it, it thrives.

- Create a dream team of like-minded colleagues who will help you make your hopes come true now.

- Serve greatly with love and a happy heart.

LES:
- Focus on what you do best. Strive to be a leader in your field of expertise. My talents are coaching, writing and creating self-awareness products.

- Look for specific opportunities that will complement and expand your greatest strengths. I created the Achievers Coaching Program for entrepreneurs because I relate easily to their challenges.

- Invest first in your own business. Stay away from deals and industries you know little about. That's why Warren Buffet has done so well.

- Surround yourself with brilliant financial mentors as previously suggested. Who you know is at least as important as what you know.

- Develop and maintain simple financial habits. Invest 10 percent of your income every month. Do not consume more than you earn. Know where your money goes. Strive to be debt-free.

GOD GIVES EVERY BIRD ITS FOOD

But He Does Not Throw It Into The Nest!

MAKE WEALTH A STUDY

To help you further, here's a list of seven great books about money and wealth creation. Set a goal to read all of them. There are literally hundreds of books on this subject. Make these a first step in your quest for financial wisdom.

1. *The Richest Man in Babylon* by George S. Clason, (Penguin Books, 1989).

2. *The Wealthy Barber* by David Chilton (Stoddart Publishing, 1989).

3. *The Millionaire Next Door* by Thomas J. Stanley and William D. Danko (Longstreet Press, Inc., 1996).

4. *Ten Golden Rules for Financial Success* by Gary Moore (Zondervan Publishing House, 1996).

5. *The 9 Steps to Financial Freedom* by Suze Orman (Random House, 1998).

6. *Think and Grow Rich* by Napoleon Hill (Fawcett Crest Books/CBS Inc., 1960).

7. *Rich Dad, Poor Dad* by Robert T. Kiyosaki with Sharon L. Lechter (Techpress Inc., 1997).

Now you have the tools for taking decisive action in your financial affairs. Our last word on this? Take the necessary steps *now*. When it comes to money, time *is* of the essence.

CONCLUSION

Here's a story about the biggest decision of all—the decision to live. It's about a remarkable man, Viktor Frankl, who found himself incarcerated in a Nazi concentration camp during World War II. A prominent psychologist before the war dramatically changed his life, Frankl suffered the fate of millions of Jews—hard labor under the most awful conditions imaginable. Every day many of his fellow prisoners would die from malnutrition, savage beatings or from being herded off to the gas chambers, the ultimate humiliation.

Despite the severity of his conditions, Viktor Frankl realized there was one element that his captors could not control—his attitude. Simply stated, he chose to live. And nothing, absolutely nothing, would shift his resolve to win this greatest of human battles.

To alleviate his terrifying circumstances, he focused on a positive picture of the future. He visualized being a successful psychologist, attending concerts and enjoying a fulfilling lifestyle. Never did he allow himself to surrender to the depravation that was going on all around him. This incredible fortitude, decisiveness, persistence and strength of character eventually paid off when the war ended. Those who had nothing to live for, and there were many, did not survive. Viktor Frankl went on to become one of the world's most renowned therapists and inspirational leaders. The book detailing his struggles, *Man's Search for Meaning*, is a classic. Make sure you read it more than once. It will uplift your soul.

WHY HESITATE?

UPON THE PLAINS OF HESITATION ARE THE
BLEACHED BONES OF COUNTLESS MILLIONS,
WHO ON THE THRESHOLD OF VICTORY SAT DOWN
TO WAIT, AND IN WAITING THEY DIED.

—Author Unknown

ACTION STEPS

The Problem Solver

Financial Certainty

When you're experiencing a significant challenge, use the Problem Solver below to help you solve it. This is a series of ten questions that will guide you step by step to the outcome you want. For best results, it's important to go through the entire written process. Use it often—your decisiveness will dramatically improve when you do.

1. What is my challenge?
Accurately define your situation. Remember to be clear, brief and specific.

_____

_____

_____

2. Decide to confront the issue and deal with it.
Making a decision to move through your fear is a major step forward. For your good health and peace of mind, decide now.

3. What is the desired result I want?

Again, clearly define the preferred outcome. Visualize closure, and describe the major benefits when you have dealt with the issue.

_____

_____

_____

_____

4. In one word, describe how you will feel when the issue is closed.

_____

5. What information do I need that will help?

Learn more by reading, researching old files, contracts, etc.

_____

_____

_____

6. What can I do myself?

_____

_____

7. Who else can help me?

_____

_____

_____

8. Now, what specific action steps am I going to take?
This is your game plan. Think through each step to final closure.

1. _____

_____

2. _____

_____

3. _____

_____

9. When am I going to start? _____ date

When am I going to bring this unfinished business to closure?_____ date

Get started!! .
Remember, peace of mind is on the other side of fear.

10. Review your results and celebrate!

THE HABIT OF FINANCIAL CERTAINTY

A Money Quiz to Clarify Your Current Position.

1. **What does money mean to you?**

   _____

   _____

   _____

2. **Do you deserve a lot of money?** ❑ yes ❑ no
   Why? or Why not?

   _____

   _____

   _____

3. **Define FINANCIAL FREEDOM as it relates to you personally.**

   _____

   _____

   _____

4. **Do you know how much you spend, and how much you earn specifically each month?** ❑ yes ❑ no

5. **Are you consumption-oriented, or do you have a clear savings and investment program that takes priority?**

   _____

   _____

   _____

6. **Are you in the habit of paying yourself every month?**

                ❑ yes   ❑ no

7. **Do you have a brilliant financial adviser or team of advisers?**

                ❑ yes   ❑ no

8. **How much money will you require when (and if) you retire, to enjoy the lifestyle you want?**

_____

_____

_____

9. **What is your present shortfall, if any?**

_____

_____

_____

10. **Are you on track to have a healthy net worth?**

This means having enough money to enjoy the quality of life you really want. To have the choice of working or not working, because you can afford it.

If you are not at this level of financial freedom yet, what do you need to change?

_____

_____

_____

_____

_____

_____

_____

LIVING ON PURPOSE

TAKING DECISIVE ACTION

CONSISTENT PERSISTENCE

ASK FOR WHAT YOU WANT

THE CONFIDENCE FACTOR

BUILDING EXCELLENT RELATIONSHIPS

CREATING OPTIMUM BALANCE

DO YOU SEE THE BIG PICTURE?

IT'S NOT HOCUS-POCUS, IT'S ALL ABOUT FOCUS

YOUR HABITS WILL DETERMINE YOUR FUTURE

Only one strategy left—you're almost there.

Living On
Purpose

"THIS IS THE TRUE JOY—THE BEING USED FOR
A PURPOSE RECOGNIZED AS A MIGHTY ONE."

—George Bernard Shaw

Craig Kielburger is a most unusual young man.
At the tender age of thirteen, a time when the majority
of his friends were more interested in playing hockey
or football, Craig was passionately telling the world
about an organization he had created called Free The
Children.[4] His schedule looks like that of a top celebrity
international speaker. From India to Washington D.C.
and New York, followed by a trip to Canada, and then
on to Haiti. Add to all of this a flattering profile on
60 Minutes lauding his crusade to stop child labor.

So what makes this five-foot-tall teenager, who
demonstrates a maturity far beyond his years, really tick?
He says, "I just feel very passionate about the issue of
child labor, and I want to do something to alleviate it."

Simply stated, Craig Kielburger is living on purpose.
He has found something that gets his juices flowing
and the adrenaline pumping. His purpose gives him

---

[4] To make a donation to Free The Children, phone 905-760-9382, or
contact their Web site at *www.freethechildren.org*.

tremendous energy. He's excited about it and relentless in its pursuit. At the same time he's normal enough to show that he's still a kid. As journalist Robert Russo noted, "After a visit to the home of Vice President Al Gore, he exclaims in wide-eyed wonderment, 'I got one of his napkins. It says Vice President of the United States on it. He has his very own napkins!' Americans have rushed to embrace this young Canadian phenomenon who appears remarkably well adjusted and who is living out his own dream, rather than that of his parents."

And that dream has instilled a steely determination, an unrelenting drive that has forced other high ranking officials to sit up and take notice. Upset by the millions of children being forced to work in India, Craig decided to go there. This coincided with a visit by Canada's Prime Minister, Jean Chretien. Young Kielburger created such a flurry of media attention that Mr. Chretien finally agreed to have a personal meeting with him. Yes, when there's a fire in your belly you can do the impossible. Here's the intriguing question. Why is it that some people have this burning desire and the vast majority do not? Most people simply go through the motions every day, caught up in routines that often become boring. If you are experiencing this mechanical approach to life, take heart. There is a better way.

Finding Your PURPOSE

Entire books have been written about this all-encompassing topic. We have condensed it down to the fundamentals. Please note, this is a vitally important chapter for you. In the following pages you will discover how essential it is to have a purpose for your life. We'll even help you create a clear definition. Most people don't have a clue about this. You'll understand why, when we share with you later a breakthrough concept called the Level of Being. We don't want you to end up like masses of other people out there, wandering generalities who are unsure of what they are doing, and why they are doing it.

Then there are those people who come to a crossroads in their life. Somewhere between thirty-five and fifty-five years of age, the famous mid-life crisis appears. Suddenly deeper questions begin to surface like, "Is this all there is?" After some serious navel-gazing, they begin to feel a void, a sense of emptiness. Something is missing, but they can't quite put their finger on it. Gradually they come to the realization that collecting material things and paying off the mortgage isn't doing it for them anymore.

LEARNING TO LIVE ON PURPOSE

Is this scenario familiar to you? Are you wondering about a lack of purpose in your own life? The ideas in this chapter go far beyond the specific daily habits you have started working on, important though these are. At some level we all hunger for meaning in our lives. We need to feel at our core that we matter, and that we are making a difference.

Adopting a lifestyle that is on purpose provides an opportunity to enrich others, by leaving your imprint in a positive way. For example, if you have a daily philosophy of being a giver and you develop the habit of helping others with no immediate thought of personal reward, you are demonstrating the beginnings of a sense of purpose. When you are able to expand this philosophy to encompass a broader vision, your purpose will crystallize. We'll show you how.

The Marathon of
HOPE

But first, to clarify this even further, here's the remarkable story of Terry Fox. When he was only eighteen years old, Terry discovered he had cancer. The diagnosis was osteosarcoma, a fast-metastasizing cancer that often strikes the legs and arms and may spread to the lungs, brain or liver. After the agony of his new reality set in, Terry basically had two choices: give up hope and wait for death, or discover something meaningful to live for. He chose the latter. The cancer meant he would lose his leg. As he lay in his hospital bed, Terry dreamed of running across Canada. That day he made a commitment to make his dream a reality. His vision was starting to take shape.

By committing his life to making a difference in the fight against cancer, he created a true purpose. The goal of his one-legged run, named the Marathon of Hope, was to raise one million dollars for cancer research. The final total was $24.6 million!

Young Terry discovered a purpose so great it uplifted him physically and mentally every day. This power of purpose drove him to remarkable heights of performance. Even though he had only one healthy leg, a prosthesis attached to the stump of his other leg enabled him to run. The action was more like a hopping movement. It created the sensation of stubbing his toe with every step. Terry wore shorts while running. This of course exposed his false leg and made some people feel uncomfortable. Terry's response was, "This is me, why hide it?" Starting out on April 12, 1980, he ran the equivalent of a marathon (twenty-six miles) almost every day, covering a total of 3,339 miles in only 143 days—an amazing feat! By doing so, he provided hope for thousands of people all over the world.

This may prompt you to ask, "What am I doing with my life? What is my life's work all about? What legacy will I leave behind when my time is over?"

Important questions, don't you think?

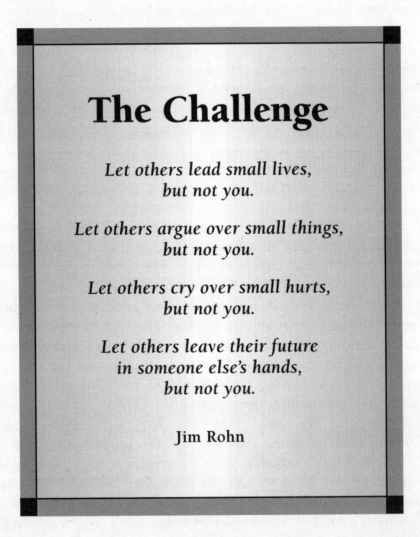

The Challenge

Let others lead small lives,
but not you.

Let others argue over small things,
but not you.

Let others cry over small hurts,
but not you.

Let others leave their future
in someone else's hands,
but not you.

Jim Rohn

Three Key POINTS

Let's take a closer look at the key points that helped Terry Fox successfully forge his new purpose. First, we need to clear up the distinction between setting goals and having a purpose. Your purpose transcends your goals. It's the Big Picture—like an all-encompassing umbrella. Goals, on the other hand, are the steps you take along the way. Terry's purpose was to help eliminate cancer. His specific goal, however, was to raise one million dollars for cancer research by running across Canada. When you align your everyday goals with a well-defined purpose, you will enjoy peace of mind and a wonderful sense of being alive. That's a rare commodity these days.

The following three key points will help you activate your own purpose:

1. Align your purpose with your natural ability.
Terry Fox aligned his purpose with something he really enjoyed—athletics. He excelled at running, so running across the country became the natural vehicle for him to achieve his goal. We have all been gifted with natural talents. Discovering what these are is part of the game of life. Often, our work is not aligned with what we do best. Our values and our actions may be at cross purposes. It's these mixed messages that cause internal conflict and uncertainty.

2. Be determined.
Every day Terry stayed true to his purpose. Despite snow, rain and sleet, he soldiered on. In the early stages there was almost no media coverage and he sometimes felt alone and misunderstood. He overcame that by keeping his purpose in the forefront of his mind. Many people lose their direction in life because they are easily distracted or influenced by other people. Consequently

they wander along bouncing from one situation to the next, like a ball in a pinball machine.

Living your purpose requires single-mindedness—a resolve to do whatever it takes. It separates the weak from the strong, the procrastinators from the truly committed. It inflames a deep passion and creates a feeling of significance. When your purpose is clear, your life will have meaning. You'll sleep at night fulfilled, instead of worrying about all the day-to-day stuff that creates stress and tension.

3. Maintain a humble attitude.

Don't allow an unhealthy ego to override your good intentions. Individuals who have the greatest and most positive impact on society are not concerned with fame and fortune. Mahatma Gandhi, Mother Teresa, and thousands of others who are not as well-known, simply got on with the work. Greed and power were not part of their formula for living on purpose.

In the later stages of his Marathon of Hope, Terry Fox attracted thousands of people in every major city. His attitude throughout was, "I'm just an average person, no better or no worse than anyone else. There are a lot of other people involved with this, and they deserve recognition too." It was this humble outlook and genuine concern for others, plus his never-give-up attitude as he battled adversity, that endeared him to millions of people. Even after the cancer spread to his lungs, he was determined to carry on. Terry never did get to finish his run. He died on June 28, 1981. However, the ongoing legacy he left continues to help cancer victims. To date, an astounding $150 million has been raised for cancer research from the annual Terry Fox Run.[5] The event is held in at least fifty countries with more than two hundred thousand people participating. At this point you may be thinking, "That is a great story, but I really don't see

[5] To make a donation to The Terry Fox Foundation for cancer research, phone 416-924-8252, or contact their Web site at *www.terryfoxrun.org*.

myself dramatically changing the world. I'm not a celebrity. My struggle is just getting to the end of the month."

That's the very reason you *are* struggling—you don't get it yet. The importance of purpose, that is. If you did, you wouldn't view your life as a struggle.

As trainers, our biggest challenge is getting people to understand how critical this is to their future. Wouldn't it be nice to have a ready-made "purpose button" on the top of your head, that you could hit and your true purpose in life would immediately become clear? Obviously there's a lot more to it than that. The remainder of this chapter will enlighten you much more.

Here's the next step to making your purpose come alive.

Discovering Your PURPOSE

As we stated earlier, most people do not have a well-defined purpose. To help you figure out yours, here are some probing questions. Take your time to think through these before answering. If you are feeling stuck, or going through a major transition, consider taking a couple of days off and going to a quiet retreat where you can really think about what you want to do with your life. It's impossible to make excellent decisions when you are caught up in the busy whirl of everyday activities. You can't think on the run! If you don't have a special sanctuary of your own, there are probably a few retreats in your area. Check the Yellow Pages or your local churches for assistance.

David McNally, bestselling author of *Even Eagles Need a Push* and *The Eagle's Secret*, is the producer of a wonderful award-winning video about Terry Fox. (See Resource Guide for details.) It is truly inspiring. David is regarded as a leading authority on how to thrive in our personal and professional lives. He created the critically important ten-question exercise called Discovering and Living Your Purpose (see Action Steps). These are essential questions. So don't sell yourself short—reserve a few minutes to complete the exercise—it could lead to a major breakthrough for you. But first, finish reading the chapter. In doing so, you will develop a greater understanding of how to determine your purpose.

Here are some key considerations: Your quest begins with recognizing your special skills and talents. What do you do best? What do you really enjoy doing? Chapter 3, Priority Focus, helped you to figure this out. Most people stagnate in their jobs. They end up bored, just going through the motions. It's very frustrating. Often, the reason is a lack of challenge. The work does not utilize their strengths and they end up stuck doing activities that deplete their energy, instead of being inspired by some magnificent project. Does this in any way describe you?

Purposeful work also means that you care deeply about something. You don't feel obligated to perform, rather you are passionate about it. Terry Fox was profoundly touched by younger cancer victims. It spurred him on every day, despite the hardships.

When you are living on purpose you feel that you are making a difference. And you don't need to be famous. You can make a significant impact in your own community. Another important factor as you explore your direction is your level of enthusiasm. Are you in Have-To mode most of the time, or Choose-To? As we mentioned earlier, living in Choose-To gives you power. You feel energized. When serving a purpose larger than yourself, your level of commitment also expands. As your purpose unfolds, you will develop a unique philosophy about life and a Big Picture viewpoint. Surface and routine tasks become less important as your work takes on new meaning. In order to live life to the fullest, your goals need to reflect your purpose. If you are focused only on making money, a large slice of life will pass you by.

DILBERT *reprinted by permission of United Feature Syndicate, Inc.*

Statement
of
PURPOSE

Many businesses have spent large sums of money developing mission statements. This usually involves the leaders of the company. Sometimes a management consultant is hired to help with the process. The result is usually three or four paragraphs of well-meaning words and clichés. These are often made into a beautiful plaque that hangs elegantly in the main entrance of the office. Sadly, this is as far as it goes for many companies. Even sadder is the fact that, when asked, most people who work in the organization cannot repeat the mission statement. It never becomes part of the culture. All too often it is just something management dreamed up, another flavor of the month.

LES:
I had a speech to deliver to the board members of a large national food chain. I knew they had a mission statement and were upgrading it. So I randomly called several of their stores and asked the person who answered the phone,

279

"Can you tell me what your company mission statement is, please?" Not one person was able to answer the question. One manager responded, "I think we have a copy of it somewhere. I'd need to check my filing cabinet." So much for living your mission!

If you own a business or are a key decision-maker, consider these suggestions: First, change the phrase "Mission Statement" to "Our Purpose." Generally speaking, employees understand this more easily than a mission. Keep it short and simple, so that everyone in the office can memorize it. One powerful sentence that everyone puts into practice every day will do more for your business than a long-winded statement dropped into some obscure filing cabinet.

An excellent example is Harry Rosen Men's Wear, a high-end clothing chain. Here's their statement: To Exceed Our Customer's Expectations. This is printed on the back of every salesperson's business card, and everyone who works there knows it. Each employee also has the authority to turn this statement into action. For example, if you bought a pair of pants that needed altering, and you had to have them tomorrow but couldn't pick them up, the salesperson would ensure that they were delivered by courier. No problem. That's going the extra mile. We suggest you keep your own personal statement of purpose to one meaningful sentence. Make it generic enough that you can serve your purpose in many everyday situations.

LES:
My purpose statement is, **To help as many people as I can during my lifetime, in a way that significantly improves their lives.** This gives me a multitude of opportunities. I can serve business people through our three-year Achievers Coaching Program. I can also share ideas by writing books and magazine articles and recording cassette albums. Or I can simply offer a word of encouragement and a smile to someone who needs a

boost—for example, a waitress who is feeling pressured because the restaurant is short-staffed. Or a parking lot attendant who rarely has a conversation with any customers because they are in too big a hurry to extend a greeting.

JACK:
My purpose statement is, **To inspire and empower people to live their highest vision in a context of love and joy.** Similar to what Les stated above, there are many opportunities and many forums for accomplishing this. I can write books, conduct seminars, give speeches, write articles, appear on radio and television shows, motivate and mentor my staff, consult with other organizations, develop a self-improvement curriculum for at-risk, inner-city high school students, or simply inspire the person sitting next to me on an airplane.

MARK:
My purpose statement is, **To inspire my audience with wisdom that will make their world work.** My audiences range from several thousand people at a large convention to a handful of people in a boardroom. Or, like Les and Jack, I can also have an audience with one person for ten minutes. It's amazing how you can touch someone with a few well-chosen words of encouragement and support. Sometimes it only takes a moment to make a positive difference.

We have also developed a statement of purpose for our *Chicken Soup for the Soul* series. It simply reads:

TO CHANGE THE WORLD, ONE STORY AT A TIME.

Developing Your PURPOSE

To help you develop your purpose to an even greater degree, you are now about to discover a unique way of expanding your awareness. It's called the Level of Being.

Earlier we mentioned the groundbreaking work of George Addair. George is a remarkable man who has dedicated his life to what he calls "The Work." This includes special study groups and self-knowledge programs that are transformational for the people who participate. By 1999, more than thirty thousand people had graduated from his Omega Vector and Delta Vector programs (see Resource Guide for more details).

George's relentless pursuit to understand life's deeper principles unearthed this unique code for living at a higher level. To fully understand how the Level of Being works, please read the next few pages several times until you grasp the true meaning. Lack of awareness about these fundamental truths will keep you stuck, unfulfilled and struggling to reap life's biggest rewards.

To facilitate the concept, we're going to break this into three specific areas. First, you'll learn how to differentiate between personal growth and the term Level of Being. Then we'll identify the fundamental stages of human evolution. Don't worry, this will not be a long, drawn-out history lesson. As bottom-line thinkers, we like to get to the heart of things quickly. Finally, you'll see how the Level of Being works in detail, and the important connection it has to the first two subjects. When you are able to synchronize all three of these elements and implement them, your success in life is pretty much guaranteed.

I'M NOT HERE JUST TO MAKE A LIVING,
I'M HERE TO MAKE A DIFFERENCE.

—Helice Bridges

Personal Growth and
LEVEL OF BEING

Look at the graphic on page 284. This shows the relationship between personal growth and time. All personal growth is vertical. It is often described by metaphors, such as *going for higher ground, reaching the top, climbing the mountain, ascending the heights* or *living up to your potential.*

Failure, on the other hand, is pointed downward with metaphors like *hitting rock bottom, in the hole, going backwards, slipping and sliding,* and so on.

On the other scale, time is horizontal. This shows that the past is behind us and the future is still out in front.

The fact is, neither scale is directional. The up and down scale represents your Level of Being. The left and right scale represents non-being, a state of illusion, because your past is already dead and your future is not yet born. Where the two scales intersect is the here and now; that is, your present circumstances. As you'll see in a few minutes, the higher up you are on the vertical scale, the better your ability to understand how life works.

The next step in this puzzle is to realize that there are three broad categories of human evolution: the Child stage; the Adult stage; and the Self-Realization stage. The Child stage is mechanical and unconscious—a land of inner sleep. Note that we are referring to grown-ups as well as to children. The Adult stage literally involves an awakening. Unfortunately, some people never wake up; they stay stuck at the lower levels of awareness. At the higher levels, people in the Self-Realization stage know what their purpose is, and have a well-defined philosophy of life. We'll expand on this concept later.

First, here is another important distinction: the difference between events and states. The outer world we experience is a series of events. It's what happens in our world every day.

However, our inner world is experienced as states. These include our wide range of emotions, instincts and intuition. These states determine our Level of Being, or awareness.

The next sentence is crucial. Only when you make a conscious distinction between events (your outer world) and states (your inner world) will you know how life really works. For example, your present lifestyle (standard of living) is determined by your inner state of being, *not* by outer events. It is impossible to have a low Level of Being on the inside and simultaneously a higher Level of Being on the outside. Most people don't understand this—they attempt to manipulate outer events to achieve success. This never works. The only way to truly enjoy a higher level of success, including financial freedom, job satisfaction and richer relationships, is by changing your inner Level of Being. To fully appreciate the range of Levels of Being, study the graphic on page 285. Each level is like the rung on a ladder. Every time you take a step up, your awareness and ability to have what you want increases.

Personal Growth and Level of Being

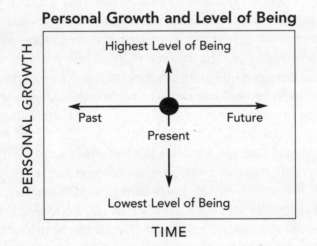

Reprinted with permission from George Addair.

The circle symbolizes your current Level of Being, in other words, your present circumstances. Lifestyle is unrelated to time. Success and failure are determined solely by one's Level of Being.

LEVELS OF BEING DEFINED

Standard of living, lifestyle, prosperity and poverty are determined not by events or circumstances in the outer world, but by one's state of Inner Being. It is impossible to have a low Level of Being on the inside and simultaneously a high level of success on the outside. Listed below are several examples of these Inner States or Levels of Being.

Examples of Being

STATE OF SELF-RELIANCE: High self-esteem and inner validation. Motivates from within. Follows "Inner Voice." Is free from all needs and gives selfless service to others. Experiences no resistance.

STATE OF ALLOWING: Accepts life unconditionally. Portrays invisible leadership skills. Harmless to all. Has personal power. Lives each day with no judgment and accepts the truth without blaming others.

Conscious and Awake

(Self-Realization stage)

DISCOVERY OF LOVE: Learns and practices unconditional giving and unconditional love. Accepts easily, is forgiving. Begins to appreciate harmlessness.

STATE OF AWAKENING: Explores win-win behavior. Becomes intuitive. Takes conscious risks. Learns to give more instead of taking. Begins to share feelings. Thinks through situations, uses reason.

Awakening (Adult stages)

SELF-LOVE AND VANITY INSTINCTS: Judges others, rationalizes and justifies why life isn't working. Often lives in denial—uses retaliation—reactive—intellectualizes. Mechanical Addictive Behavior.

SAFETY INSTINCTS: Defensive—fearful—tendency to worry—jealous—blames others and events for lack of success. Does things for approval—attention-seeking. Portrays mechanical addictive behavior.

SURVIVAL INSTINCTS: Possessive—territorial—controlling and aggressive behavior. Uses attacking and threatening methods to stay in charge. Mechanical addictive behavior.

Mechanical and Asleep (Child stages)

Reprinted with permission from George Addair.

Let's take a closer look at the Levels of Being from a practical point of view. The lowest rungs on the ladder are called the Mechanical or Asleep level, also known as the Child stage. People at this level usually have no interest in learning more, or in significantly improving their lifestyle. They have a limited level of awareness. In a sense they are unconscious of a higher level. For them life is pretty routine and basic. Their main concern is for security and survival. As long as they can preserve the status quo, hold down a job, watch a little TV and pay the bills, they'll survive. They tend to blame situations and others for their lack of success, but aren't prepared to change themselves. Consequently, they stay stuck. Do you know anyone like this?

Please understand, we're not saying this is wrong. As you know, everything in life is a choice. If you choose this Level of Being, then you will remain there. To make a transition requires a vertical movement. It has nothing to do with time. This concept is fundamental. Working harder and longer each day will simply bring you more of what you already have. Moving to a higher Level of Being first requires that you become conscious of how life really works.

Moving up the ladder a little, we find people who are held back by guilt and self-doubt. Often, people at this Level of Being live their lives for other people's approval. They have a low self-worth so they tend not to complete goals or finish what they start. Interestingly, they have all sorts of justification for their lack of progress. Other characteristics include a need to be right and a tendency to be very self-centered.

Moving further up the ladder into the Adult stage, the awakening process begins. When you are at this Level of Being, your life involves taking conscious risks, starting to understand win-win and becoming a giver instead of a taker. You are now able to share your feelings with confidence and the search for a meaningful existence becomes apparent.

Transcending into even higher Levels of Being, you come to the stage of Self-Realization. Here you are fully conscious and awake, which requires you to demonstrate total integrity in everything you do. This is not easy. Very few people live their lives in this rarefied atmosphere. As you become more aware, you become less attached to events and the need for so many material things. Service to others becomes more important and you experience no resistance.

At the highest level you are constantly fine-tuning your special talents. This creates additional opportunities for you to serve. Your life starts to flow, instead of being a series of disjointed events and pressure situations. You intuitively know the right decisions to make and which direction to follow. In turn, this helps you to become increasingly more self-reliant and guided by your own sense of destiny.

Here's the big question: Where are you on the ladder? What Level of Being do you currently represent? A word of caution here. It would be easy to say that you fluctuate from top to bottom depending on the day of the week. The truth is, you consistently demonstrate certain behaviors more than others. These are your dominant habits—your true Level of Being.

Please understand one thing. Before you can move up to the next rung on the ladder, you must let go of the one you are on. Remember, there is a transition stage here. At one point you have stepped off the rung, but you can't quite reach the next one. This is the scariest part—the uncertainty of not knowing if you'll reach the next step. This produces doubt. Fear mixed with doubt is a potent combination that can ensure that you stay stuck on the ladder. The only way to move up is to embrace change and take the risk. It's like jumping into the swimming pool for the first time. If you can't swim, your fear of not coming up again may keep you out of the water forever. The simple reality is that you will come up, but you must jump to find out.

Make A STOP LIST

You can accelerate your move to a higher Level of Being by making a Stop List. There is an exercise at the end of this chapter called Your Personal Stopping List, to help you. This is a list of all the things you are doing that are self-limiting, that keep you stuck on the ladder. Remember, nothing will change until you change. Place emphasis on the habit of consistently changing your habits. By doing so, you will start to appreciate the joy of living life at these higher levels.

LIFE'S FUNDAMENTALS

KNOW WHAT YOU WANT
KNOW WHY YOU WANT IT

DISCOVER YOUR TALENTS
USE THEM DAILY

WORK HARD
WORK SMART

GIVE UNCONDITIONALLY
LOVE UNCONDITIONALLY

FIND YOUR PURPOSE
LIVE YOUR PURPOSE

© Les Hewitt

CONCLUSION

Living your true purpose at the highest Level of Being indicates that you want to make a difference. It is the most fulfilling place you can be, and offers magnificent rewards. Your life will be joyful, you will have peace of mind and you will be expressing your God-given talents in the most meaningful way possible.

So press on with the search. Strive to understand more about yourself and the role you were designed to play. It's a journey that will take you a lifetime. Along the way you will need to become more accountable. This requires making different choices, some of which will undoubtedly be difficult. As you'll see in our Final Words following this chapter, it's the ultimate commitment . . . the commitment to change.

LIFE IS SHORT. FOCUS FROM THIS DAY FORWARD ON MAKING A DIFFERENCE.

ACTION STEPS

Discovering and
Living
Your Purpose

The ten questions below were formulated to help you determine if your life is centered around purpose. In combination with the key points in this chapter, they will help you clarify a definition of purpose that works for you. Before responding, think about each question and read the comments. Then simply check "yes"; "don't know/not sure"; or "no."

1. Do you recognize what you are good at and what energizes you?

❑ yes　　❑ don't know/not sure　　❑ no

Many people never find their niche because they avoid analyzing their career objectives. They fall into jobs and never actually ask themselves, "What do I do well? What type of life do I want to lead? What type of work creates positive energy for me?" It's important for you to know and use your special skills.

2. Do you fully utilize your most-enjoyed skills?

❑ yes　　❑ don't know/not sure　　❑ no

Many people stagnate in their jobs. They are capable of doing so much more, yet they are afraid to challenge themselves. There are four separate categories of job expectations. Unfortunately, most people fall into the first three.

A. "It's just a job. Any job is okay as long as the pay is good and I can do my own thing after work."

B. "Work has to be regular. I need the benefits, vacations and security of a permanent job."

C. "I want substance and content in my profession, trade or vocation. I want to use my talents and be challenged."

D. "Work is not related to money; work is a path to further learning and personal growth. Work focuses me on something that I really believe needs doing in this organization, community, or world."

3. Does your work further some interest or issue that you care deeply about?

❑ **yes**   ❑ **don't know/not sure**   ❑ **no**

Caring is the basis of all purpose. It requires an openness to everything around you. To develop care, you need awareness. You should not be burdened by a sense of duty or obligation. When you care naturally, it's because something has profoundly touched and moved you.

4. Do you see yourself, through work, as making a difference in the world?

❑ **yes**   ❑ **don't know/not sure**   ❑ **no**

The "rust-out syndrome" is prevalent in today's society. Because so many people find work to be meaningless, they lose motivation. Work must offer more than money and status; it must offer you the chance to make a difference.

5. Do you view most days with a sense of enthusiasm?

❏ yes   ❏ don't know/not sure   ❏ no

When you are serving a purpose larger than yourself, you will feel more committed and become more enthusiastic. Remember, the years fly by quickly, so approach each day and each task with zeal.

6. Have you developed your own philosophy of life and success?

❏ yes   ❏ don't know/not sure   ❏ no

Everyone needs a set of principles to live by. Too many people, however, accept the values of others and never develop their own. They do not reflect enough upon their lives; instead, they worry about getting approval from others. Real power comes from acting out your deep, personal values.

7. Are you taking the necessary risks to live your philosophy?

❏ yes   ❏ don't know/not sure   ❏ no

No one is ever completely sure of the path to follow, but those with the courage to believe in themselves and their ideas, with the potential of some loss involved, are the true individuals. You must take the risk—have the courage, to be true to yourself.

8. Do you feel a sense of meaning and purpose for your life?

❏ yes   ❏ don't know/not sure   ❏ no

Terry Fox is a wonderful example of someone who had a deeply felt purpose in life. His memory spurs us to raise our own expectations of what we can be. You can choose to focus your vigor on what gives you the deepest feeling. You can occupy your time and talents with people, commitments, ideas and challenges that feel purposeful.

9. Do you have active goals this year relating to your purpose?

❏ yes   ❏ don't know/not sure   ❏ no

Purpose as a part of our lives serves as inspiration. But it is really our goals that motivate us on a day-to-day basis. Our lives are empty when we do not have something to strive for. Goals, though not always easy to achieve, provide the satisfaction of accomplishment, which in turn enhances our sense of self-worth.

10. Are you living your life to the fullest now instead of hoping that things will work out someday?

❑ yes   ❑ don't know/not sure   ❑ no

Why wait for the lottery? Use your potential now instead of taking it to the grave. Now is the time to live within your values, and with purpose.

SOURCE: *The Power of Purpose*

Score your results as follows:

- For each **yes** answer give yourself a **0**
- **Not sure** or **don't know** scores a **1**
- Each **no** answer scores a **2**

Now add up your score. As these questions are subjective, there are no right or wrong answers. However, use the scoring analysis as a general guideline. Here's how it works:

If you scored between 0–7, your life is pretty focused, you have a sense of direction, and you are intent on making a difference.

If you scored between 8–15, you have a sense of purpose, but you need to clarify your commitment. Are you really living your values and "walking the talk" every day?

If your score was between 16–20, you run the risk of not using your potential and just wasting your life. Please note: This high score may also mean that you are in the middle of a crisis or major transition.

Now that you have had an opportunity to think about what purpose means to you, construct a one-sentence statement that captures the essence of your life's purpose as you currently see it.

Choose your words carefully, and as always, be specific.

_____

_____

_____

To reinforce your purpose, embrace this statement every day. Print it on a special card that you can keep close to you. Develop the habit of re-affirming your statement of purpose until it becomes totally ingrained in your consciousness. This is the catalyst that will change your behavior and allow you to actually enjoy living your life on purpose.

If you are not able to create a meaningful statement after doing this questionnaire, don't be too concerned. Often it takes months (and sometimes years) to clarify this. What will help is to keep searching and thinking about what you are doing and why. The answers will eventually present themselves to you.

Your Personal Stopping List.
Make a list of all the things you need to stop doing or let go of to facilitate your move to the next Level of Being. Be specific. Consider your career, finances, relationships, health, philosophy and attitude.

Here are a few examples:

1. Stop overspending.

2. Stop being late.

3. Stop toxic relationships.

4. Stop blaming others for what you don't have.

5. Stop putting yourself down with negative self-talk.

LIVING ON PURPOSE

TAKING DECISIVE ACTION

CONSISTENT PERSISTENCE

ASK FOR WHAT YOU WANT

THE CONFIDENCE FACTOR

BUILDING EXCELLENT RELATIONSHIPS

CREATING OPTIMUM BALANCE

DO YOU SEE THE BIG PICTURE?

IT'S NOT HOCUS-POCUS, IT'S ALL ABOUT FOCUS

YOUR HABITS WILL DETERMINE YOUR FUTURE

Congratulations—you did it!
Now use your power of focus to help others.

FINAL WORDS

It's Your Life . . .
Accept The Challenge!

"To laugh often and much;
to win the respect of intelligent people
and affection of children; to earn the
appreciation of honest critics and endure
the betrayal of false friends;
to appreciate beauty, to find the best in others;
to leave the world a bit better, whether by a
healthy child, a garden patch or a
redeemed social condition; to know even
one life has breathed easier because you
have lived. This is to have succeeded."

—Ralph Waldo Emerson

If you've read this book all the way through, congratulations. If you're one of those people who likes to skip to the last few pages to see how it ends—well, you probably do this with a lot of things in your life. Understand, there are no shortcuts to building a life of substance. It's an ongoing process. It takes time, real effort and a desire to become more than you already are. It's a worthy challenge. However, your biggest challenge starts tomorrow. How will you apply what you have learned between the covers of this book? All the strategies we have shared with you really work. They can dramatically change your life for the better. But only if you choose to use them.

We are all faced with tough decisions. It's part of the human dilemma. Which path do you take, this one or that one? Certainly, there are no absolute guarantees when it comes to charting your personal course for a better future. However, the fundamental habits we have shared with you throughout this book will go a long way to ensuring that your business and personal life will be blessed beyond measure. They have worked for us and for thousands of others. So take up the challenge. Make a decision now to refocus and become the best you can be, one day at a time.

Now is the time to step up and be counted. The alternative is to say, "That was interesting information," and then put this book on a shelf and carry on with your old habits. That would be sad, because nothing much in your life will change. And if you took the time to read this book, you obviously want to improve some things.

Because of what you have read, you are now more aware of how life works. So you have no more excuses for future failure, unless you don't push yourself to make the necessary changes. There are thousands of people, just like you, who have turned their lives into wonderful success stories simply because they decided to change.

You can do the same. You really can. Believe in yourself. Soak up the knowledge you have gleaned from these pages and focus on taking the first step, whatever that may be. Make that a priority. Then take another, and pretty soon your life *will* change. We guarantee it. With a little practice and persistence, new habits will become a part of you. A year from now you'll say, "Look how much I've changed, and look at the results—I can hardly believe it."

Refer back to these strategies often. Use them as an ongoing guide to help you. And remember, you *can* really make a difference in this world. It's your responsibility to do so, and also your destiny. Go forward now with courage and new hope. Your future awaits you—seize it boldly!

We wish you an abundance of health, joy and prosperity in the years ahead.

P.S. We'd love to know how these strategies are working for you. Please send your success story to: Achievers, P.O. Box 30880, Santa Barbara, CA 93130. Fax us at 001 (403) 730-4548 or e-mail *achievers@nucleus.com*.

ACCELERATE YOUR PROGRESS WITH EXPERT COACHING!

THE  **ACHIEVERS**
COACHING PROGRAM

**A proven system to help you focus on
your strengths, so you can maximize income
and have a lot more time for fun.**

The Achievers Coaching Program consists of small groups of qualified business people who are keen to jump to an even higher level of performance and income. Each group meets every two months for a whole day under the leadership of an experienced *Achievers Coach.*

The purpose of this regular time-out is to rethink, refocus, and review your progress as well as brainstorm with other participants. We'll also show you how to create "Big Picture" action plans, that will triple your income and double your time off. In addition, you'll learn how to eliminate procrastination, time pressures and unnecessary stress.

The Achievers Coaching Program will help you implement the focusing strategies you have learned in this book.

Call today for your FREE copy of *The Achievers Scorecard*—an eye-opening sixteen point checklist that will clearly identify your strengths and weaknesses.

PHONE: 001 403-295-0500 FAX: 001 403-730-4548
E-MAIL: *achievers@nucleus.com* WEB SITE: *www.achievers.com*

For examples of the results you can expect from this leading edge coaching program, please turn to page 300.

DOES **COACHING**

REALLY WORK?

The best answer is to show you some results.

"Achievers has helped me see the big picture. I'm really tracking results now, and surrounding myself with experts. During the last two years my income has more than doubled."

John Dafoe
managing partner, Tomko Sports Systems

"I'm nearing the end of my business career and contemplating retirement. Achievers has helped me change many business habits and given me a new focus for the rest of my life."

Dale Tufts
founder, Winterhawk Petroleum Consulting Services Ltd.

"Thanks to your sales strategies, we increased our revenues by $200,000 and that was only one client!"

Lori Greer
director of national sales, Company's Coming Publishing Ltd.

"It's great to have a day every couple of months for thoughtful reflection and self-analysis. The Achievers process has helped me to simplify things and enjoy a better quality of life."

Rob Hunt
vice president, Akita Drilling Ltd.

"This is our thirtieth year in business. My biggest challenge was creating a better balance between work and home. Achievers challenged me to make changes. It works. Last year I took three months off. Interestingly, our total sales increased 52 percent."

Phyllis Arnold
president, Arnold Publishing Ltd. (winner, ITV's Women of Vision Award)

"Achievers has helped me develop better organizational skills and all around focus. We now selectively target the clients we want to work with in our law practice. I also delegate more effectively and that's given me more personal time."

Daniel Smith
partner, Gordon, Smith and Company

"Thanks to Achievers, I'm more focused than I've ever been before. Our business has grown at least 25 percent, and I've doubled my personal time off. The workshop discussions have helped me to be more accountable and open to making changes."

Barry Lloyd
regional manager, Royal & Sun Alliance Financial

"I'm much more focused on activities that produce results. We adapted one strategy from the 'Building Relationships' workshop that will add $120,000 to our bottom line. That's what I call a good return on investment."

Ralph Puertas
president, Zep Manufacturing Company, Canada

You too can receive similiar results . . . and more!

*The Power
of
FOCUS*

ONE-DAY WORKSHOP
conducted *in person* by Les Hewitt

Now you and your key people can learn the most important focusing strategies in a "live" setting. Ideal for in-house meetings, conferences, sales conventions, corporate retreats, etc.

This dynamic one-day program includes:

- An in-depth session on how to set and achieve your business, personal and financial goals, complete with Action Plans!
- How to master the habit of Priority Focus—learn to spend 90 percent of your time on what you do best and let go of everything that is keeping you stuck.
- A proven system that ensures you will enjoy an excellent balance between work and family—guilt free!

Additional Bonus:

THE ACHIEVERS SCORECARD—Discover the sixteen best strategies used by the Top Achievers in business today. Check your score against the best of the best.

Please Note: Limited dates available. To avoid disappointment, reserve well in advance.

For details and scheduling information please call (001) 877-678-0234

Phone: (001) 403-295-0500 / Fax: (001) 403-730-4548
E-mail: *achievers@nucleus.com;* **Web Site:** *www.achievers.com*

RESOURCE GUIDE

The following is a list of recommended books, tapes, videos and courses that will enhance the ten focusing strategies we have outlined. All of the references previously mentioned in *The Power of Focus* are included. (*see asterisks*)

RECOMMENDED READING

Atlas Shrugged by Ayn Rand. New York, New York: Division of Penguin Putnam, Plume, 1999.

*Bits & Pieces (booklets). Fairfield, New Jersey: The Economic Press Inc.

*Chicken Soup for the Soul by Jack Canfield and Mark Victor Hansen. Deerfield Beach, Florida: Health Communications, Inc., 1993.

*Chicken Soup for the Soul at Work by Jack Canfield, Mark Victor Hansen, Martin Rutte, Maida Rogerson and Tim Clauss. Deerfield Beach, Florida: Health Communications, Inc., 1996.

*Chicken Soup for the Unsinkable Soul by Jack Canfield, Mark Victor Hansen and Heather McNamara. Deerfield Beach, Florida: Health Communications, Inc., 1999.

*Don't Sweat the Small Stuff... and it's all small stuff by Richard Carlson. Bolton, Ontario: H.B. Fenn & Co., 1997.

*Don't Worry, Make Money by Richard Carlson. New York, New York: Hyperion, 1997.

*Even Eagles Need a Push by David McNally. Eden Prairie, Minnesota: Transform Press, 1990.

Future Diary by Mark Victor Hansen. Costa Mesa, California: Mark Victor Hansen and Associates, 1985.

How to Handle a Major Crisis by Peter J. Daniels. Ann Arbor, Michigan: Tabor House Publishing, 1987.

How to Reach Your Life Goals by Peter J. Daniels. Ann Arbor, Michigan: Tabor House Publishing, 1985.

In Search of The Invisible Forces by George Addair. Phoenix, Arizona: Vector Publications, 1995.

It's Not What Happens to You, It's What You Do About It by W. Mitchell. San Franciso, California: Phoenix Press, 1999.

Leading an Inspired Life by Jim Rohn. Niles, Illinois: Nightingale-Conant Corporation, 1997.

*Live and Learn and Pass It On by H. Jackson Brown, Jr. Los Angeles, California: Rutledge Press, Inc., 1991.

Love is Letting Go of Fear by Gerald Jampolski, M.D. New York, New York: Simon & Schuster, 1995.

*Man's Search for Meaning by Viktor Frankl. New York, New York: Pocket Books, 1984.

*NLP: The New Art and Science of Getting What You Want by Dr. Harry Alder: London, England: Judy Piatkus Ltd., 1994.

*Putting Your Faith into Action Today! by Dr. Robert H. Schuller. Garden Grove, California: Cathedral Ministries, 1998.

Reclaiming Higher Ground by Lance H. K. Secretan. Toronto, Ontario: MacMillan Canada, 1996.

Relationship Selling by Jim Cathcart. New York, New York: Berkeley Publishing Group, Division of Penguin, 1990.

*Rich Dad, Poor Dad by Robert Kiyosaki with Sharon L. Lechter. Paradise Valley, Arizona: Tech Press Inc., 1997.

Success System That Never Fails by W. Clement Stone. New York, New York: Simon & Schuster, 1991.

*Success Through a Positive Mental Attitiude by Napoleon Hill and W. Clement Stone. Paramus, New Jersey: Prentice-Hall, 1977.

*Swim with the Sharks Without Being Eaten Alive by Harvey Mackay. New York, New York: Ballantine Books, 1996.

Take This Job and Love It! The Joys of Professional Selling by Tim Breithaupt. Calgary, Alberta: The Professional Equity Group Ltd., 1999.

*Ten Golden Rules for Financial Success by Gary Moore. Grand Rapids, Michigan: Zondervan Publishing House, 1996.

*The Aladdin Factor by Jack Canfield and Mark Victor Hansen. New York, New York: Berkeley Books, Division of Penguin Putnam, 1995.

*The Bible.

*The Eagle's Secret by David McNally. New York, New York: Delacorte Press, 1998.

The E-Myth Revisited by Michael Gerber. New York, New York: Harper Business, 1995.

The Great Crossover by Dan Sullivan. Toronto, Ontario: The Strategic Coach Inc., 1994.

The Greatest Secret in the World by Og Mandino. New York, New York: Bantam Books, 1972.

The 7 Habits of Highly Effective People by Stephen R. Covey.
New York, New York: Simon & Schuster, 1989.

The Lexus and the Olive Tree by Thomas L. Friedman. New York, New York:
Faraar, Strauss and Groux, 1999.

*The Millionaire Next Door by Thomas J. Stanley and William D. Danko.
Marietta, Georgia: Longstreet Press, Inc., 1996.

*The On-Purpose Person by Kevin W. McCarthy. Colorado Springs, Colorado:
Navpress, 1992.

*The Richest Man in Babylon by George S. Clason. New York, New York:
Penguin Books, 1989.

The Seasons of Life by Jim Rohn. Austin, Texas: Discovery Publications, 1981.

*The 9 Steps to Financial Freedom by Suze Orman. New York, New York:
Random House, 1998.

*The Tomorrow Trap by Karen E. Peterson. Deerfield Beach, Florida:
Health Communications, Inc., 1996.

*The Wealthy Barber by David Chilton. Don Mills, Ontario:
Stoddart Publishing, 1989.

There Are No Limits by Danny Cox. Franklin Lakes, New Jersey:
Career Press, 1998.

*Think & Grow Rich by Napoleon Hill. New York, New York: Fawcett Crest
Books/CBS Inc., Division of Ballantine Books, 1960.

Unlimited Power by Anthony Robbins. New York, New York:
Simon & Schuster, 1986.

1001 Ways to Reward Employees by Bob Nelson. New York, New York:
Workman Publishing Co., 1994.

Work for a Living and Still Be Free to Live by Eileen McDargh. New York,
New York: Time Books, Division of Random House, 1985.

AUTOBIOGRAPHY/BIOGRAPHY

Buffet: The Making of an American Capitalist by Roger Lowenstein. New York,
New York: Random House, 1995.

Hammer by Armand Hammer. New York, New York: Perigee Books,
Division of Penguin Putnam, 1988.

Losing My Virginity by Richard Branson. London, England:
Virgin Publishing Ltd., 1998.

Made in America by Sam Walton. New York, New York: Bantam Books, 1993.

Muhammad Ali: His Life and Times by Thomas Hauser. New York, New York:
Simon & Schuster, 1991.

AUDIOTAPES

Happy, Healthy and Terrific by Ed Foreman. Dallas, Texas: Executive Development Systems. (001) 800-955-7353

How to Build High Self-Esteem by Jack Canfield. Niles, Illinois: Nightingale-Conant Corp., 1989. (001) 800-323-5552

Magic Words That Grow Your Business by Ted Nicholas. Niles, Illinois: Nightingale-Conant Corp. (001) 800-323-5552

Relationship Strategies by Jim Cathcart and Tony Alessandra. Niles Illinois: Nightingale-Conant Corp. (001) 800-323-5552

Self-Esteem and Peak Performance by Jack Canfield. Boulder, Colorado: Career Track Publications and Fred Pryor Seminars, 1995. (001) 800-255-6278

*The Aladdin Factor: How to Ask for and Get What You Want in Every Area of Your Life by Jack Canfield and Mark Victor Hansen. Niles, Illinois: Nightingale-Conant Corp., 1999. (001) 800-323-5552

The Challenge to Succeed by Jim Rohn. Dallas, Texas: Jim Rohn International. (001) 800-929-0434

Unlimited Power: The New Science of Personal Achievement by Anthony Robbins. San Diego, California: Robbins Research International, 1986. (001) 800-898-8669

VIDEOTAPES

*Chicken Soup for the Soul by Jack Canfield and Mark Victor Hansen. Boulder, Colorado: Career Track Publications and Fred Pryor Seminars, 1996. (001) 800-255-6278

How to Have Your Best Year Ever by Jim Rohn. Dallas, Texas: Jim Rohn International. (001) 800-929-0434

Phone Power by George Walther. Niles, Illinois: Nightingale-Conant Corp. (001) 800-323-5552

Self-Esteem and Peak Performance by Jack Canfield. Boulder, Colorado: Career Track Publications and Fred Pryor Seminars, 1995. (001) 800-255-6278

The Man Who Would Not Be Defeated by W. Mitchell. Santa Barbara, California: W. Mitchell. (001) 800-421-4840

*The Power of Purpose (the story of Terry Fox) by David McNally. Eden Prairie, Minnesota: Wilson Learning Corp. (001) 612-944-2880

COURSES

Business Coaching

The Achievers Coaching Program. Contact: Les Hewitt.
(001) 877-678-0234 Canada: (001) 403-295-0500 U.S.A.: (001) 408-357-0616, United Kingdom and Ireland: 0846-667227 *www.achievers.com*

The Strategic Coach Program.
(001) 800-387-3206 Canada: (001) 416-531-7399
U.S.A.: (001) 847-699-5767 *www.strategiccoach.com*

Personal Development

Insight Training Seminars. Santa Monica, California. (001) 310-829-7402

STAR/Success Through Action & Responsibility. Santa Barbara, California.
(001) 805-563-2935

The Dale Carnegie Course. Garden City, New York. (001) 516-248-5100

The Delta Vector. Contact: George Addair, Phoenix, Arizona.
(001) 602-943-7799

The Forum – Landmark Education. San Francisco, California.
(001) 415-981-8850

The Facilitating Skills Seminar. Santa Barbara, California. (001) 805-563-2935

The Hoffman Quadrinity Process. Cambridge, Ontario. (001) 800-741-3449

The Successful Life Course. Contact: Ed Foreman.
Dallas, Texas. (001) 800-955-7353 or (001) 214-351-0055

Personality Profiles

Kolbe Concepts Inc. Phoenix, Arizona. (001) 602-840-9770

Personality Plus. St. Paul, Minnesota. (001) 651-483-3597

Public/Professional Speaking

The National Speakers Association. Tempe, Arizona. (001) 602-968-2552

Toastmasters International. Rancho Santa Margarita, California
(001) 949-858-8255

ADDITIONAL REFERENCES

"Agassi Returns to Top." Brian Hutchinson. *Calgary Herald*, August 7, 1998, E-5.

"Canadian Kid Wins U.S. Fans." Robert Russo. *Calgary Herald*, May 3, 1996, A-7.

"A New Course of Commitment." Robin Brownlee. *Calgary Herald*, January 25, 1996, C-1.

"An Extraordinary Capacity to Forgive." Patricia Chisholm. *Maclean's*, February 10, 1997.

PERMISSIONS

ABOUT THE AUTHORS

 **Jack Canfield** has shared *The Power of Focus* strategies in twelve countries at his *Self Esteem* and *Peak Performance* workshops. His clients include Campbell Soup Company, Clairol, Coldwell Banker, General Electric, ITT, Hartford Insurance, Federal Express, Johnson & Johnson, NCR, Sony Pictures, TRW and Virgin Records, plus other organizations such as the Million Dollar Round Table, the Young Presidents Organization, and the World Business Council.

For further information about Jack's books, tapes and training programs, or to schedule him for a presentation, please contact:

The Canfield Training Group, P.O. Box 30880, Santa Barbara, CA 93130, phone (001) 800-237-8336, fax (001) 805-563-2945, Web site: *www.chickensoup.com*, to send e-mail: *soup4soul@aol.com,* to receive information via e-mail: *chickensoup@zoom.com*

 **Mark Victor Hansen** has taught these successful strategies to millions of people, covering thirty-seven countries in the past twenty-five years. He has appeared on CNN, *Eye to Eye*, QVC, the *Today Show*, PBS and *Oprah*, and has been featured in dozens of national magazines and newspapers such as *Entrepreneur, Success, Time, U.S. News & World Report, USA Today, New York Times, Washington Post* and *The Los Angeles Times*. Mark is also receiving the prestigious Horatio Alger Award in May, 2000.

Jack and Mark are also coauthors of the highly successful *Chicken Soup for the Soul* series, which *Time* magazine calls the publishing phenomenon of the decade, with more than 50 million copies currently sold worldwide!

You can contact Mark at:

P.O. Box 7665, Newport Beach, CA 92658, phone (001) 714-759-9304 or (001) 800-433-2314, fax (001) 714-722-6912

 **Les Hewitt**, originally from Northern Ireland, is one of the top performance coaches in North America. He is the founder of the highly successful *Achievers Coaching Program*. Currently operating in the United States, Canada, United Kingdom, and the Republic of Ireland, this unique three-year process has been the catalyst for many of his clients' remarkable transformations. Since its inception in 1983, Achievers has conducted training programs for thousands of businesspeople from a wide variety of industries.

Les is a dynamic speaker, business coach, sales trainer, writer, and entrepreneur. For the past twenty years he has personally coached hundreds of entrepreneurs to achieve exceptional profits and productivity.

To contact Les, or obtain information about volume discounts, The Achievers Coaching Program, licensing partnership opportunities, speeches, seminars and *The Power of Focus* one-day workshops contact:

Achievers Canada, 5160 Skyline Way NE, Calgary, AB T2E 6V1, toll free (001) 877-678-0234 or phone (001) 403-295-0500, fax (001) 403-730-4548, Web site: *www.achievers.com*, e-mail: *achievers@nucleus.com*

A B O U T